THE QURAN
UNCHALLENGEABLE MIRACLE

By CANER TASLAMAN

TRANSLATED BY ENDER GÜROL

© Nettleberry / Çitlembik Publications, 2006

Library of Congress Cataloging-in-Publication Data

Taslaman, Caner
    The Quran: Unchallengeable Miracle/Caner Taslaman; çev. Ender Gürol
    Includes bibliographical references.
    ISBN: 975-6663-94-4
1. Koran and science. I. Title.— II. Gürol, Ender
BP134.S3 2006
297.1228

Cover art: Ozan Balki
Cover design: Devrim Gülşen
Layout: Tarkan Togo
Translation: Ender Gürol

Printed at Berdan Matbaası:
Davutpaşa Cad. Güven San. Sit.
C-Blok No: 215-216 Topkapı Istanbul, Turkey
Tel: (0212) 613 12 11 - 613 11 12

In the USA:
Nettleberry, LLC
44030 123rd St.
Eden, South Dakota 57232
www.nettleberry.com

In Turkey: Çitlembik Publications
Şeyh Bender Sokak 18/5
Asmalımescit - Tünel
80050 Istanbul
www.citlembik.com.tr

THE QURAN

UNCHALLENGEABLE MIRACLE

By CANER TASLAMAN

TRANSLATED BY ENDER GÜROL

Nettleberry/Çitlembik Publications

For my Grandmother,
Müyesser Taslaman

TABLE OF CONTENTS

INTRODUCTION

The word "miracle" expresses an event that is beyond the capacity of man or society. The appearance of a prophet invariably incited people to demand testimonials-miracles-as proof that he was a truly a heaven-ordained messenger. Moses, Christ and Muhammad were no exceptions.

50- For they say: "How is it no signs were sent down to him from his Lord?"

29-The Spider, 50

To work miracles is no great matter for God. But miracles are not performed according to the expectations of disbelievers. A prophet's mission, in his capacity as God's messenger, is to warn mankind. No prophet can work miracles, nor can he produce evidence of prophethood, unless God says so. The answer to the disbelievers' skeptic attitude is provided in the same verse:

50- ...Say: "The signs are with God. I am only a plain warner."

29-The Spider, 50

THE QURAN IS ITSELF A MIRACLE

The proofs generally demanded by unbelievers are "God's manifestation" in one way or another, or the "descent of angels from above." But miracles are not meant to conform to the wishes of disbelievers. God announces, immediately after the above-mentioned verse, that the Quran He has sent is miracle enough:

51- "Is it not sufficient for them that We have sent down to you the Book being read to them? It is indeed a grace and reminder for people who believe."

29-The Spider, 51

15

The Prophet insistently repeated: "I am but a slave of God," "The Signs are with God," "I demand from you neither emolument nor recompense," "Here is the Book sent by God, so act accordingly." God asks, in referring to the Quran's descent: **"Is it not sufficient for them?"** Nevertheless, the dissatisfaction and insistence of unbelievers could not be curbed as they refuted all evidences produced. They claimed that the Quran was the word of man:

25- "This is nothing, but the word of a human."

74-The Hidden, 25

FROM THE BOTTOM OF THE SEA TO THE LOFTY HEIGHTS OF SPACE

In the course of our journey through this book we shall study the revelations of the Quran, a journey that will take us from the bottom of the sea to the heights of space, from the creation of the universe to the latest discovery on the firmament, from the embryo to the life of bees and from the most probing questions of philosophy to the most complicated problems of physics. In this expedition we shall try to assess the unbelievers' contention that "The Quran is the word of a human" as opposed to "The Quran is the word of God."

We shall witness that the Quran is exempt from all errors, despite the vast range of subjects it covers, and that it reveals information that was not - and could not possibly be - known at the time. There are so many revelations succinctly communicated in the Quran - in four or five words - that man had to have recourse to knowledge accumulated over millennia in order to be able to understand the meanings hidden in them (for example, the verse related to the expansion of the universe that we shall presently be discussing). It is only due to the highly developed telescopes, sophisticated microscopes, systematical observation, computer-aided analysis, and huge research resources and sums of money that we have been able to derive that knowledge today.

As we proceed, we shall realize that the verses of the Quran could not have been produced by men alone, even if all of humanity at the time of Muhammad succeeded in devising a "collective mind." Supposing that the population of the world, one hundred years ago, had succeeded in creating such a "collective intelligence;" the data we shall be discussing in the first seventy chapters of the present book would still be beyond the reach of the human mind. The revelation of so many miraculous predictions at the time of the Prophet is inconceivable. It is an injustice to truth to ignore this evidence, which neither can be explained by probability, nor by the knowledge and scientific level of the time.

> **49- To the contrary, these are clear signs in the hearts of those who are granted knowledge. None deny Our messages except the unjust.**
>
> *29-The Spider, 49*

FROM DESERT BEDOUINS TO PROFESSORS

We shall witness that the knowledge that modern science has achieved had already been foretold by the Quran 1400 years earlier. The lore of the Quran is presented in a somewhat different form than in the textbooks of physics, chemistry and biology, which are based on scientific methods. The Quran follows a beeline in communicating information, while the knowledge that books on science conveys to us is attained after long accumulation of data. The source of the Quran is the Creator of the universe. He has no need for accumulation of knowledge. He is the Knower of everything and can succinctly say what He wants to communicate to men.

His address is to humanity in its entirety, from the Bedouins of the desert to the professors of universities and scholars of great erudition. As the Quran addresses humanity in its entirety, it makes a distinction between the ignorant and the knowledgeable.

> **9- Say: "Are those who know equal to those who do not know? Only men of understanding take heed."**
>
> *39-The Throngs, 9*

WILL MIRACLES BE PERFORMED FOR US?

In the first section of the present book, I shall dwell particularly on the scientific miracles predicted in the Quran. The second section will deal with mathematical miracles. Mathematics is the common language of natural sciences and a science that cannot be refuted. As a matter of fact, the extraordinary mathematical structure of the Quran shows that it cannot possibly be the work of a human being and that the Quran has been exactly preserved. The literary style of the Quran is also excellent, but those who do not know Arabic cannot appreciate this. Therefore, it is our intention here to limit our discussion in this book to an examination of the miracles in the fields of natural sciences and mathematics, the common languages of humanity. We shall witness the universal miracles contained in the Quran that address mankind.

In an age when people were immersed in witchcraft, Moses triumphed over the conjurers of Pharaoh by performing miracles, with God's assistance. At a time when healers were honored, Christ performed miracles and cured the sick. We observe today that considerable effort is spent to show that religion is superseded by science, while in reality, science is the body of rules that God - originator of the universe and its laws - instilled into matter. At such a critical point, we cannot help observing the unfolding of scientific and mathematical miracles. The fact that they are made manifest at such a transitional period of history is astounding indeed.

These miracles show that God's scientific laws running the universe cannot and will not contradict religion He has established. The Quran is not self-contradictory; neither is it inconsistent with the universe that God has created:

82- Will they not then ponder on the Quran? And if it were from any other than God, they would have found in it many discrepancies.

4-The Women, 82

The question, "Why are miracles performed for ancient communities not witnessed or performed for us?" has thus been answered. Only God decides to work miracles and the time when they shall be demonstrated.

We will try to realize the scope of God's miracles, ranging from physics to chemistry and from biology to mathematics. Those who seek God's help without negotiating conditions have always been rewarded. We must be thankful for His guidance. At a time when religion is being confronted by science, God is displaying His miracles by pulling our attention to the scientific facts expressed or embedded in His scripture. This vindicates God's religion and demonstrates that the controversy between religion and science is irrelevant.

CHALLENGE

After reading this book, those who contend that religion and science are adversaries must accept one of the following alternatives:

1) Either what is asserted as religion has nothing to do with religious truth, thus, fabrications extraneous to religion must be purged; or,

2) The so-called scientific data or assumptions are false. One should inquire then, by systematic observation and logical deduction, where the errors lie and then search for scientific truth.

Religion, as a system devised by God, cannot contradict the universal natural laws imposed by the same God. However, bigoted fundamentalists, styling themselves as God's spokesmen, and orthodox scientists who deny the Creator of all sciences, do their utmost to prove the so-called contradiction.

The self-confidence of the Quran is unprecedented. The language of the Quran is so confident and assertive that both believers and disbelievers have no choice but to acknowledge it either as the greatest reality or the biggest lie. Even the disbelievers, however, must still concede the extraordinary character of the Quran.

> **13- Or, they say: "He has forged it." Say: "Then bring ten forged suras like it, and call upon whom you can besides God, if you are truthful."**
> **14- But if they fail to answer you, then know that it is revealed with God's knowledge, and that there is no God but He. Will you then submit?**
> *11-Hud, 13-14.*

Ten chapters (suras) ... Ten forged chapters ... Had they been able to forge ten chapters, they might be in a position to hold sway over masses of people and forestall the spread of the influence of the Quran. The Quran's assertion goes even further.

23- If you are in doubt of what We have revealed to Our Servant, then bring a sura like this, and call any witness, apart from God, you like, if you are truthful.
24- But if you cannot, as indeed you cannot, then guard yourselves against the fire whose fuel is men and rocks, which has been prepared for the disbelievers.

2-The Cow, 23-24

Could they forge one, let alone ten like it? How about facing this challenge? History bears testimony against it. Had they been able to emulate even one single sura of the Quran, the wrongdoers would have most willingly liked to do it and forestall the spread of Islam. They could not. They were incapable of it. Perverse that they were, they opted for an ill-favored alternative. The villains preferred to have recourse to arms and thus they drew their swords during the lifetime of the Prophet and fought against the believers. Had there been an easier way to settle things, everything would have been different, of course. To write was easy but to emulate the style of the Quran was impossible.

88- Say, "If all the humans and jinns came together in order to produce a Quran like this, they would surely fail, no matter how much assistance they lent one another."

17-The Children of Israel, 88

A formidable challenge indeed! But the miracles we shall behold as we proceed will bear witness to the truth of this fact.

THE FUNDAMENTAL QUESTION

We must not lose sight of the question raised by the Quran. The question is: "What is the state of our being?" Supposing for an instant that there was no such thing as the Quran (this argument is valid, of course, for all divine religions), questions such as "Where do I come from?" or "Where do I go?" would be left unanswered. Finding answers to these questions is even more important than finding our daily food. Eating and drinking are acts in our brief span of life that are insignificant compared to eternity, the ultimate desire of every human being.

The miracles contained in the Quran provide answers to our questions about our state of being. The revelations will lead us to the eternal bliss anticipated by man. Nothing can prevail over immortality. Eternal existence will certainly carry the day and will overshadow the transient.

Questions regarding our existence are addressed not only by the Quran, but also by all the other books previously sent. The message of the Quran promising eternal life can be matched by no other written human record. These miracles vindicate the teaching of the Quran. The Quran guides mankind to immortality, gives them hope and saves them from leading a life devoid of meaning.

What I am trying to achieve here is not the guidance of perplexed souls to a blindfolded credulity but rather to trigger their intelligence in order that they may end up in believing in the existence of God. The promises made in the Quran are eventually to our benefit, as those endowed with intelligence will readily see their scheme.

The fundamental truth is God's existence and His revealed religion as propounded by the Quran. Conceiving God's existence justifies the truth of religion that enables us to experience God, and refutes all counter arguments and teaches His ways. Perceiving the truth of religion confirms God's existence, as the fundamental issue is the experience of God. Thus God and religion coalesce.

The Quran furnishes convincing proofs of God's existence, as it also speaks of morals and religion and man's view of life. In fact, the Quran is religion. The miracles of the Quran are not only compelling evidence of the existence of religion; they are also evidence of God's existence. In addition to this, our cumulative knowledge derived from meticulous study of science also provides evidence for God's existence, since it shows us God's power and knowledge. For example, the description in the Quran, 1400 years ago, of the gestation of the fetus in the mother's womb is a miracle and it corroborates God's existence through the miraculousness of the Quran. The process of gestation, a proof of God's omnipotence and providence, confirms

God's existence not only by its miraculous conception in the Quran, but also by showing the perfection of His creation. The convergence of these two paths, separate from each other, also gives substance to the irrefutable truth of the deduction made. In examining these miracles, we shall benefit from the opportunity to meditate on God's wonderful creation. The Quran is God's book as it elucidates in the best possible manner God's existence and places Him in the core of man's life, honoring him. Thus, the miracles in the Quran prove the existence of God through proving the existence of religion while it proves the existence of religion by proving the existence of God through pointing to His creations.

PURE TRUTH

The miracles in the Quran reflect pure truth. Because these miracles were incomprehensible at the time of the descent of the Quran, the disbelievers tried to use them against the Quran. For instance, in the fourth chapter I refer to the sura Elucidated, verse 11. How incredible it must have been for the people of the Medieval Ages to read that, in the beginning, our world was in the form of gas. How incredible it must have been to imagine that the mountains, seas, stars, the sun and the moon had once been gaseous in form. Today our deductions are based on systematic observations rendered possible by the help of telescopes and the assistance of the accumulation of astronomic data, their computation and evaluation. This scientific information was not available at the time of the revelation of the Quran and did not serve as an advantage to its dissemination. As a matter of fact, because these assertions could not be substantiated, some of the believers were held in derision. But the revelation did not swerve from its declared aim: the announcement of the truth. This is but one historical example compelling us to believe in the revelation of the Quran, even though we may be unable to unravel all its mysteries. The Quran has never shaken the belief of its followers and points that were not clear at first, came in due time to be actualized in the form of miracles.

No intelligent, thinking human would conceive of communicating information to his own detriment while he was still alive, information that would only prove beneficial after the lapse of a millennium. It is true that at the time, man was in no position to understand these facts, but supposing that even if he had been, human qualifications would obviate the proper use of these data.

REMINDERS

While examining the miraculous predictions in the Quran, our book does not rely on the viewpoint of any particular sect or religious order or go against the creeds of it, and does not set boundaries between schools of religious law like Hanefiyah, Shafiyah, Malikiyah, Hanbeliah, Alevi, Caferi, Zahiriyah, Shi'ah, etc. Religious controversies, historical issues are not within the purview of our work. The existence of God and religion, the magnificence of God's power, art and science are particularly stressed. It is our wish and expectation that our book finds favor with all of its readers, regardless of their creeds.

In the preparation of this work, I have had recourse to many sources, regardless of the religion in question or the religious order to which their authors belong. I divided the first section of our book into 70 chapters. Among the subjects treated are astronomy, physics, chemistry, biology, archaeology and geology. The second part of the book analyzes the mathematical miracles and is divided into 50 MMLC (the Mathematical Miracle in Lexical Concordance). The "code 19" in the Quran has been our last domain of research. The subdivisions of the book make reading easier. Reference numbers are given under the verses quoted. I have been particular in giving the clearest translation of the Quran. Here is a list of the suras mentioned throughout our work, with the original titles.

NAMES OF THE SURAS

1. The Prologue   *Al-Fatihah*
2. The Cow   *Al-Baqarah*
3. The Family of Imran *Ali-Imran*
4. The Women   *An-Nisa*
5. The Feast   *Al-Maidah*
6. The Cattle   *Al-Anam*
7. The Purgatory   *Al-Araf*
8. The Spoils of War   *Al-Anfal*
9. Repentance   *At-Taubah*

10. Jonah   *Yunus*
11. Hud   *Hud*
12. Joseph   *Yusuf*
13. The Thunder   *Ar-Rad*
14. Abraham   *Ibrahim*
15. Hijr   *Al-Hijr*
16. The Honeybee   *An-Nahl*
17. The Children of Israel *Bani Israel*
18. The Cave   *Al-Kahf*
19. Mary   *Maryam*
20. Ta-He   *Ta-He*
21. The Prophets   *Al-Anbiya*
22. The Pilgrimage   *Al-Hajj*
23. The Believers   *Al-Muminun*
24. The Light   *An-Nur*
25. The Distinguisher   *Al-Furqan*
26. The Poets   *Ash-Shuara*
27. The Ant   *An-Naml*
28. The History   *Al-Qasas*
29. The Spider   *Al-Ankabut*
30. The Romans   *Ar-Rum*
31. Luqmaan   *Luqman*
32. The Prostration   *As-Sajdah*
33. The Parties   *Al-Ahzab*
34. Sheba   *Saba*
35. The Originator   *Al-Fatir*
36. Ya-Seen   *Ya-Seen*
37. Who Stand in Row   *As-Saffat*
38. Sad   *Sad*
39. The Throngs   *Az-Zumar*
40. The Believer   *Al-Mumin*
41. Elucidated   *Fussilat*
42. Consultation   *Ash-Shura*
43. Vanity   *Az-Zukhruf*
44. Smoke   *Ad-Dukhan*
45. Kneeling   *Al-Jathiyah*
46. The Dunes   *Al-Ahqaf*
47. Muhammad   *Muhammad*
48. Victory   *Al-Fath*

88.	Overwhelming	*Al-Ghashiyah*
89.	The Dawn	*Al-Fajr*
90.	The Town	*Al-Balad*
91.	The Sun	*Ash-Shams*
92.	The Night	*Al-Layl*
93.	Early Hours of Morning	*Ad-Duha*
94.	Cooling the Temper	*Al-Inshirah*
95.	The Fig	*At-Tin*
96.	The Hanging	*Al-Alaq*
97.	Determination	*Al-Qadr*
98.	Proof	*Al-Bayyinah*
99.	The Earthquake	*Az-Zalzalah*
100.	The Gallopers	*Al-Adiyat*
101.	The Shocker	*Al-Qariah*
102.	Plenitude	*At-Takaathur*
103.	Time	*Al-Asr*
104.	The Backbiter	*Al-Humazah*
105.	The Elephant	*Al-Fil*
106.	The Quraish	*Al-Quraish*
107.	Charity	*Al-Maun*
108.	Bounty	*Al-Kauthar*
109.	The Disbelievers	*Al-Kafirun*
110.	Help	*An-Nasr*
111.	The Father of Flame	*Al-Lahab*
112.	Absoluteness	*Al-Ikhlas*
113.	The Day Break	*Al-Falaq*
114.	People	*An-Naas*

CHAPTER 1

WE LIVE IN
AN EXPANDING UNIVERSE

47- With power did We construct heaven. Verily, We are expanding it.

51-The Dispersing, 47

Is the universe infinite? Or is it finite in a steady state? From the very beginning this has been a subject of debate between great minds. Hot debates and ratiocination of all kinds failed to clarify this dilemma. This had once been the subject of philosophical speculations before it yielded its place to the science of physics. Some of the great minds argued that the universe was not a confined space, while others contended that its boundaries were drawn. The Quran describes it as a continuously expanding and dynamic universe. According to this description, the universe has a new aspect every instant that deviates from the concept of an infinite space; its perpetual expansion defies the concept of a confined and steady state universe. Thus, the Quran propounds a third alternative, leaving the heated controversy of thinkers in abeyance.

This may contribute to the formulation of a judgment for the inquiring minds, probing whether the Quran is God's revelation or not. We have, on the one hand, Muhammad in the desert, neither a philosopher nor a physicist, and, on the other hand, the assumptions of great thinkers and philosophers such as Aristotle, Ptolemy, Giordano Bruno, Galileo Galilei and Isaac Newton, to name but a few. The greatest minds in history, basing their arguments on observations and formulas they had ingeniously devised, claimed either that the universe had its confines or that it was an endless space, but it occurred to none of them to think of a dynamic expanding universe, until the 20th century when Edwin Hubble, by means of a telescope, demonstrated that the universe was expanding. The theory of expansion of the universe was first advanced in the 1920s. Until the descent of the Quran no other source had made such an assertion!

MUHAMMAD'S TELESCOPE

Unbelievers contended that the Quran was Muhammad's own fabrication and not the revelation of God. How then would these dissenters explain the fact that Muhammad had been the only person who was aware of the expanding universe long before the 1920s. Could it be that in the 600s he had invented a telescope similar to the one contrived in the 1900s? Could it be that he had been familiar with the handling of such a telescope and acquainted with the motion of stars and that he had concealed it from his fellow men? If those who accused the Prophet of lunacy and alleged that in his delusional states he imagined himself the messenger of God were justified in their claims, how would they account for the fact that he knew facts not known to his contemporaries, facts that were to be discovered 1300 years after his revelation of them? If those people assert that the Prophet had devised a religion to serve his own ends, how can they explain that his so-called delusions materialized after a lapse of 1300 years? His pronouncements at the time did not promote his interests in any way; quite the reverse was the case, since he unwittingly gave his enemies a hint they might take advantage of. Can a person whose own interests prevail over the interests of others declare something not to his own advantage that was sure to be bitterly censured and much derided by those whose naked eyes failed to observe the expansion of the universe? If, despite this, a person came up with the contention that Muhammad was an intelligent man who might have perceived this truth, what sort of an intelligence might this have been? And, instead of boasting of having been the depository of such knowledge, why would he have preferred to tell an untruth and claim that this was not his own discovery but the revelation by God? While the inventor or discoverer of a pin is inclined to brag about his breakthrough, why on earth would Muhammad choose to be modest and categorically declare that the Quran was not his own production, but the revelation of God? Was this due to humility? Would these people

- who had denied his prophethood and accused him of having been an impostor - have dared qualify him with the laudable attribute of "humility?"

DISCOVERY OF THE EXPANDING UNIVERSE

There was a gap in Newton's physics. Newton believed in an endlessly vast and static universe. His law of gravity encountered a problem. How was it that the physical bodies, in the course of eons, defied their mutual attractions and did not collapse into a unity? The formula that Einstein devised abandoned the absolute notions of space and time as reference points for all objects in the universe. Basing his studies on Einstein's formulas, Alexander Friedmann, a Russian physicist, discovered that the universe must be expanding. Georges Lemaître, a Belgian cleric, astronomer and cosmologist, formulated that the universe had begun in a cataclysmic explosion of a small, primeval super-atom, like the growing of an oak tree from an acorn. This theory explained the recession of galaxies within the framework of Albert Einstein's theory of general relativity. This idea was so incredible that even Einstein had problems accepting it, despite the fact that this all had originated from his own formulas. Einstein, rather, countered that physics was not the forte of Lemaître, and the universe was an infinite expanse and in a steady state.

Lemaître's theory posited that the universe was expanding. This was a statement that no philosopher and no scientist had ever before set forth. Kant had said in his *Critique of Pure Reason* that this was an enigma unsolvable by human intelligence. This theory fit everything and explained the reason why the universe did not collapse in spite of gravity. The key had fit into the lock. It was the correct explanation of the enigma. However, this statement met with the usual adverse reaction: "No, it is not the truth..."

Remaining outside the sphere of theoretical controversy, American astronomer Hubble was, about the same time, making observations with his sophisticated telescope in the Mount Wilson observatory. He observed that galaxies were receding from each other, which proved that the universe was expanding. In answer to those who said they could not believe in things their eyes had not witnessed, Hubble's discovery led to the following declaration: "Now that you see it, you have got to believe it." Hubble showed this by the Doppler Effect. Thus the wavelengths of receding bodies prolonged in the spectrum of light waves would shift to red, while, if the bodies approached each other, the wavelengths would shorten, shifting to blue. The light that came from galaxies that shifted to red showed that the galaxies were receding. In line with this observation, Hubble discovered a striking law: the speed of galaxies that receded was directly proportional to the distance between galaxies. The farther away a galaxy stood, the more its speed of recession accelerated. The result was tested again and again. In 1950, a high-magnification telescope was installed on Mount Palomar in the USA, the largest instrument of its kind. The new tests and controls justified this observation. The measurements made pointed to the fact that the creation of the universe occurred about 10-15 billion years ago.

Both Einstein and Lemaître took an interest in Hubble's work; Einstein, who did not agree with Lemaître at first, eventually acknowledged during a conference that Lemaître was right after all. He confessed that his failure to endorse these findings had been the gravest error in his life. Thus it was that the fact that the universe was of a dynamic nature and expanding, confirmed by observations, was also validated by the great physicist Einstein.

In the examples presented by Hubble and Lemaître, we see illustrated how a physicist arrives at a conclusion both in theory and through observation. While Lemaître demonstrated how he had made inferences from Einstein's formulas to substantiate his theoretical discoveries, Hubble presented the data of his observations and his conclusions. As we see, the result obtained by physicists is the consequence of cumulative and collective bits of knowledge and research. The Creator of physical laws provides the answer in the Quran to the issues of towering importance throughout human history. The Quran's presentation of scientific facts is clear, direct, and concise; it is different than the presentation of scientists, which tends to be complicated by scientific methods and procedures. The provider of this answer does not have to go through all the labyrinths a scientist has to. The Quran's method is perfectly straightforward, unswerving and explicit.

If we had the possibility of looking at the universe from above and somebody asked us to describe what we saw, our answer would be that it was expanding. To achieve the Quran's revelation of this fact

1400 years ago, man would have needed access to the assistance of accumulated scientific data acquired throughout long years and to sophisticated telescopes. When people claim that science and religion oppose each other, the Quran furnishes answers to the most complicated scientific problems. Observations made by sophisticated telescopes today confirm the statements of the Quran.

The Quran, perfectly aware of the human psyche with its pre-science, states that nonbelievers will insist on their convictions regardless how many miracles are presented to them. Some ask: "Why did the people also not believe in Jesus, who had performed miracles and healed the sick and the blind?" This example demonstrates why the majority of people did not believe in Christ and the other prophets, despite their miracles. Miracles change in fact as time goes by, but the negative attitude of most humans remains unchanged.

REASON FOR THE USE OF THE ROYAL PLURAL

I think it advisable to explain the reason for the use of "We" in the verse analyzed in this chapter. God uses both the royal plural "We" and the first person singular "I." Some languages use the first person plural "we" to express grandeur and exalted rank.

In the hundreds of references addressing God in the second person, the pronoun used is "Thou" and never the plural "You" or "Ye." The thousands of references made to Him as a third person always use the pronoun "He" and never "They." References in the Quran to God always use either the second or the third person, and none of them as a second or third person plural. Thousands of times in the Quran, God is referred to as "Allah," "Gracious (*Rahman*)," Merciful (*Raheem*)," and "Lord (*Rab*)" and all of these words are in the singular, never the plural.

CHAPTER 2

THE POINT OF DEPARTURE OF OUR ODYSSEY

> **30- Do not these disbelievers see that the heavens and the earth were an integrated mass, which We then split, and from water We made all living things? Will they not believe even then?**
>
> *21-The Prophets, 30*

We deduce from the contents of this verse that it admonishes the unbelievers for ignoring the apparent miracles. The atheists' basic contention is that matter has no beginning and that it is the matter that has generated everything, both living and inanimate things, by fortuitous act. The Big Bang theory refutes the basic assertion of atheism in positing that the universe and time had a beginning. **"Do not these disbelievers see that...?"** is significant. And as it is implied by this verse, the fact that the heavens and the earth were in a state of unity before they were rent asunder was something indeed conceivable by the human mind. The 1900s were the years during which scientific discoveries succeeded each other. Those were the years in which some people tried to point out the contradiction between science and religion. It was presumptuous of them as their whims had been indulged by the prosperity generated by the industrial revolution to idolize matter, daring to substitute it for God. The fact that matter was created - that it had had beginning - as proven by the Big Bang theory, was a blow for unbelievers. The concluding sentence of the verse **"Will they not believe even then?"** is significant in that history confirmed the truth of this and the unbelievers remained adamant despite evidence produced.

Nevertheless, the arguments of this verse refute the unbelievers' thesis of eternal matter and compel them to believe. This truth that was to be taken for a fact 1300 years after the revelation of the Quran was another warning for unbelievers. In history, there has been no one, other than the God through Quran, who claimed that the universe had been expanding and that the heavens and the earth had been split asunder. Ancient Greece, the Middle Ages, the Modern Age, Plato, Thales - all those who had attempted to explain natural phenomena in natural terms - Ptolemy, Copernicus, Kepler and Kant, none of humanity's great minds, had had an inkling of an expanding universe and of the fact that before creation the heavens and the earth had been an indivisible whole. Without the sophisticated equipment of the twentieth century at their disposal, and devoid of all accumulated scientific data, all of these celebrated philosophers and physicists had failed to take cognizance of this fact. The Creator of the universe communicated such important facts about His creation in His book and shed light on the celestial bodies, also proving thereby that the Quran had been His revelation. God unfolded to man the evidences of His creation, the creation that had originated from a single point in which man stood as another point. It is significant to note that while pointing at the comprehensibility of this revelation in the verse, **"Do not these disbelievers see...?"** He prefigures the stubbornness of unbelievers: **"Will they not believe even then?"** Einstein himself said that what astounded him was the comprehensibility of his discoveries about the universe, rather than the discoveries themselves. This shows how significant it was to stress the fact that these phenomena were in fact within the reach of man's mental capacity.

COSMIC BACKGROUND RADIATION

The original unity of the universe is expressed by the Arabic word *"ratq,"* meaning the integrated state and the word *"fatq,"* signifying disintegration by separation. I have already mentioned that when Lemaître had posited this separation as described in the Quranic verse, his theory was first refuted. One of the contenders of this argument was Fred Hoyle. In the 1940s Fred Hoyle contended that if the Big Bang had effectively taken place there should have been a residue of the explosion, and asked that this fossil be shown. This satirical criticism led to the discovery of much evidence in support of the Big Bang theory. The expression "fossil" which was mockingly uttered by

Hoyle became the scientific word for real evidence discovered later. While he was trying to debunk the theory of the Big Bang in a humorous way, he had unwittingly contributed to the confirmation of the Big Bang theory.

In 1948, George Gamow and his student Ralph Adler concluded that if the Big Bang theory were true, it must have had a fossil left behind as Hoyle had claimed. According to their logic, the low-level background radiation must have existed in every direction since the universe had begun expanding in every direction following the Big Bang. Radiation other than that caused by the Big Bang must have had particular points in space from which it departed. But the radiation generated by such an explosion could not be traced back to a point. With the universe's dynamic expansion radiation must have scattered in every direction. In the 1960s, the form of radiation imagined by Gamow and Adler was made the subject of research by a group of scientists with precision instruments at their disposal at Princeton University. However, what they had been looking for was to be discovered by others in a very interesting way. Arno Penzias and Robert Wilson were researchers at the Bell Telephone Company. One day, quite unexpectedly, they detected a uniform microwave radiation that suggested a residual thermal energy throughout the universe of about 3 Kelvin, which is a temperature of 3 degree Celsius above absolute 0. At first Penzias and Wilson could not unravel the mystery and had to call their colleagues Robert Dicke and his team. When he hung up, Dicke understood that he had lost the cause as he took cognizance of the fact that the discovery that was to bring the Nobel Prize award had been the lot of others. Surveys of the cosmic 3-Kelvin radiation indicated that it was perfectly uniform in all directions. The residue that Hoyle believed nonexistent had been found. So the Nobel Prize went to Penzias and Wilson.

SATELLITE IN SUPPORT OF BIG BANG

After Penzias and Wilson shared the Nobel Prize in 1965, the Cosmic Background Explorer (COBE), was rocketed into the sky in 1989. The data received from COBE confirmed the discovery of Penzias and Wilson. A great number of scientists evaluated the data produced by COBE as conclusive proof. Thus the process initiated by Lemaître in the 1920s was substantiated once again with new discoveries in the 1990s. 1400 years had elapsed since the revelation of the Quran and the satellite's findings validated its statements. Supposing that we landed on a desert island and stumbled upon ashes: no one

The remnants of radiation that dispersed throughout the universe following the Big Bang were discovered by the COBE.

would doubt the fact that there had once been a fire on this island. The residue radiation that Penzias and Wilson ran across, and the COBE's data, indicated the existence of the Big Bang. The contention by dissenters that the radiation scattered all over space had to be perfectly uniform in all directions is another indicator of the soundness of this evidence.

One of the proofs substantiating the Big Bang theory is related to the hydrogen-helium ratio in the universe. In the 1930s, astronomers, basing their studies on the fact that every celestial object emits a particular light, had recourse to a spectroscope to analyze the composition of the stars and galaxies. Calculations made by means of the spectroscope and mathematical formulas demonstrated that the universe, at its initial stage, comprised an average of 73% hydrogen and 25% helium and 2% other gases like carbon and oxygen. Stars did not generate hydrogen and that much helium. Calculations made by scientists made it clear that 20%-30% of the helium must have been produced before the evolution of stars. Only the primordial fireball at the outset of the Big Bang could have generated such a light synthesis; the expectations in the wake of the Big Bang and the quantity of hydrogen and helium in space are just a few of the proofs validating the theory.

Although the available scientific evidence is in itself sufficient to prove the Big Bang theory, we are witnessing a steady increase of this evidence. A Big Bang medium was created in Switzerland at CERN (*Conseil Européen pour la Recherche Nucléaire*), the famous center that has the most powerful and versatile facilities of their kind in the world. The findings of the research carried out here lends further support to the theory.

The law of thermodynamics supports the theory according to which the universe must have had a beginning; the second law of thermodynamics states that some processes in nature are irreversible and unidirectional, the direction being dictated by an overall increase in entropy. Thus, the energy grows less and less utilizable until it becomes of no profit. If the universe and matter had existed from eternity, the movement would have come to a standstill in eternal time. On the other hand, eternity does not pass; if it does, then it is no longer an eternity. In brief, the very fact that we happen to be at this point connotes the existence of a beginning. If we think that time was not created, the contradiction is inevitable and ends up with a dilemma. The only solution to the dilemma would be positing that time was created and that the universe must have had a beginning; these, as proved by the Big Bang Theory, are mutually validating evidences.

COULD MUHAMMAD HAVE SENT A SATELLITE TO SPACE?

We have witnessed the verification of data received from the satellites sent into space. How did it happen that the Prophet had an insight into the fact that the earth and the heavens were an integrated mass before they were split? We asked whether the Prophet could have had a telescope concealed under the sand dunes, a telescope as sophisticated as the Hubble telescope? Are the unbelievers going to claim now that Muhammad discovered the primeval unity of the heavens and the earth by having recourse to calculations of the cosmic background radiation, and that he had sent his satellite long before the launch of COBE, 1400 years ago? Penzias and Wilson shared the Nobel Prize for the discovery. Would the unbelievers nominate Muhammad for the Nobel Prize for physics for having announced 1400 years ago that the universe had once been a whole before space began expanding?

It is evident that anyone who contended that the Quran had not been sent by God, but was the work of the Prophet, would necessarily become an object of ridicule. However, those resolved to remain unbelievers would insist on their convictions regardless of all evidence being brought forth. So had it been with Abraham and Moses and Christ and so was it with Muhammad. The psychology of unbelievers has never changed throughout history.

Those who opposed Moses declared that they would adhere to their own conviction, no matter what signs Moses would produce.

132- They said: "No matter what kind of sign you show us, to bewitch us, we will not believe in you."

7-The Purgatory, 132

BIG BANG:
SIGN OF GOD'S UNITY

Polytheistic beliefs have exhibited structures that differ according to the communities and times in which they have evolved. The polytheistic beliefs in ancient Egypt differ greatly from the polytheism of India. However, these systems have something in common. Every god has his apportioned domain where he exerts his sovereignty. The sun is a god, so is the moon, and the divinity whose sanctuary is the hills is another such being. Some of these control the rains, others the winds; some have control over the mountains, some over the rivers... In opposition to belief-systems that parcel out the universe, the monotheistic religions, namely Judaism, Christianity and Islam, saw the universe as a whole. These religions professed that severance and sundering could not be imagined in a universe created by one God. According to these religions what seems to be divided is but in appearance only, while the essence of the universe is one whole; the universe ruled over by God is one entity, with every one of its points being interrelated with all the other points.

Famous philosophers of the past, from Kindî, Farabi, Averroes and Avicenna to Christian scholars, had announced that "One comes out of one," positing thus the unity of God. These thinkers had tried to find a correlation between the occurrences in the universe whose logical conclusion would be the unity of God. In the aftermath of the Big Bang, this unity was once again proven. The origin of the universe was irrefutably one single composition. Considering that everything evolved out of this single entity, all elements should be in correlation with each other. No one could henceforth declare that the sun, the moon, man, the serpent or a plant had its respective creators. Unity lay beneath everything, and the Creator of this unity was also the Creator of the sun, the moon, the beasts and the plants that emerged from this unity. Even before the Big Bang theory, the irrationality of the idea that attributed different creators to different objects was evident. However, the Big-Bang proved with new evidence that God is One.

1- Say: He, God, is One.
2- God is He on Whom all depend.
3- He begets not, nor is He begotten;
4- And none equals Him.

112-Absoluteness, 1-4

CHAPTER 3

WE ARE CREATED OUT OF NOTHING

117- Creator of the heavens and the earth from nothing-ness, He has only to say when He wills a thing, "Be," and it is.

2-The Cow, 117

The Arabic word "*beda'a*" means creation of something out of nothing. This word also connotes the fact that something is created not on a pattern previously designed of something but as a completely new entity having no precedence. The greatest marvel of the creation is the creation of all concepts out of nothing. Think of the spectrum of colors. None of us can visualize a color that we have not already seen, nor can we produce that color. We are familiar with colors that already exist, but we cannot possibly create a new color. God, on the other hand, created all colors at a time when the concept of color did not exist, just as the universe did not exist before. To create a concept and its range of contents out of nothing is beyond human imagination and power.

Atheists contend that matter existed from eternity, that it had no beginning and that all formations evolved fortuitously. For example, in his books, famous materialist theoretician George Politzer contends that the universe was not created; had it been so, the universe would have been the work of a God who would have created it at a given moment out of nothing, that in order to be able to accept the theory of creation, one had to posit the existence of a moment when there was no universe, as it was to emerge from the void.

Atheism is the belief that God does not exist and materialism is the belief that only physical things have reality. These two words are often used as synonyms. Atheists who refute God's existence accept the infinite existence of matter, and are, consequently, materialists. Atheists contend that matter was not created but existed from eternity. The postulate of the eternal existence of God and that matter was created goes back to the monotheistic religions. All the monotheistic religions postulate that God existed from eternity and that matter was created by God. The fact that matter was created also proves the existence of God and that Judaism and Christianity and Islam are religions revealed by God.

It is true that there are still some people today who worship the sun, the moon and fire. They carry on their practices and rituals without any logical, scientific or philosophical justification. It is futile to logically or scientifically refute beliefs that do not value reason, logic and science. Such people need evidence that would break down their prejudices and relieve them of their obsessions. Throughout history there have been three separate viewpoints that allege to be in conformity with reason and science. These viewpoints at least declare that they accept reason, logic and science as criteria. In the present book, I shall try to expound on these ideas and analyze their relevancy.

These three views are:

1) Monotheism: There is but one God, He that created this magnificent physical universe and everything in it, living or inanimate.
2) Atheistic materialism: Matter has been in existence since eternity. Everything is made of matter from a chain of fortuitous events.
3) Agnosticism: We cannot know which of these two viewpoints is correct. Both may be justified in their postulates.

Essentially there are two fundamental alternatives. For the third announces that none of these views can be proved rather than propounding a new view. The agnostic point of view contends that we cannot know whether matter and things were created or not. For instance in his *Dialogues Concerning Natural Religion,* David Hume's (1711-1776) three interlocutors exhibit contrasts, namely "the accurate philosophical turn of Cleanthes" with "the careless skepticism of

Philo" and "the rigid inflexible orthodoxy of Demea;" the words of Philo reflect the agnostic attitude. Kant (1724-1804) in *The Critique of Pure Reason* asserts that we cannot know whether matter was created or not. (Although his ideas were agnostic in character, Kant believed in God.)

THE BIG BANG INVALIDATES BOTH AGNOSTICISM AND ATHEISM

The agnostic's assertion may be expressed by the sentence, "We cannot know whether there is a God or not, and we cannot know whether the universe has been in existence since eternity or not." He believes that nothing is or can be known. If the hypothesis "Matter had a beginning" is confirmed, the assertion that "Matter had no beginning" would be refuted and the contention "We cannot know whether it had a beginning or not" will be proved wrong. Thus, demonstration of the fact that matter had a beginning is a blow not only to atheism but also to agnosticism and skepticism. Once the hypothesis of the beginning and creation of matter has been confirmed, the atheists should abandon their disbelief and the agnostics their skepticism. If you remember the words in the sura The Prophets, verse 30, **"Will they not believe even then?"** this statement in the verse that described the Big Bang is a sign according to which the unbelievers will stick to their own convictions, or lack of conviction. It has become clear that an agnostic is no different than a man who worships the cow and the denial of the atheist is tantamount to the adoration of fire; these people base their philosophies on absolute lack of evidence, sheer delusion, total lack of logic and scientific reasoning. The claims of rationality and the so-called scientific approach of the atheists and agnostics have been debunked. In the coming pages we shall see that both in the creation of the universe, in things created within the universe and in the creation of living beings, an intelligently designed process is going on, and we shall demonstrate that the objections of agnostics and skeptics to this assertion are merely delusions.

BEFORE THE BIG BANG

It was understood that time existed in relation to the movements of matter. As matter and its movements did not exist prior to the Big Bang, time did not exist before the Big Bang. Matter and time came into being after the Big Bang. Their existence depends on each other. Roger Penrose and Stephen Hawking conclusively proved in mathematical terms that the universe had had a beginning. The Big Bang theory confirmed the hypothetical alternative suggested by atheists that the universe had to have a beginning if it had been created. In brief, the claims of atheists have been proven wrong in scientific terms and in terms of logic and reason; and yet the atheistic attitude is still prevalent today due to reasons like stubbornness, delusion and arbitrariness.

If there are two theses that negate each other, the substantiation of either of them disproves the other's argument. The contention of atheists that matter existed from eternity having thus been falsified, the fact that it was created becomes the incontestable truth, discrediting the conviction of unbelievers. Insistence of denial of this proven fact is a gross mistake and an example of inexcusable dogmatism.

> **49- To the contrary, these are clear signs in the hearts of those who are granted knowledge. None deny Our messages except the unjust.**
>
> *29-The Spider, 49*

TEACHINGS OF THE BIG BANG

The Big Bang theory confirmed that the universe and time had a beginning and that matter did not exist from eternity but was created. The assertion that the universe existed from eternity was thus debunked.

The Big Bang not only demonstrated that the universe was created by the Creator, but at the same time the false beliefs like the distribution of sovereignties among divinities, each having under his command the earth, the sun, the moon and the mountains respectively, were proved wrong. It became clear that whoever He was Who had devised the initial composition of the universe, having recourse to the Big Bang, was the Creator of everything. Thus the universe was under the exclusive control of One Single Power and this power was not shared. The universe evolved from a single point; the Author of that point was also the Originator of men, rivers, stars, butterflies, supernovas, colors, suffering and happiness, music and aesthetics. Since everything came into being emerging from the oneness, He must be the Author of that "oneness."

The Big Bang showed that the matter idolized by atheists, and the matter that makes up the entire universe is but an insignificant speck of dust, so to say. Those who witnessed that from that insignificant speck there have emerged men, beasts, plants, and the universe in its glowing colors understand that the genius was not inherent in the matter itself but in something exterior to it, i.e., in the Creator. Close your eyes and try to imagine the void and open them to behold the trees, the seas, the heavens, your own image reflected in the mirror, the food put at your disposal for your consumption and the works of art. . . . How could all these glorious things have emerged all by themselves from the dark and from one single point in the void? For intelligent minds, the creation unfolds itself not only in artistic aesthetics but also in mathematical terms. The velocity of expansion of the universe is of such a critical point that, according to the expression of a scientist, had the velocity been different at the primeval explosion less than $1/10^{18}$, the universe would have collapsed, sinking unto itself and never coming into being as it is. Likewise had the quantity of matter been less than it actually was, the universe would have scattered around, rendering the formation of the celestial bodies impossible. The force applied in the disintegration of the initial composition at the moment of creation is not only incommensurably great, but the design behind it is infinitely ingenious. Thus everything was designed by our Creator to make possible the existence of the universe. All these events are meant to show the blindfolded the infinite power of our Creator and the fact that He designed everything to the most infinitesimal detail perfectly. We are witnessing another fact through these phenomena: impossibility does not exist in the vocabulary of the Creator; it suffices Him to wish that something come about, and there it is.

CHAPTER 4

THE UNIVERSE IN GASEOUS STATE

11- Then He turned to the heavens, and it was in a gaseous state. And said to it, and the earth; "Come into existence, willingly or unwillingly." They said, "We come willingly."

41-Elucidated, 11

"*Dukhan*" is the word used in Arabic for smoke, vapor and gaseous matter. It appears that the universe was a gaseous mass before it reached the state - by the will of God - from which the universe and the earth came to be.

We know that our world, the sun and the stars did not come about immediately after the primeval explosion. For the universe was in a gaseous state before the formation of the stars. This gaseous state was initially made of hydrogen and helium. Condensation and compression shaped the planets, the earth, the sun and the stars that were but products of the gaseous state. The discovery of these phenomena has been rendered possible thanks to successive findings as a result of observations and theoretical developments. The knowledge of all contemporary communities during the time of the Prophet would not suffice for the assertion that the universe had once been in a gaseous state. The Prophet himself did not claim to be the author of the statements in the Quran as it often reminded, declaring that he is simply a messenger of God.

44

49- This is news of the unseen which we reveal to you, which neither you nor your people knew before. So, be patient. Surely the end is for the dutiful.

11-Hud, 49

VOLATILE GASES TO ONE DAY BE TRANSFORMED INTO MAGNOLIAS

It is evident that the aim of the scientific miracles expounded in the Quran was not only to perform miracles, or to teach us some scientific facts. The knowledge provided by the Quran is of paramount importance. The Book focuses our attention on the ingenuity of the creation full of marvels. The fact that it miraculously predicted events, the knowledge of which was unattainable at the time of the revelation of the Quran, is not the only important point. It also provides consequential knowledge. Take for instance sura 41, verse 11: the fact that the Quran revealed 1400 years ago that the universe was previously in a gaseous state is a miracle. But the fact that the universe was not confined to its original state, but expanded in the wake of the primeval explosion and from this there emerged - within the framework of laws imposed by God - the stars, the planets, human beings and the magnolias are also part of His miraculous creation. In witnessing these miracles unfolded in the Quran we must not lose sight of the level of knowledge of the time and what is concealed behind the expressions.

We witness perfect operation of the physical laws in creation as the smoke of gas compressed formed the stars. Gravitational power caused the smoke to contract and the stars to be born, but the gravitational force does not go to extremes, and prevents the star from becoming a black hole. What can be the agent behind this process involving infinitesimal calculations, if not the Creator? Natural laws that encompass the entire universe also apply to the formation of stars. The objectives were targeted by the Creator on the eve of creation. Gravitation is not something intelligent and sentient and cannot be the author of all these formations. What a grotesque sight we would behold had the Creator had recourse to a chain to hold fast all the celestial bodies instead of the gravitation he devised. The problem was solved by His ingenious creation of gravity. Isaac Newton (1642-1724), who considered gravity the natural law imposed by the Creator, was the first scientist to discover laws of gravity. But neither he nor any other scientist could discover the fact that the universe was in a gaseous state in the beginning, neither before the revelation of the Quran, nor 1000 years afterwards. The sun that warms us, the blue oceans, the musical notes, the taste of our dishes have their origin in that gaseous state.

11- Indeed this is a reminder,
12- For anyone who desires to bear it in mind.

80-He Frowned, 11-12

CHAPTER 5

PERFECT ORBITS

7- By the Sky with its ingeniously devised paths (orbits).
51-The Dispersing, 7

The Arabic expression *"zat-ul hubuk"* means ingeniously devised paths (orbits). The expression connotes beautifully designed formations.

The scintillating brilliance of the stars that has enchanted us ever since the beginning of our existence, the incomparable sight unfolded across the sky has always attracted our attention, overwhelming us. Numerous poems and prose works describe the charming sensations that the sky generates in the human breast. The rising and setting of the sun, the phases of the moon, the sky studded with stars give the picture of a steady state universe. The universe full of its orbits is not visible to the naked eye. Stars that move at incredible speeds seem stationary to us. The fact that all stars and heavenly bodies are in motion was only scientifically established after the discovery of the telescope and the advance of science. The number of galaxies in the universe exceeds hundreds of millions, each comprising more than one hundred million stars, some larger and some smaller than the sun. Our sun is comparably of middle size. These stars have many planets like the earth and the planets have their satellites like our moon. All these have come about after having detached from one single point. All these stars and planets and satellites have their respective orbits.

The omnipotence of God is conspicuous in His creation. God who originated everything from a single point demonstrated that the skill involved was not inherent in that point; having generated from it billions of celestial bodies displayed the endlessness of His power and

47

facility. Every one of these bodies moves in its own orbit so that the state of the universe changes every second. This variation takes place by the motion within the respective orbit of every star, planet and satellite. Every moment in the universe is a new occurrence: so is every instant of a star, a planet and a satellite.

ARGUMENT FROM MOTION

The process of motion has been the subject of study by many thinkers throughout history. Plato said that the source of motion must have been God and described the universe as being governed by a Designer who was good and beneficent. Aristotle inferred that God must be the Prime Mover, that He was the original source and cause of motion in the universe. Farabi, representative of the Islamic world, concluded that the Prime Mover was the source of all existence and that He, the Unmoved Mover, had generated the movement. The *Ihvan-ı Safa*, a philosophical-religious association of the 10th century, produced encyclopedic works. This association underlined the motion of the universe, confirmed the process of creation out of nothing, drawing attention to the order reigning in the universe and the perpetual movement that proved the existence of God. A great many Christian thinkers like Thomas Aquinas saw the motion of the universe as an evidence of a Supreme Being.

The fact that the motion in the universe is not limited to our solar system or to a handful of stars but is spread all over space is a very important point since it is also a proof of the endlessness of the power of God. The attention that the verse draws to the orbits in space is also meaningful. Galaxies move in perpetual motion; their constituent billions of stars float in their respective pathways; the planets trace elliptical orbits around the stars; and the satellites make their rounds about the planets, motion inside motion. If motion had not been devised to be an intrinsic part of matter we could not have sat comfortably in our chairs to watch TV. Nor would the sun, the earth or our very selves exist. All these formations owe their existence to the moving objects. The movement of stars in their orbits, the movement of planets around the stars have rendered our existence possible and our sipping coffee while watching television. The creation of motion in an ingenious and regular order generating chain reactions, and our observation of precise, ordered and perfect movements in galaxies of macrocosm and in atoms of microcosm are flamboyant invitations to conceive God's power and knowledge. There will certainly be people who will turn a deaf ear to these invitations. Verse 7 of the sura The Dispersing that draws our attention to the orbits is followed by the following verses:

8- You are surely caught in contradictions
9- Deviating therefrom are the deviators.

51-The Dispersing, 8-9

CHAPTER 6

ATOM AND SUBATOMIC PARTICLES

3- Not even an atom's weight in the heavens and the earth, or something smaller or greater than it is hidden from Him, but all are in a clear record.

34-Sheba, 3

The atom is the smallest particle of matter. God drew attention to the existence of the atom, laying emphasis on the importance of its knowledge. A naked eye looking at a table, a carpet, a wall or a stone cannot fully grasp the importance of the atom and the knowledge it contains. While the Quran stresses the importance of the atom, it emphasizes also the subatomic particles, **"Or something smaller or greater than."** In the expression **"greater than"** is comprised the knowledge of the greater compositions like molecules, the entirety of which is within God's ken. Men contemporary with the Prophet could not possibly have known that in the atom and subatomic particles and their compounds different types of knowledge were comprised. The Quran asserts the omniscience of God. Drawing attention to the existence of the atom and the subatomic particles is relevant to the present day information that physics has discovered. The knowledge obtained today by means of cosmological physics studying the science of the origin and structure of the universe are interrelated with the data of atomic physics. Another miraculous sign of the Quran is its referring to the weight (*miskale* in Arabic) of the atom wherever the word *"zerre"* (atom) is mentioned.

FROM VAST TO SMALLEST MAGNITUDES

Imagine you are eating a pizza with great relish. What are its ingredients? Sausage, cheese, mushrooms, tomatoes and flour. What are the constituents of these sausages, cheeses, mushrooms and tomatoes and what are the constituents of the constituents? This series of questions leads us to molecules. The molecules themselves are made up of atoms such as oxygen, hydrogen and carbon. Then come protons and electrons, together forming eventually the nucleus of the atom...

The entire universe is made of matter or energy. From the trunk of a tree to its leaves, from the hands of a human being to his eyes, from golden ornaments to cotton dresses, everything is matter. The atom is the individual structure that constitutes the basic unit of any chemical element. The proton is an elementary particle that is the positively charged constituent of ordinary matter, and, like the neutron, is the building stone of atomic nuclei. The electron is an elementary particle that is the negatively charged constituent of ordinary matter. These are the recent discoveries of science that led us to the discovery of the television, computer, Internet, etc. Take, for instance, a grain of sand in the palm, which is assumed to be the simplest matter, and think of the quadrillion of atoms it contains; quadrillions of atoms you could not finish counting throughout the span of your lifetime. Imagine that each of these atoms has its electrons moving around the nuclei, like the planets making their rounds around the sun. A quadrillion solar systems contained within a grain of sand or piece of rock in your palm. An intelligent mind will readily conceive that there is nothing simple in the universe. Be it a pizza or a rock, suppose that you fancy recomposing them. To embark on such a huge project, you must go back to the very beginning, to the primeval explosion, and repeat the process. In this odyssey, you will run into atoms, cornerstones of the universe, entailing the existence of protons, electrons and neutrons; then you will be faced by the gaseous substance made of hydrogen and helium; these will be followed by stars and atoms produced in these stars which will one day be transformed into the mushrooms, cheese and tomatoes of our pizza. In order to really make a pizza, we need to create the entire universe with all the stages it had.

The more you delve into the study of the atom the greater becomes your wonder. Suppose a penny on the table is the nucleus of an atom. The orbit that the electron would trace around it would be at a distance of 2-3 km. What is in between? The distance between the two, i.e., the nucleus and the electrons, is a vacuum. In other words, a piece of rock held in our hand contains in it quadrillions of solar systems, but 99.99% of it is a vacuum. Interesting, isn't it?

While we observed the fact that the universe was replete with orbits as described in the verse (51-The Dispersing, 7), we witnessed the infinitude of God's power and magnitude. This divine power is demonstrated through more than one hundred million galaxies, more than a hundred million stars contained in each, countless planets and satellites and their quadrillions of devised orbits. A grain of sand, then, contains quadrillions of miniature replicas of the solar system where electrons dance around the nuclei of quadrillions of atoms. What should one deduce from this? To begin with, the incommensurable magnitude of our Creator's power is also observed in the depth of matter. Endless vastness has been created from these particles. The motion of the atom is the same movement around the center of limitless magnitudes. The system in any given galaxy and the one forming a particle of dust is the same system. The Author of that speck of dust is also the Author of the universe. All these phenomena point to the immensity of His power and to the order reigning in the universe, as well as to the fact that nothing is casual in His creation. The creation of the smallest and of the biggest is equal for Him. The creation of a point containing trillions of atoms and of immense space is equal for Him and difficulty is a notion not applicable for Him. There is no limit to His wisdom and power.

27- And if all the trees on earth were made into pens, and the ocean supplied the ink, augmented by seven more oceans, the words of God would not run out. God is indeed Almighty and Wise.

31-Luqmaan, 27

INFINITESIMAL CONTENTS OF ATOMS

The nucleus of the atom contains protons charged with positive electricity. These positive charges repel each other. The miracle of creation occurs when protons adhere to each other forming a single point. The power that confines the protons repelling each other and the neutrons within a single point is immense; it is called strong nuclear force. The elementary particles containing this force are referred to with the French epithet *"gluons"* meaning "sticky" (The immense destructive energy of the atomic bomb was obtained by the use of this force). God, who devised everything in the universe with mathematical precision, has also conceived this immense force with mathematical exactitude. This force adheres the mutually repelling protons to each other; had the power been weaker or stronger, the protons could disintegrate or it could cause the intrusion of protons and neutrons into each other.

The atomic bomb demonstrated tragically the immense power of the atom. It also showed that one of the factors that contributed to our worldly existence is its intrinsic balance. Thanks to the well-adjusted order reigning in this field, matter does not disintegrate all of a sudden, giving rise to noxious effects of radiation. Another important factor that contributes to the stability of the atom is the weak force inherent in it. This force is particularly important in establishing the balance of the nuclei that comprise an excessive number of neutrons and protons.

Electromagnetic force is another factor contributing to the existence of atom. It is this force that brings about the attraction of oppositely charged particles and the repulsion of particles having like electric charges. This has made possible the coming together of the protons and electrons. However, this coming together has its limits. Electrons do not stick to the protons while they move at a breathtaking speed around the nucleus in their orbits. The repulsion of negatively charged electrons turning in succession, and the attraction of the electrons by the protons changes nothing. In this way, the electron does not stick to the proton that attracts it, nor is it moved away. The Creator of this system, of these electrons, deprived of consciousness, is undoubtedly the Creator of matter, atoms, electrons, etc. Let us make an experiment as conscious human beings. Imagine tying a rope around the waists of three or four people while others stand in the middle of the circle. Let those in the middle try to pull the tied people towards themselves while the outside people are circumnavigating the center, and let the people making the circle push each other and those in the center as well, resembling the movement within the nucleus of an atom. We certainly do not expect them to make thousands of rotations per second like an electron. Can reasonable human beings continue to imitate the motion of an atom for the length of one minute? And imagine for an instant that we venture to imitate the model of an atom with 3 or 4 orbits and that there are three or four rotations around the symbolic nucleus. In addition to this, suppose that sumo wrestlers representing the *gluons* with adhesive properties within the nucleus try to keep those pulling the rope while pushing each other at their places. What an awkward experience this would be! How have the protons and electrons been performing this feast over and over again endlessly for eons and eons with the quadrillions of atoms contained in a small rock?

These atoms existing in the universe and in our bodies were produced long ago in supernovas. The calcium in our teeth, the carbon that our pizza contains, and the iron atoms in our body are products of stars of high temperatures. These raw materials of the universe are prepared in the laboratory of these stars before being transformed into pizzas, water, blood, flesh, teeth and eyes.

This is not a story of an adventure taking place far away from us. Our hands, hair, eyes, our very food and the chair we sit on, everything is performing this process indiscriminately. Our Creator is perpetuating this process incessantly with His omnipotence and omniscience. All these movements of the atom and the energy inherent in it are what perpetuate our existence.

2- To Him belongs the dominion of the heavens and the earth. No son has He begotten, nor has He a partner in His dominion. It is He who created all things, and ordered them in exact measure.

25-The Distinguisher, 2

WHAT ELSE?

It is estimated that there are some 10^{80} particles in the universe. Add 80 zeros after 1 to have an idea of this magnitude. These particles function thanks to complex, ingeniously devised and balanced forces. So do the comets, supernovas and planets, a consequence of the harmonious interaction of these particles. What else must one bring forth to give an idea of the power and design lying behind all these?

In this chapter, I tried to outline the structure of an atom and emphasize that it was extremely complex, perfect and ingeniously devised. Were we to push our exploration further, our wonder would be much greater. The emergence of elementary particles in the wake of the Big Bang is the result of an intelligent design. The heat at every instant during the explosion, the number of atomic particles, the forces involved in every stage and their intensities have been carefully planned. Any change in these values would be the end of existence, of galaxies and atoms, and would end up in chaos. The consequence of this primeval explosion was not chaos as might be expected, but a perfect harmony, the work of the Creator, governed by physical laws, a perfect order reigning among galaxies and atoms.

Tiny units of split seconds had their function to perform in the creation of the universe. Had the particles and anti-particles been created in equal number, all of them would be destroyed when the temperature fell below one billion degrees, leaving behind nothing but radiation. The very fact of our existence is evidence to the contrary. The number of electrons had to be somewhat more than the number of positrons and the number of protons should exceed the number of anti-protons and the figure representing the neutrons should be superior to the number of anti-neutrons.

Every particle had to come into being at a predetermined velocity, temperature and time sequence. The primeval explosion was designed in such a way that it was followed by an evolution that reflected the Creator's ingenious artistry. We have touched on the structure of the atom and the formation of atomic particles after the primeval explosion. The more one delves into the mystery of creation the more one's wonder and amazement increase. The actual magnificence of the atom, the creation of particles of the atom by an intelligent design and the transformation of the particles into atoms are beyond the grasp of the intellect. If 10^{80} particles, with mutually attracting and repulsing electricity charges, had not been transformed into atoms in a finely balanced manner, neither the human ego, nor the book we read, nor the earth we inhabit would exist.

Whether we ascend to the heavens or descend to the microscopic depths, we encounter the same perfection and immensity of God's work and design.

120- To God do belong the dominion of the heavens and the earth, and all that there is therein, and it is He who has power over all things.

5-The Feast, 120

CHAPTER 7

BLACK HOLES:
MIGHTY OATH

75- So, I swear by the place where the stars fall.
76- And that is indeed a mighty oath, if you but knew.
56-The Inevitable, 75-76

The expression "place where... fall" (*mawqi*) also mentioned in the sura, The Cave (*Kehf*), verse 53, means the place where the sinners fall, i.e., hell. The root of this word is "*WaQa'Aa*" and it means the action of falling, a happening and an incidence.

Stars perpetuate their existence with hydrogen bombs exploding in them. During these explosions a portion of matter is transferred into energy, emitting heat of immeasurably high temperature. Conversion of one gram of matter into energy may be obtained by burning two million kilograms of coal. For instance, in our sun-which is but a star of medium size-four billion kilograms of matter are converted into energy every second. A star uses but a small portion of its matter as fuel, and when this fuel is exhausted, it dies off. The lifetime that God designed for the living had also been apportioned for the stars. As new stars are born somewhere in the universe, the old ones bid farewell, as if saying: "We pass away, but our Creator is for ever abiding and his Creation is perpetual."

FALLING OF STARS AND MIGHTY OATH

The place where the stars fall is stressed by an oath coupled with the epithet "mighty." We shall see incommensurately great mathematical figures in connection with the death of stars whose fuel is exhausted.

56

The great numerical values in the universe come about at the death of stars to which reference is made with the following words in the Quran, **"And that is indeed a mighty oath, if you but knew."**

Everybody versed in physics knows that one of the most interesting phenomena in the universe is the black hole that comes about in the wake of the death of massive stars whose magnitudes are greater than three times the size of our sun. Having depleted their fuel, these cosmic bodies die, collapsing inward upon themselves. The giant stars that contract possess a great gravitational force. This force is so immense that even light, with its velocity of approximately 300,000 km/sec, cannot escape it; these black holes absorb even the light that passes by. Later on, a great many planets and stars are attracted by this gravitational force. Black holes also constitute **"the place where the stars fall."** The existence of black holes is deduced from the fact that they attract as whirlpools the matter of other nearby stars and emit X-rays, swallowing all the lights and stars around. The most interesting studies of Stephen Hawking are on black holes. Stephen Hawking discovered the radiation that came to be called the Hawking Radiation by establishing the fact that a black hole could emit radiation while conforming to the physical laws of energy.

The black holes formed by the collapse of stars by their gravitational force are in perfect conformity with verses 75-76 of the sura, The Inevitable. At the time of the descent of the Quran, the end of a star by being transformed into a black hole was something unknown. A star turning into a black hole and the stages it goes through are very interesting phenomena.

Stars that run out of fuel do not immediately collapse. They grow in size at first, as if inflated. Their temperature, around 15 million degrees, rises up to 100 million degrees. They are first transformed into red giants or super giants. The area covered by a super giant is so vast that it can easily contain more than sixty million suns. The immensity of these numerical values is reminiscent of the magnitudes indicated in 76th verse of the sura.

Some of the supernovas contract and turn into white dwarf stars whose mass equal the size of a human being but weigh 10 million kilograms. Still greater stars become neutron stars (pulsars), stars supposed to form in the final stage of the stellar evolution; these consist of a super dense mass mainly of neutrons having a strong attractive force. The matter in the neutron stars is extremely dense. Just to give you an idea, a teaspoonful of this matter would weigh one billion tons.

While all these spectacular events are taking place, we, on our planet, continue to sleep, run and talk, quite unaware of them. So is our life: rendered possible by forces beyond our ken.

CHAPTER 8

PULSARS

1- By the heavens and The Knocker.
2- How will you comprehend what the The Knocker is?
3- It's a piercing star.

86-The Knocker, 1-3

The word "*Tariq*" stems from the root "*TaRaQa*" meaning "knocking, striking." In many translations of the Quran this word was taken for a name and left untranslated. The word may also mean "to pulsate" like a beating heart, from which the word "pulsar" is derived, denoting an object that is far away in space, and like a star produces a regular radio signal.

LITTLE GREEN MEN OF THE UNIVERSE

In 1967 Jocellyn Bell accidentally stumbled on a gravity time warp a million times greater than that produced by the sun. The object she detected was emitting regular pulses. These pulses were reminiscent of heart-beats. At the time, such a pulsating object was not known to exist in space. At first, it was concluded that these signals might well have been propagated by intelligent beings, inhabitants of other planets. Invitation cards were printed, the media were notified and a seminar was arranged. LGM (Little Green Men) signified that intelligent creatures had been detected and were contacted by radio signals. Not long after, the source of the signals in question was discovered: it was a spinning neutron star, an object whose velocity was incommensurably great. The neutron star had another name: "pulsar." Bell's discovery failed to establish contact with the inhabitants of space, but she had found pulsars. The words "pulsar" and "pulsating" seem to accord with the word *Tariq* of the Quran, which means "knocker."

CAN YOU COMPREHEND WHAT A PULSAR IS?

In the second verse of the sura, The Knocker, we read: **"How will you comprehend what The Knocker is?"** A spoonful of matter taken from a pulsar would weigh one billion tons. Were we to depose a small particle of it on earth, the particle would pierce it and end up in its center. Just think of it, a spoonful of any matter on earth hardly weighing more than a few grams! This shows how difficult it is to conceive of a pulsar. A pulsar is produced by the compression of stars a couple of times bigger than the sun. The diameter of a pulsar can be about 15-20 km. Were we to compress our world in a like manner, we would have a sphere of 100 meters of diameter. It takes the earth 24 hours to rotate around its own axis, whereas the pulsar rotates around its own axis many times per second; all these things show how difficult it is to comprehend this striking, pulsating star.

LET'S SEE IF YOU CAN WORK A MIRACLE

Some have tried to identify the star mentioned in the verse and have claimed it to be a certain celestial body, like Saturn or Venus. Mustafa Mlivo, who claims these assumptions are not correct and that *"Tariq"* is none other than a pulsar, says the following:
Characteristics of the celestial object mentioned in 86:1-3 are:

1- It pulsates (knocks);
2- It is a star;
3- It penetrates, pierces, drills.

None of the solar system planets meets all those criteria because:

A- None of the planets produces pulsations that give the impression of knocking, beating.
B- None of them is a star. They are cold celestial bodies.

C- None of them produces such an intensive radiation.

As one can see, the Quran had already mentioned a star that was to be discovered. This star was indeed discovered, but in the year 1970. Since the concept of a "pulsating star" could not be imagined at that time, it was rendered in translation as it stood, i.e., "*Tariq*," the meaning of it being explained in footnotes, in dictionaries and interpretations.

The Quran whose every sentence, every word is based on the finest of meanings, wherein lie hidden realms still to be discovered. The more we study the Quran, the more we are enlightened, the more we learn.

CHAPTER 9

ATTRACTION AND MOTION

15- I swear by those that recede
16- By flowing that goes to nest

81-The Rolling, 15-16

To gain clearer insight into the meaning of these verses, let us see first the signification of the words used in Arabic. The Arabic word *"hunnes"* that we translate with the expression "Those that recede" also has the connotation of "shrinking," "sinking," "retrogression" and "regression." On the other hand, the Arabic word *"kunnes"* means "to follow a definite itinerary," "to return home" and also "nest of a moving object." And the word "flowing" in the 16th verse is expressed by the word *"jariye."*

We are inextricably bound by an indefinite number of scientific laws in our daily life, among which are the law of gravitation, the law of motion, the law of thermodynamics, etc. While we eat or relieve ourselves we are subject to the law of gravitation. When astronauts eat and relieve themselves in space, they have to take recourse to special arrangements in order to satisfy their demands, because their bodies were created according to the standards of the earth gravitation.

Discoveries of scientists are not discoveries of the nonexistent, as their function is to throw light on those things that already exist. Gravitational force has always existed in the universe. But it fell to the lot of Isaac Newton (1642-1727) to clarify it by describing it with mathematical formulas. Newton demonstrated by the law of gravitation that God's creation was based on the law of gravity, which governs the stars, the earth, the moon, and that man's erect posture was not a haphazard development, but was related to the gravitational force inherent in matter.

Referring to the fine balances of the universe, Isaac Newton said that the author of this extremely sensitive system, composed of the sun, the planets and the comets, can only be a Creator endowed with intelligence and power. He, whom we call our omniscient Lord, is the ruler of all these things, His dominion embraces all.

UNIVERSAL MATHEMATICS

The Quran often speaks of the fact that God created everything within a given measure. This means that everything in the universe is governed by mathematics. The thing made to measure is commensurable, measurable by a given standard and can be expressed in mathematical terms. Newton corrected the results that Kepler and Galileo had reached, gave them precision and proved that the material universe could be explained in mathematical terms.

In the 1700s science took cognizance of the importance of the gravitational force. God alluded in the Quran in the 600s to the law of gravitation, to which He had had recourse in His creation. In the verses mentioned at the head of this chapter, one can see the allusion to attraction and to the balance between attraction and motion. The sun and the nucleus of the atom are in states of recession and retrogression, the nucleus attracting electrons and the sun attracting planets. The nuclei, which have already retrograded in the center, want to integrate the electrons, and the sun acts likewise by drawing the planets unto themselves by applying forces that cause them to recede. The word "*hunnes*" mentioned in verse 15 of the sura, The Rolling, can easily be claimed to be signifying attraction.

Despite the attraction by the nucleus of the atom, electrons do not adhere to the nucleus. Likewise, the planets do not come into contact with the sun despite the latter's gravitational force. It is the motion of electrons and planets that prevent the electrons from fusing to the nucleus and the planets to the sun. The word "*jariye*" used in verse 16 of sura The Rolling signifies flowing, and is a perfect choice since it is the factor that prevents adhesion. Had the electrons and planets tended to adhere to the nucleus and to the sun respectively, no planet, no solar system, no orbit, no vital energy, and no majesty in the creation would exist. If the electrons and planets were to scatter in defiance of the "*hunnes*," having been released from the gravitational force, again, neither galaxies, nor the animal kingdom, nor vegetation, nor we would exist. Thanks to these two separate phenomena, electrons return to their orbits, their homes, and planets where they belong, to move in their orbits. This is marvelously expressed with the word "*kunnes*" in verse 16. The Quran uses the word "*hunnes*" to signify attraction, and motion by the word "*jariye*" that resists against the force of attraction and to be within the orbit again by the word "*kunnes.*" Thus, in a period when there was no term to express attraction, the Quran had already revealed the phenomena that depended on attraction.

MARVELS FROM ATOMS TO STARS

As we already have seen, God testifies under oath to pull our attention to certain events or phenomena. The oaths we see pronounced in verses point to the flawless creations of God, and the miraculous announcements in the Quran for minds cleansed from stubbornness.

Protons exert attraction in the innumerable nuclei of atoms in our body while the electrons oppose this force while remaining within the orbit. These happenings in the atom are in continuous and harmonious activity thanks to the electromagnetic force and to the other forces of the atom. If the atoms of our body we call "I" were to stick to the chair we are sitting in and to integrate with the ground upon which we stretch out, there would no longer be an entity called "I." Again, if the electrons of the chair we are sitting on collided with the electrons of our body, giving rise to chaos, could we have ever existed? No. The gravitational force and the motion, as well as other forces, harmoniously contribute to our being.

Forces that have come about, and everything in Creation, remind us of God.

CHAPTER 10

ALL AFLOAT IN ORBITS

33- It is He who created the night and the day, and the sun, and the moon; each of them floating in an orbit.

21-The Prophets, 33

The word expressing totality in the Arabic language is "*kullu*" while the Arabic expression "*tasniya*" refers to any two objects. In the verse reference is made to the motion of two celestial bodies, namely the sun and the moon. However, the reason why "*tasniya*" is not used indicates that there should be more than two objects. If we suppose that the night and the day take place on the earth, the other object should be the earth. The Arabic word "*falak*" is used in Arabic to denote the orbit traced by stars and planets.

THE MIRACLE IN THE USE OF
EVERY SINGLE WORD

As one can see, every single word and suffix has been carefully selected. The Arabic equivalent of the expression "to float" is "*sabaha.*" Maurice Bucaille says the harmony of the movements of the sun, the moon and the earth can be expressed as follows: "*The Arabic verb 'sabaha' refers to displacement of an object by its own movement. The meanings of this verb converge on displacement referring to the motion of the object by itself. When displacement takes place in water, the movement refers to the act of floating; when it is on land the displacement takes place by the movement of the object's own legs. If, on the other hand, this displacement occurs in space, the motion intended can be described*

only by the etymological sense of the word. Thus, 'sabaha' should be con-
ceived as a motion in a self-generating act. The moon rotates around its
axis within a space of time equal to its revolution around the earth; that
is 29.5 days. So what we see is always the same face of the moon. The sun
turns about its axis within 25 days approximately. The word 'sabaha'
that describes the motions of the sun and the moon conforms to the find-
ings of recent scientific data. This fact could not have been fancied by a
human being in the 7th century, regardless of his erudition."

THE SOLAR SYSTEM

The motions of the sun and the moon and the earth continue without
the slightest interference with our life. On the other hand, all the phenomena are brought about to make life on earth and diversity possible.
The earth revolves about the sun, at an angle of inclination of 23
degrees and 27 minutes. The seasons evolve upon the earth thanks to
this inclination upon which depends also the system of growth of plants.

The velocity of rotation of the earth about its axis attains 1670 km.
If the earth did not rotate, its surface facing the sun would be exposed
to continuous light while the rear would be in perpetual darkness. In
such a world, neither vegetation nor beings could exist.

**40- Neither can the sun overtake the moon, nor does the
night precede the day. Each of them is floating in an orbit.**

36-Ya-Seen, 40

All the motions of the sun, the moon and the earth continue in
perfect harmony. Everything is so excellently arranged that even
Jupiter, the largest planet in the solar system, contributes to the life
on earth. Astronomer George Wetherill, in his article on Jupiter, says
that had there been no planet of a magnitude equal to the size of
Jupiter, the earth would have had one thousand times more exposure
to stray meteors and comets, and that if Jupiter were not at the place
where it happened to be, we could not have been here now to probe
into the mystery of the origin of the solar system.

No matter where we turn, we come across splendors, infinitesimal
calculations and works of art provided. Of course, we meditate on

God's creation using our intelligence. Our Creator displays the evidences of His omnipotence and omniscience and His compassion everywhere in the universe.

190- Surely, in the creation of the heavens and the earth, and the alteration of night and day, there are signs for those who posses intelligence.

191- They remember God while standing, sitting, and lying on their sides. And contemplate on the creation of the heavens and the earth: "Our Lord, You did not create all this in vain. Be You glorified. Protect us from the torment of the fire."

3-The Family of Imran, 190-191

CHAPTER 11

CREATION IN PAIRS

36- Glory be to the One, who created in pairs all things that the earth produces, as well as themselves, and other things they do not know.

36-Ya-Seen, 36

The Arabic word *"azvaj"* is the plural of *"zavj"* meaning "pairs," "matches," "partners." There are three sorts of pairs in the Creation as described in the verse:

a- Pairs that grow from the earth, i.e., plants that have species of differentiated sex;

b- Human pairs, males and females. Also some included human characteristics like bravery / cowardice; love / hate; generosity / stinginess, etc.

c- Pairs unknown: men did not know anything about the creation in pairs at the time of the descent of the Quran. In this section we shall be dealing with the latter in particular.

THE DISCOVERY THAT WON
THE NOBEL PRIZE AWARD

The atom lies at the basis of all matter in the universe. A study of this smallest piece of matter may give an idea about the creation of everything in pairs (partners). As research conducted on the structure of the atom gained momentum, it became clear that the constituents of elementary particles were not limited to protons, neutrons and electrons and that their compositions were of a more complex nature and an unerring precision. Creation in pairs is also valid for elementary particles.

A proton has its anti-proton, an electron is coupled with a positron, and a neutron possesses an anti-neutron. The creation of matter in pairs is one of the discoveries of towering importance of physics. Paul Dirac, a British scientist, was awarded the Nobel Prize in 1933 for his discovery in this field. His discovery (Parity) led to the discovery of the fact that matter has an anti-matter.

God's ingenious calculation is also seen in the numbers of protons, electrons, and neutrons, and of their respective pairs. Let us take as an example the electron and its counterpart, the positron. When these two get together, energy is generated. If there were 15 units of positron versus 10 units of electrons, 10 units of electrons and 10 units of positrons would be eliminated leaving behind 5 units of positron. If their numbers were equal, there would emerge only energy, leaving behind no electrons or positrons. The survival of protons, electrons and neutrons depends on the quantities higher than their respective pairs, while the numerical balance between electrons, protons and neutrons is also important. For example, if the number of electrons were less than the number of protons, there would be no life in the universe. All the fine calculations in our existence are based on this fact. Had one single formation of thousands of phenomena been left to chance, we would not have been on our planet today. We exist thanks to the omniscience of our Creator Who controls everything through His omnipotence.

CONTRIBUTION TO UNITY OF POLARITY

As I have already pointed out, the fact that the description of scientific phenomena in the Quran could not be accounted for by the knowledge acquired at the time of the Prophet is not the only outstanding point. This fact is certainly very important. However, our wonder becomes even greater when we examine the scientific data provided in the verses of the Quran which reflect God's omnipotence, art, science and design.

For instance, the statement in sura 21, verse 30 that the universe was created from an integrated mass, as the raw material of the heavens and the earth were closed up before God split them, could not possibly be the word of a mortal at the time of the Prophet. This also proved that God had created the matter, the universe and that He had preset objectives in His mind. Therefore, as we proceed, I shall try to point to the scientific miracles in the verses of the Quran as well as to the fact that these things testified to His existence and the splendor of His art. In brief, as important as the existence of the miracles themselves is the inspiration displayed by the miracles.

This also holds true of course for the verses announcing that the material world was created in pairs. At the time of the descent of the Quran the creation of the universe in pairs and the significant role of this phenomenon could not possibly have been known. Important as this is, the gamut of wonders ranging from the forces to the balance between the protons and anti-protons, between neutrons and anti-neutrons are also important. The Quran's concern is not merely to stress the miracle as such, but also to draw attention to the creation in pairs so that we may have a better insight into the wonders of the creation.

The importance of creation in pairs in the universe gained momentum with the discovery of quarks within the protons and neutrons as well. Laboratory research has made it clear that quarks and leptons (another subatomic particle) emerged in pairs. When the quark called "Bottom" was discovered after such quarks as "Up," "Down," "Charm" and "Strange," the consciousness of creation in pairs was so widespread among scientists that the name "Top" was given to a quark before even it was discovered. In the year 1994, the discovery of the quark "Top" was announced. The research carried out in the Fermi labs in the USA resulted in the discovery of "Top," that paired up with the quark called "Bottom."

All paired creations contribute to the integral order of the universe. The quarks "Up" and "Down," the protons and antiprotons, the positive and negative electricity charges in the universe have no consciousness. All these well-ordered and predetermined formations are created in a microcosm that, in turn, renders possible the formation of galaxies, stars, planets, plants, the animal kingdom and humankind. Opposite pairs of forces and opposite pairs of particles owe their existence to an Omnipotent Power. The colorful and marvelous universe based on the formation of opposite pairs of force bars the possibility of chaos. Whoever the author of the creation and the designer of ultimate ends may have been, it was He who generated the pairs of particles and forces and set these opposite particles and forces to operate in a harmonious unity until the targets are reached. For those who take heed the evidence is clear.

49- And We created pairs of everything that you may contemplate.

51-The Dispersing, 49

CHAPTER 12

RELATIVITY OF TIME
ANNOUNCED 1400
YEARS AGO

4- To Him ascend the angels and the spirit in a day the measure of which is fifty thousand years.

70-The Heights, 4

5- He regulates all affairs from the heaven to the earth. Then they ascend to Him in a day, the measure of which is a thousand years as you count.

32-The Prostration, 5

Throughout history, "time" was assumed to apply equally in every imaginable spot in the universe and in every medium. If we consider this conception, we can see the radical change that the above verses brought. The Quran said that, according to circumstances, the "day" concept might equal even up to fifty thousand years. These verses which must have encountered objections have been elucidated in the twentieth century and shed light on important truths.

The theory of relativity is Einstein's best known discovery. However, many people whose interests are not in any way related to physics are at a loss to understand what this theory signifies. The Quran had already touched on these facts 1400 years ago. Einstein's theory of relativity has two main divisions, namely the special theory of relativity and the general theory of relativity.

According to Einstein, time would pass more slowly for somebody driving a vehicle at a speed close to the velocity of light. In a medium in which an inhabitant of the earth passes one hundred days, it may take a person fifty days to displace at a speed nearing the propagation speed of light. This finding is the most interesting fact of the relativity theory. Time slows down in direct proportion with speed. Time is therefore a relative conception, as indicated in the Quran. Hours differ and days are conceived differently according to the medium, place and speed involved.

The general theory of relativity deals with gravitational fields and tries to demonstrate that time is slower in the fields of greater gravitation. A man walking on the surface of the sun will see that his clock runs more slowly, as do the biological and anatomical functions and all the motions in terms of his atoms. Recent experiments have corroborated this fact. One of these experiments was conducted in the British National Institute of Physics. John Laverty, researcher, synchronized two clocks indicating the exact time (two clocks of optimum perfection; error of precision in the course of a space of time of 300,000 years would be not more than 1 second). One of these clocks was kept at a laboratory in London; the other was taken aboard an airplane shuttling between London and China. The high altitude at which the aircraft flies is subject to a lower gravitational force. In other words, time was expected to pass at a faster rate aboard a plane in conformity with the general relativity theory. There is not so great a difference in terms of gravity between someone treading upon the earth and someone flying in the air. This difference could only be established by a precision instrument. It was established that the clock aboard the aircraft had a greater speed, one per fifty five billion seconds. This experiment is one of the proofs of the relativity of time. According to the prevailing prejudice, there should not be any difference between the two clocks. This supports the dispelling of prejudices as foreseen in the Quran. Had it been possible to make this experiment on a planet with greater gravitational force, there would be no need for precision instruments to measure the difference, since normal watches could do the job.

THE USE OF THE WORD "DAY" IN THE QURAN

Verse 5 of the sura The Prostration and Verse 4 of the sura The Heights not only point to the relativity of time, but give also a clear meaning of the Arabic word "*yawm*" that denotes not only the space of time of one day - which comprises 24 hours - but also a certain period of time. This makes it easier to understand the six "*yawm*"s mentioned in the Quran (See: 7-The Purgatory, 54; 11-Hud, 7; 10-Jonah, 3; 25-The Distinguisher, 59; 32-The Prostration, 4; 57-Iron, 4.) Before the creation of the universe and the world there was no notion of "day," a period of 24 hours. Therefore, the six "*yawm*"s must be understood as six "periods."

This gives a clue to the Jews and Christians for the interpretation of the Biblical account according to which the world was created in six days. Findings in the domain of space physics show that the universe and our world passed through many stages, from a gaseous state to galaxies, to the formation of the atmosphere surrounding the Earth, and of waters and metals. The fact that the Quran refers to the stages that the process of creation went through is also better understood by modern cosmology.

If we remember the stories of creation of ancient Egypt, China and India, we encounter wild fancies such as a universe standing on a tortoise or as an eternally existing entity. None of the past civilizations had made any reference to the stages of this evolution. This message of the Quran contributes to a correct interpretation of Biblical exegeses of the concept of day.

The message in the Bible that reads: "*And on the seventh day God finished His work that He had done, and He rested on the seventh day from all His work that He had done.*" (Genesis 2, 2) was thus corrected, as fatigue was certainly out of the question for God.

38- We created the heavens and the earth, and all that lies between them in six days, and no fatigue touched us.

50-Qaf, 38

CONTRIBUTION OF THE RELATIVITY THEORY

Einstein postulated that the concept of time was relative. For Kant time was an innate function of reason. He contended that the perception of time was an *a priori* category. Einstein's physics was henceforth the science that integrated time and space, so that, instead of space we had now space-time.

There is something that must not escape attention, however: the perception of time is achieved by the intellect. Since according to our estimation, just as the special relativity theory establishes that velocity makes time relative and the general relativity theory postulates that gravity makes time relative, one should elaborate on "the intellect's relativity" which posits that the intellect's perception manner would render the relative perception of time. Like a key that fits the lock, our intellect also has the capacity of perceiving time and the universe. That is (1) time exists in the universe, (2) and the intellect is created with *a priori abilities to perceive time and the universe.* The two processes are coexistent, just like the coexistence of the world seen by us and the eyes.

It seems to us only fair to add the intellect's perception factor to Einstein's concepts relating velocity and gravity and time. Comprehension of time's relativity will contribute to a better understanding of the Quran. For instance, it is said in the Quran that the dead will think when resurrected that their span on the earth had been very brief. Once time's relativity has been conceived, the puzzling question of the time to elapse from one's death till the Day of Judgment will be clear. Such questions for the inquisitive mind that sees the time upon the earth as the only valid time regardless of the attending circumstances will find their answer, once time's relativity is understood. Given the fact that a deceased person is outside the confines of the temporal dimensions of the earth, the time to elapse after his death, regardless of its actual duration, would be of no consequence.

45- On the day when He gathers them, it will appear to them as if they had tarried an hour of a day...

10-Jonah, 45

112- He said: "How many years did you stay on earth?"
113- They said: "We stayed a day or part of a day, ask those who account."

23-The Believers, 112-113

ANYONE AMONG US TIRED OF WAITING FOR EONS?

The reason why the fifteen billion years that elapsed from the moment the universe was created until the creation of man was made clear by time's relativity. In a different context, fifteen billion years may be conceived as one minute or even less. The length of its duration depends on our perception and standpoint.

Scientists, based on the most recent and accurate calculations, assert that approximately fifteen billion years have elapsed since the creation of the universe until this very moment. Is there anyone who feels tired of waiting for eons? The evident answer being in the negative, the time the departed will have to wait as from their decease until resurrection will not cause anxiety in them. Comprehension of time's relativity renders possible the solution of many problems believed to be beyond the grasp of the intellect.

PROOF FROM NECESSARY VERSUS POSSIBLE BEING

A host of celebrated philosophers like Avicenna, Farabi, Taftazani and Jurjani had recourse to this argument in proving God's existence. They asserted that all the possible creatures upon the earth could not exist by themselves as they owed their existence to a Creator. "The created" requires a Creator while God, "the Self-Existent" (whose existence is a necessity) does not need a creator. The created is a product of causality; their existence or non-existence are within the confines of possibility. To think of the non-existence of the existent poses no contradiction. However, this does not hold true for the Self-Existing, God; otherwise the contradiction would be evident. Philosophers like Leibniz argued in like manner the principle of "Sufficient Reason." According to him, the universe is made of possible beings. The universe itself is a possibility. If we try to trace back the chain of causality (which is impossible) until the infinite this would not explain the universe. Yes, the universe is a possibility but requires a Sufficient Reason outside its confines.

To allege that the reasons may be traced back to the infinite would mean that we were created after eternity. But since eternity is endless there would be no question of any lapse of time after eternity; if there has been a chain of causality, it would necessarily follow that it had had an end. If there had been a chain of causality that came to an end, it would prove the existence of a "first cause." There may be persons who would find the existence of a first cause difficult to grasp. On the other hand, an eternal chain of causes would be a self-contradiction. Absurd and incomprehensible are not the same thing. For instance, the structure of a space-shuttle may be incomprehensible for us, but we cannot deny its existence. The number 5 cannot be higher than the number 10; that is absurd. As the contrary is absurd (that the eternal chain of causes has led to this point), the existence of a first cause is a necessity (although there are those who contend that this argument is "beyond comprehension").

What I propose to do is to reformulate the approaches of a series of thinkers from Avicenna to Leibniz in the light of scientific data obtained in the twentieth century in a richer and more scientific context. Findings related to the relativity theory may be used for this end. That the perfect use of time existing only in relative terms in the universe, in the formation of the universal targets, can only be grasped by the existence of an Absolute and Indispensable Regulator, that the existence of time can only be explained in a satisfactory way by the Cause behind the creation of time, that the harmony existing between time and intellect can be imagined to exist by the presence of a Regulator outside the confines of time and intellect and that even time is a possibility depending on a Creator should be integrated for use with the explanation of the "proof from necessary versus possible beings."

81- And He shows you His signs: Then which of the signs of God will you deny?

40-The Believer, 81

CHAPTER 13

THE SUN ALSO MOVES ALONG

38- And the Sun moves on to its destination. That is the ordinance of the Mighty, the Knower.

36-Ya-Seen, 38

For a long time in the past men thought that the earth was stationary and that the sun revolved around the earth. Later Copernicus, Kepler and Galileo postulated the theory that the sun was stationary and that the earth revolved about the sun.

It was even later, thanks to sophisticated telescopes and the accumulation of cosmological data, that it was concluded that the sun was moving as well and the earth revolved about the sun in motion. Despite the fact that it took science this long, this motion of the sun had already been told 1400 years ago in the Quran. Contrary to the assertion that the sun traced a vicious circle about the earth or that it was stationary, the 38th verse of the sura Ya-Seen stated correctly that it moved on to its destination. As in other subjects, in this one also the Quran is the source that gave a correct account of the sun's motion.

THE METHOD OF THE QURAN AND THE METHOD OF SCIENCE

A book of science purports to demonstrate the theses it advances and the points of reference. The Quran is the message from the Creator of the Universe and describes the Universe in the word of its Creator, in a style different from that of a book on science. The fact that basic statements about the universe in the Quran were destined to come to

78

light after the lapse of more than a millennium, that none of its statements referring to various scientific issues contained errors, shows that
the Quran is the book of the Creator of the Universe. Unlike a scien
tific treatise that tries to find answers to such inquiries into the whys,
wherefores and hows and seeks corroborative proofs to theories
advanced, the Quran makes final statements. The scientific method
has to follow a well-known path before it formulates the postulates
toward which the Quran draws a beeline.

We see that the methodological ways of science differ from the
direct communications of the Quran. Regardless of statements made,
science must follow its own path consisting of stages. This is a consequence of the structure of scientific knowledge. As a matter of fact,
the Quran promotes scientific research both upon the earth and in
space. On the other hand, I am not trying to create a contest between
science and the Quran by juxtaposing the Quranic statements and the
secular scientific conclusions. What I have been trying to do is to draw
attention to the fact that the straightforward statements made in the
Quran tally with the conclusions of science arrived at by following
predetermined stages of research, thus proving the realization of what
has been predicted in the Quran. The Quran's origin is the Creator,
who is the Knower of Everything. The information directly communicated by the Quran was inaccessible through scientific methods
which would have recourse to the accumulation of data, formulas,
observations and technical findings. The Creator of both the universe
and the rules governing it had already communicated the findings of
science in the Quran.

THE SPEED OF THE SUN

The sun moves at a speed of 700,000 km/h in the direction of the star
Vega, following its orbital path referred to as the Solar Apex. The
Earth rotates around its own axis while revolving about the sun, mov-
ing along with the Solar System.

The sun rises every morning and sets every night. However, the
points where it rises and sets are never the same. The earth travels
around the sun, which moves in the universe without ever passing
through the same point. To imagine that in the course of time elapsed
from the time at which we started reading our book until now that we

are reading this very page, the sun, along with our world, have traveled a few million kilometers, and that we have not been adversely affected by this motion in any way whatsoever, may give use a clue of God's system.

RISING POINTS OF THE SUN

5- The Lord of the heavens, and the earth, and all that lies between them, and the Lord of the easts (places where the sun rise).

37-Who Stand in Row, 5

Because the earth has a spherical shape, the sun that rises somewhere sets simultaneously somewhere else. Night and day chase each other. Therefore we cannot speak of a given point from which the sun rises, but rather of different points. The hour of dawn is different at every single point of our sphere. Every spot on the earth expects the rise of the sun while it is "rising" at different spots in space.

The sun we behold every morning is a giant nuclear reactor. This reactor, generated by the conversion of hydrogen atoms into helium, performs its task marvelously. We continue our journey in space unaware of the immense speed of our source of life toward our predestined point. God's omnipotence and the Quran's miracles will unfold to those who take heed, who have an inquiring mind and are truthful in their approach to the Quranic verses.

43- And such are the parables we set forth for the people, but only those understand them who have knowledge.

29-The Spider, 43

CHAPTER 14

DIFFERENCE BETWEEN THE SUN AND THE MOON

5- It is He who made the sun to be a radiant and the moon to be a light ...

10-Jonah, 5

The sun as a nuclear reactor is our world's source of light and heat. The quantity of radiation reaching our world from the sun that warms our world in the cold of space is two per billion of the sun's total quantity of radiation. The moon is not a source of heat and light like the sun. This difference between the sun and the moon finds its description in the Quran, i.e., the sun's light is expressed by the Arabic word *"ziya"* (radiant) and the moon's light is expressed by the word *"noor"* (light). The word *"ziya"* meaning radiation has the connotation of light and heat, while *"noor"* does not have such a connotation.

Other attributes of the sun in the Quran are similes such as *"seraj"* (torch) or *"wahhaj"* (lamp). Both *"seraj"* and *"wahhaj"* emit heat and light through the fire burning within them. The fact that such attributes are not used for the light of the moon shows how refined the style of the Quran is.

AMENITIES OF THE SUN

The energy generated by the sun in just one second is equal to the energy that three billion power stations would generate on earth in a year. The world receives but two per billion parts of the overall radiation coming from the sun. The slightest decrease in this quantity would turn our world into a place no longer habitable by human beings, as ice age

81

would reign. The distance of our world from the sun, the size of the sun, and the power of reactions within the sun are all calculated infinitesimally. We are part of these calculations. The slightest change in the figures would make life on earth impossible. The creation and the perpetuation of these critical values are the *sine qua non* of our lives. The sun rotates around its own axis while moving towards a particular destination; the earth, on the other hand, has a variety of movements; it rotates around its own axis, revolves about the sun, being dependent on it, and is affected by the moon. In all the rapid movements, our world changes all the time according to the position of the solar system and galaxies. None of the movements affects our position in relation to the sun nor puts an end to our life on earth.

Life requires carbon-based molecules. These are only generated between -20 degrees Celsius and +120 degrees Celsius. The range of temperatures is vast in the universe, the heat in stars rises to millions of degrees and falls until -273.15 degrees Celsius is reached. The bracket for the ideal medium for the formation of carbon-based molecules is just a thin slice, one per one hundred thousand of the existing heat differences. Had the world failed to conserve its existing heat and quit the bracket it is in, that would be the end of us. But our Creator is ever conscious of our actual needs and everything is controlled by Him.

2- ...He has subjected the sun and the moon. Each one runs for an appointed term. He regulates all affairs, and explains the signs in detail that you may believe with certainty in the meeting with your Lord.

13-The Thunder, 2

The sun, about 150 million kilometers distant from us, renders life on earth possible. An aircraft traveling at 1000 km/hour would have trouble covering this distance in seventeen years. The temperature in the center of the sun, whose surface temperature is six thousand degrees Celsius, is 15 million degrees Celsius. Not even on the surface of this incandescent gaseous sphere can life be imagined. But at a reasonable distance for us, it is our planet's closest friend and source of life.

98- Your only god is God. There is no other god but He. His knowledge encompasses all things.

20-Ta-He, 98

CHAPTER 15

THE ORBIT OF THE MOON

39- And the moon. We have measured for it mansions. Till it returns like an old curved palm tree branch.

36-Ya-Seen, 39

In comparison with other satellites of the solar system, the moon is a very large one. Competing theories have been developed regarding the formation of the moon. According to the one most widely accepted, the earth must have collided with a celestial body, the impact parceling out a big mass from the earth's crust that was eventually to turn into the moon. Although this may not be the true story, recent data obtained - with the help of the Lunar Prospector, the American probing instrument - seem to corroborate this theory.

There are, in the Quran, many references to the moon and its movements. The data provided by modern scientific findings demonstrated how necessary the moon is for life on earth. The moon with its great volume, a well-designed distance in terms of proportions of a satellite, fixes the earth's center of rotation. This makes possible the climatic conditions of our planet, creating the ideal medium for life on it. This situation has been going on for billions of years. There are scientists who contend that the core of our world preserves its liquid form thanks to the gravity exerted by the moon. This protects our planet's magnetic field (We shall come back to this in Chapters 18 & 19). Had there been no magnetic field, the cosmic radiation would destroy life on the earth. Had it not been for the moon, it is estimated that the earth would have rotated about its axis in ten hours, which would seriously affect the life on earth. The moon's exerting its attraction on oceans slowed down its rotation.

All these formations, including the mass and the spinning velocity of the moon, are the result of infinitesimal calculations made at the time of creation by God. God used the word "*qadar*" (measured) for the mathematics to which He had recourse. We are not going to dwell on the erroneous interpretation of this concept haphazardly contrived in the name of religion. In Verse 39 of the sura Ya-Seen, the mathematical arrangement is expressed by the word "*qadar*." The moon's distance from the earth, its mass and the velocity of its revolution, its position in relation to the sun and gravity are calculated with mathematical precision. Its "*qadar*" has been predetermined. The slightest variation in these calculations would bring life on earth to an end. The moon is not only the actor of romantic nights, the object of inspiration of poets, but also the *sine qua non* friend of life on earth.

OLD CURVED PALM TREE BRANCH

The moon orbits earth in 27 days, 7 hours, 43 minutes and 11 seconds. The Arabic word "*qamar*" meaning "moon" is used 27 times in the Quran. (The miraculous character of this shall be dealt with in the coming pages.) The moon's orbit around the earth traces a sinuosity. While the earth travels around the sun, the moon revolves about the earth in a variable orbit, tracing a curvature, a sinuosity, a spiral. The same face is always presented to the earth. The curve it traces is reminiscent of a curved branch. The Arabic word used to designate the orbit of the moon is "*urjun*," the curved palm tree branch. This branch is qualified by the attribute "old" that denotes a thinner and more curved branch. The simile beautifully describes the orbit traced by the moon about the earth.

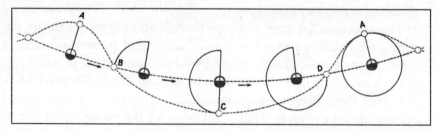

As the moon orbits around the earth it has a sinuous orbit that looks like an old curved palm tree branch. The illustration here demonstrates the moon's orbit through space.

MOON'S DEPENDENCE ON THE SUN

1- By the sun and its brightness
2- And the moon that follows it.

91-The Sun, 1-2

In the verses above, the moon's relation to the sun is described. The Arabic word "*talaa*" means a "follower," "a hanger-on." The moon revolves around the sun together with the earth of which it is a satellite; they follow in the footsteps of the sun. Both the moon and our world are dependent on the sun's motion. They displace while pursuing the sun. The moon and the earth revolve around a moving sun. The Quran's revelation about the moon's dependence on the sun is another miracle that leaves us in awe.

CHAPTER 16

JOURNEY TO THE MOON

18- And the Moon when it is full
19- You will surely ride from stage to stage
20- So, why do they not believe?

84-The Splitting, 18-20

The moon is associated in our minds with beautiful scenes and romantic landscapes. For those who use the lunar calendar, it is a precision calculator. The ebb and tide it causes have always been a mystery for men. It is used to symbolize mathematics, astronomy, art and romanticism. Throughout history the moon has been the symbol of the unattainable. All these features also existed at the time of the Prophet. For 1400 years the meaning of the above quoted verses remained unraveled. In the Quran, the conjunction "and" (*wa*) is frequently used to stress a point; sometimes it is rendered in English by the preposition "by" when making serious promises, taking an oath or calling someone to witness. Commentators dealt differently with the "ride from stage to stage." The reason was the inaccessibility of the moon at the time. Going to the moon was beyond imagination.

This "riding from stage to stage" had the association for some of spiritual ascension, symbolizing the passage from this world to the other world, the stages of development of man from an embryo to adolescence and senescence. Yet, the verse foresees that human beings will pass from stage to stage in the future. Spiritual ascension and man's biological development were nothing new. Therefore, I am of the opinion that these interpretations of the past do not reflect reality. The context of the verse connotes the anticipation that a particular phenomenon will take place in the future and the verse questions the reason why the people do not believe when this event takes place. The Arabic word *"tabaq"* (stage) also mentioned in the sura 67, 3rd verse, and the sura 71, 15th verse, refers not to spiritual, but concrete things. The use of the word "ride" clearly connotes a journey.

Having thus explained the 19th verse in this fashion, the thing that our attention is drawn to, the moon in the 18th verse, supports the idea that "riding from stage to stage" is done by means of a shuttle from the earth to the moon.

WHY DO THEY NOT BELIEVE?

The Russian spacecraft Luna 2 was the first probe to hit the moon (September 12, 1959), and Luna 3 took the first photographs of the far side of the moon. But the most important event was the landing on the moon on July, 21, 1969 by Neil Armstrong and his companions aboard the Apollo 11. The scene of landing on the blurred TV screen was surely one of the most spectacular events in human history. What had been thought impossible had come true. There were positivists, however, who pointed to this event as a scientific achievement and used it as an argument against religion. Certain bigoted scholars of Islam contended that it was a lie that there had been such an event, and that anybody who claimed that man was on the moon would be cursed.

The miraculous prediction had come true, showing once again God's art and power. Photographs taken from the moon reflect once more the splendor of God's design. The mass of the moon, the moon's distance from the earth point to God's splendid design. Had the mass of the moon been larger or had the moon been nearer the earth, the continents would be flooded following the tide, rendering our survival impossible.

Verse 20 that comes after verses 18 & 19 in which the journey to the moon is predicted, which reads: **"So, why do they not believe?"** may refer to the unbelievers and atheists who remained blind to God's splendor and wisdom, considering this a victory of science over religion. This misconception accounts for the misinterpretation of God's ways, namely the fact that science is nothing but the entirety of rules He infused into matter. They labor under the delusion that science and religion vie for supremacy. The origin of science and religion is God. Two things that emanate from God cannot be contradictory. Any contradiction may have been due either to scientific errors or to bigoted theologians who dared to make announcements in the name of God. Verse 21, coming after the verses that I have analyzed in this section, is as follows:

21- And when the Quran is read to them, they do not fall prostrate.

84-The Splitting, 21

THE MOON HAS SPLIT

1- The Hour has come closer and the moon has split (shaqqa).

54-The Moon, 1

There is another indication in the Quran in the above verse referring to the landing on the moon. In order to have a better insight into this, let us dwell on the connotation of the Arabic word *"shaqqa"* which, among its multifarious meanings, signifies "rending asunder," "splitting," "fissuring;" it may also signify plowing the soil.

25- We pour forth water in abundance.
26- And We split (*shaqqa*) the earth in fragments.

80-He Frowned, 25-26

As we see, to describe the fissures made by water on the earth's soil, the same word *"shaqqa"* is used. One of the most important events that occasioned man's visit to the moon was the sampling of the soil on the surface of the moon. The surface of the moon was fissured by man for the first time in history. The term *"shaqqa"* may refer to this cleavage.

We have examined the 1st verse of the sura "The Moon." The 2nd verse of the same sura addresses the wrongdoers who preferred to ignore the evidences of God.

2- Yet if they see a sign they turn away and they say, "A continuous sorcery!"

54-The Moon, 2

CHAPTER 17

LAYERS OF HEAVENS

3- He created the seven heavens (skies) in layers. You do not see any imperfection in the creation by the Gracious. Turn your eyes again. Do you see any flaw?

67-The Kingdom, 3

The statement in the Quran about seven heavens may be interpreted as seven different strata, seven different dimensions or seven different fields of attraction. A closer analysis of the atmosphere, which, to the naked eye may present uniformity, makes it clear that it is not actually so.

The different layers of our atmosphere could not have been known at the time of the Prophet. This fact cannot have been established fortuitously. The Quran refers to different layers in the atmosphere in perfect accord with each other. One can also conjecture that such layers can exist in space. The creation of these harmonious layers is a phenomenon visible from the microcosm of the atom to the macrocosm of the universe. Let us remember the layers and orbits of the electron around the nucleus of the atom. The fact that the maximum number of orbits in the atom is seven may also be significant.

The number seven has special connotations in the Quran. As a matter of fact, "seven" in Arabic, also expresses a plurality; the expression "seven heavens," may either mean the number seven as the actual number of heavens, or a plurality of heavens. This usage of "seven" in the Arabic has been commented upon throughout history by many exegetics. In the sura *Luqmaan*, 27th verse, the expression "seven seas" is used and in the sura Repentance, verse 80 states that: "**Even if you ask forgiveness for them seventy times, God will not for-**

give them." So, it is said that both "seven" and "seventy" express a plurality. A similar usage of the number "seven" expressing a plurality may also be seen in ancient Greek and Roman.

LAYERS OF THE ATMOSPHERE AND THE OBJECTIVES THEY SERVE

We know now that atmosphere is made of layers that make life on earth possible. The absence of any one of these layers would be the end of life on earth. God, whose flawless art is conspicuous everywhere, displays once again His design by drawing attention - in the Quran - to atmospheric layers. Each of these layers dutifully performs its function contributing to the perfect performance of the whole. The fact that the lifeless atoms of the atmosphere are in the service of man, as if forming a conscious entity, is a consequence of God's compassion.

The atmosphere is divided into layers, of which the (1) Troposphere is the lowest layer, closest to the surface of the earth. The Troposphere, which is as low as six km, extends to a height of 12 km at the equator. Atmospheric phenomena take place within the portion of three to four kilometers from the surface. 75% of atmospheric gases are in this layer. Above the Troposphere is the (2) Stratosphere extending about 50 km up. The third is (3) the Ozonosphere, the ozone layer in other words, which is the protector from ultraviolet rays having lethal effects on living beings. Above lies the (4) Mesosphere which in turn, is topped by the (5) Thermosphere followed by the (6) Ionosphere, the upper layer reaching to a height of 500 km from the earth. Radio waves are reflected from this layer, rendering communication possible. Above 500 km lies the fringe region known as the (7) Exosphere, extending up to 10,000 km. The proportion of gases in this layer is very low and divided into ions. We can thus divide the atmosphere into 7 layers. The number 7 may change of course, if researchers prefer examining these layers by different groupings. However it is interesting to find that the commonly agreed classification of atmospheric layers supports the Quranic information and it is beyond mere interest when we evaluate it together with all other scientific remarks in the Quran. Even if the reader does not find this classification persuasive, then he or she may subscribe to the alternative understanding that the figure seven expresses a plurality, without bringing any change in the miraculous significance of the verse. This double meaning of "seven layers" thus leaves no loopholes.

Separating the atmosphere into harmonious layers is a modern discovery. The level of scientific knowledge at the time of the descent of the Quran did not permit making differentiation between the layers of atmosphere. Verse 12 of sura 41 reads: **"So He ordained them seven heavens (skies) in two days (periods) and revealed in every heaven its affair..."** making it clear that every layer served a different purpose, thanks to which life on earth was possible.

CHAPTER 18

LAYERS OF EARTH

**12- It is God who created the seven heavens and of the
earth the same number. The commands flow among them
that you may know that God has power over everything
and everything is held within the knowledge of God.**

65-Divorce, 12

The 12th verse of sura 65 mentions the seven heavens and as many
layers in the earth. We already saw that the seven layers of the heavens were in perfect harmony with each other, each performing its duty
impeccably. The 12th verse of the 65th sura establishes a similarity
between the heavens and the earth.

Our earth is also stratified as the heavens are, and our life on earth
depends on these layers. In the Arabic community of the Prophet's
time, the surface of the earth was an expanse full of mystery. The
knowledge prevalent at the time did not permit man to have an
inkling of the stratigraphy. The fact that the statement in the Quran
of the atmospheric layers is almost a replica of this stratification of the
earth is another miracle.

LIFE DEPENDENT ON TERRESTRIAL STRATA

As I have already pointed out in previous chapters, the Quran's statements are not meant to be miracles as such. But the fact that these
statements reflect at the same time actualities beyond the grasp of the
scientific lore of the Prophet's time points to announcements of
miraculous dimensions. Our aim is not only to establish truths

92

expressed therein, but rather to meditate upon the wonderful designs of God. Thanks to the matter forming the substance of the core that is one of the layers of our sphere, a magnetic field is produced around our world, making life on earth possible. Had the dynamo in the center of the earth been a little bit weaker, the magnetic field around the earth known as the Van Allen belts (belts of intense radiation in space about the earth formed by high-energy charged particles which are trapped by the geomagnetic field) would fail to form an obstacle sufficient enough to stop the lethal radiation threatening our world. The harmony in the concentration of such substances as nickel and iron in liquid form within the core of the earth renders possible the function of the Van Allen belts. All these minutely calculated designs are created in perfect order by our Creator in preparation for man's emergence upon the earth.

It took our earth billions of years to cool (it is estimated that the earth formed about 4.5 billion years ago). Despite this fact, the core of the earth contains lava, the temperature of which is extremely high. The proportion of the upper crust of the earth, of the soil - on which we live - to the world, may be likened to the ratio of the peel of an apple to its mass. The proportion of the crust of the earth to the diameter of the world is less than 1%. We are far from being conscious of this fact as we read our book, go on a walk, eat and talk. The terrific phenomena occurring in the core of our earth have little unwanted effect on our condition upon the earth where we continue to live as if by the side of a calm lake. These occurrences we qualify as terrific because the high temperatures and magnetic phenomena are in actual fact necessary for our survival. Our existence depends on these phenomena without being adversely effected. The phenomena in question are far from fortuitous and beyond our control. God is the Author of all these correlated phenomena. It is incumbent upon us to give thanks to our Creator in full consciousness of our human frailty for all the beauties and perfection we are witnessing.

NUMBER OF LAYERS

The earth is made of many different and distinct layers. The deeper layers are composed of heavier metals; they are hotter, denser and under much greater pressure than the outer limits. One of the layers is the Oceanic Crust (1), and another one is the Continental Crust (2). Beneath is the Upper Mantle (3). Another layer is the Asthenosphere (4) that exhibits plastic properties. Beneath is the Lower Mantle (5). The Outer Core (6) is underneath; its liquid content with the dynamo effect generated by the rotating of the earth forms the protective magnetic field around it. And the last layer is the Inner Core (7).

We see that our world is made of layers whose raw material and function vary. The figure 7 is again indicated in the Quran for the layers of the earth. If the two layers are integrated into a single layer for study purposes, changing the figure 7, then the meaning of 7 in the Arabic language must be taken as a plurality. A detailed examination of God's wonderful world shows that God has power over all things and that God comprehends all things in His knowledge, as it is said in the verse which we examined in this chapter.

CHAPTER 19

WELL PROTECTED ROOF

32- And We made the sky a well protected roof. Still they turn away from its signs.

21-The Prophets, 32

The atmosphere is a gaseous envelope of 10,000 km surrounding our planet, invisible to the eye. Millions of meteorites of varying sizes keep falling from space in the direction of our world. Despite its transparent structure, our atmosphere puts up a bold front against this meteorite bombardment like a steel shield. Had it not been for this feature, there would have been no life on earth, and our world would have been riddled with holes. We witnessed a sample of it when we landed on the moon. Meteor showers kept hitting the surface and the meteoric bodies of greater volume penetrated the crust of the moon, digging deep holes on it. Meteors strike the molecules in the atmosphere with a great speed, and the heat generated turns them into dust particles before disappearing in the air.

The atmosphere also has the function filtering the harmful rays of the sun, protecting life on earth against extinction. This ingenious design partially absorbs incident electromagnetic radiation. Thus, the atmosphere filters the rays harmful to life while letting the rays that foster life on earth pass through. The heavens perfectly perform the duties and functions apportioned to them by God, and unfold before the eyes of those able to discriminate intelligent and teleological creation. The verse refers once more to the dogmatic disbelievers blind to these marvels. All these formations in the atmosphere show the design behind them, namely, the creation and perpetuation of life.

The approximate temperature in space is -270 degrees Celsius. Our earth is protected against this cold thanks to the atmosphere. The atmosphere prevents the energy directed to the earth from going back to space. The atmosphere arranges an even distribution of heat on earth by meteorological phenomena. A hot air mass is thus carried to parts less warm in the atmosphere, establishing a balance between the overheated equatorial and the cold polar regions. Protection from the lethal cold and heat is secured thanks to the perfect design of the atmosphere. The Arabic word "*sema*" (meaning sky, heaven in addition to its signification of atmosphere) may have the connotation of the entirety of space and the phenomena taking place in it, as well.

VAN ALLEN BELTS

The Van Allen belts protect us against radiation bombardment. Had it not been for this, life on earth would have been impossible. The lethal cosmic rays coming from the stars other than the sun cannot penetrate this shield. These plasma clouds can reach 100 billion-fold the value of the atom bomb dropped over Hiroshima. Thanks to the Van Allen belts at a distance of 60,000 km from the world, the solar winds cannot penetrate the earth we live in. The "Well protected roof" in the verse 21:32 was the result of the speed of rotation of our world, its position in relation to the sun, the structure, the shape and thickness of atmospheric layers, the structure of the core of the earth, the proportion of the constituents in its composition and the perfect and harmonious combinations of a multitude of parameters have made this possible. The Author of all these prerequisites for our life cannot be other than the Creator Himself. Logic and conscience cannot accept that all these protective measures in the sky have come about fortuitously and that the Quran was the product of a human intellect and genius.

CHAPTER 20

RETURNED BY THE SKY

11- By the sky that returns

86-The Knocker, 11

The Arabic word *"raj"* means "to return, to turn." Rain is a prerequisite for the perpetuation of life on earth. The water that the sun's rays causes to evaporate does not disappear into space. Rain and water also returned to earth at the time of the Prophet, but scientific knowledge to explain the process was lacking. Once the layers of the atmosphere came to be differentiated, it was understood that the Troposphere, which is one of these layers, prevented the escape of vapor into space and contributed to the perpetuation of life on earth. This layer sends the condensed vapor back to earth in the form of precipitation.

Most of the phenomena that we have studied during our examination of the verse and in which the sky was likened to "a well protected roof" occur thanks to the sky's return of certain things. The sky protects our world by sending back the radioactive particles, radiation and harmful ultraviolet rays coming from the space. While it reflects back to space what is harmful for man, it prevents the evaporated water necessary for life on earth from leaving the atmosphere. The Quran's reference to this characteristic of sky, explored only in the last century, cannot be explained by the lore of the contemporaries of the Prophet.

UMBRELLA UNAFFECTED BY ADVERSE CIRCUMSTANCES

If the atmosphere had not been endowed with this capacity, the maintenance of a desired temperature to foster life on earth would be impossible. Life is possible only within a narrow temperature bracket. In the spectrum of heat ranging from the temperature in the sun to absolute zero, life thrives only in a span of less than 1%. Once attained, maintenance of this 1% span is difficult. A sudden fall and rise in temperatures would also be deadly. For instance, when we feel comfortable, say at an ambient temperature of 20 degrees Celsius, we witness a sudden increase of temperature, rising as high as 100 degrees Celsius or there is a sudden fall to -100 degrees Celsius, destruction would be imminent. The atmosphere's returning power maintains stability.

The composition of the atmosphere is as follows: 78% nitrogen, 21% oxygen and 1% carbon dioxide plus other gases. These rates are ideal for life on earth. If, for instance, the proportion of oxygen rose from 21% up to 22%, the chance of lightning likely to start a forest fire would increase by 70%. Had the oxygen and nitrogen rates in the atmosphere been in excess of what they actually are, vital functions gaining momentum would be to the detriment of life. Had these been inferior, these vital functions would sensibly slow down again, causing great damage to living beings. The steady maintenance of these rates has been possible by a series of phenomena of which the atmosphere's property of reflection is but one; but the lack of this one characteristic would be fatal. Who would claim that this perfect umbrella immune to all adverse circumstances was a fortuitous event? Who would assert that our being protected and well guarded is the result of happy coincidences that duly perform their duties in keeping for us the water and the air vital for our survival? Our Creator has beyond doubt designed everything to serve its purpose before infusing life to us. The Quran He has sent was meant to enable us to behold His wonderful creation.

27- Not without purpose did We create heaven and earth and all between! Such is the thinking of those who disbelieve.

38-Sad, 27

CHAPTER 21

HEAVENS NOT SUPPORTED BY PILLARS

2- God is He who raised the heavens without any pillars...
13-The Thunder, 2

The fact that the Quran speaks of scientific phenomena that could not be accessible to the level of knowledge at the time of the Prophet is a miracle in itself. While trying to emphasize this feature of the Quran, we often stressed that the Quran had, 1400 years ago, spoken of scientific facts that have only come to light in recent years, if not in the course of the twentieth century. One of the facts that could not possibly be attained by observations and research at the time of the Prophet is given in the verse quoted above. However, this discovery is certainly not of recent date. But at the time of the descent of the Quran, there was no general consensus about this. Even after the time of the Quran's descent there were still people who believed that the world abutted mountains at both extremities.

For instance, in the New American Bible, a picture is drawn to show how the authors of the Bible imagined the world. In that picture, the sky resembles an overturned bowl and is supported by columns (The New American Bible, St Joseph's Medium Size Edition, and pp. 4-5). Ibn Abbas (d. 687 AD), Mujahid (d. 718 AD) and Ikrima (d. 733 AD) believed in the existence of pillars (mountains) supporting the sky, too. These persons asserted that the Quran's verses referred only to what was visible and that in the portion of space invisible to the eye the pillars held up the sky. This had also been the contention of the Babylonians who believed that the sky abutted on mountains at its extremities. At the time of the Prophet, mankind did not know that the earth was spherical and that traveling in opposing directions led two people to the same spot. Therefore, the said subject of debate could not scientifically be accounted for at the time of the Prophet. Moreover, such a bold statement would have had deleterious effects on the Prophet's credibility, and objections would not tarry to arrive. Those who claimed that Muhammad was the author of the Quran would not be in a position to account for such a statement.

To appreciate better the value of these statements in the Quran, our imagination must go back to the time of the Prophet and try to guess at the mentality of the people. The Quran was revealed at a time when the airplane and the automobile did not exist, when the actual shape of the earth was unknown, when there was no such thing as a world map and when the majority of Arabs were illiterate. This is to remind the persons who claim that the authorship of the Quran should be attributed to the Prophet or to other writers at the time of the Prophet. So, if one considers that the statements of the Quran had been revealed in such a situation, the miraculous character of the explanations may gain a different dimension.

HEAVEN'S SUPPORT

In the long history of the world, man benefited from the atmosphere's characteristics and advantages without being cognizant of the mystery behind this boon. How did this mass of gases come into being then? How is it that its stability is maintained? The fact that the sky had a "well protected roof" (Ch 19), that it possessed returning and reflecting properties (Ch 20), that it was made of layers, each having its proper function (Ch 17) and that its maintenance was without pillars, all point to the glorious design of God.

Research conducted on planets of the solar system led us to conclude that none of them was surrounded by an atmosphere like the one that surrounds our world; and the way it is designed to make life on earth possible was a proof of the fact that God had decided that life thrives on earth.

The gas molecules upon the surface of the planet move at a tremendous speed. If the gravitational force of the planet overcomes this motion, the planet would attract the gas molecules and the surface of the planet would absorb the gas molecules. On the other hand, if the gas molecules moved rapidly and could escape the planet's gravitational field, they would pursue their travel in space. So, both the atmosphere and the balances established took place at a stage after the creation of the earth. The expression in the Quran, **"He raised the sky, and set the balance"** (*55-Gracious, 7*) is in perfect accord with the formation of the sky and the establishment of balance in it after the creation of the world. The formation of gas molecules in the form of the atmosphere and its fixation was possible only by the establishment of a balance, a balance between the gravitational force of the sphere and the speed at which the gas molecules travel. God contrived a precise balance in order to raise the sky high without pillars. However, this design had to be coupled with what was necessary for its perpetuity.

41- Verily, God is the One who holds the heavens and the earth, lest they cease.

35-The Originator, 41

The establishment of this balance depends on the synchronization of a variety of data. For instance, the heat balance of the surface of the earth depends on the position of the earth in relation to the sun, which, in turn, will affect the motion of gas molecules. The rotation of the earth is an important factor for the homogeneity of heat. If there is an increase in this speed, the atmosphere will scatter; if, on the other hand, this speed slows down, the homogeneity will be upset, for the atmosphere will be absorbed by the soil. For the maintenance of the atmosphere, the difference in temperature between the equator and the polar regions and the chains of mountains like the Himalayas, the Taurus Mountains and the Alps that forestall the terrible consequences that air currents would generate are also important. The chain of mountains contributes to the preservation of the balance by blocking the winds blowing upon the surface of our sphere and gathering the cold air at heights. The gases in the atmosphere also play an important role in the maintenance of the atmosphere. Carbon dioxide, whose proportion in the atmosphere is insignificant, has the function of covering the earth as a blanket, thus preventing the loss of heat at night. From the *raison d'être* of the mountain range to the creation of carbon dioxide, from the magnitude of the earth to the position of the sun, from the balance of heat on the surface of the earth to the characteristics and speeds of gases in the atmosphere, everything has been designed with an unerring precision in perfect conformity. An atmosphere can function without adhering to the earth, without getting scattered in every possible direction, thanks to innumerable conditions.

4- Verily in these things there are signs for those who understand.

13-The Thunder, 4

CHAPTER 22

GEOIDAL FORM OF THE WORLD

30- He made the earth egg-shaped.

79-The Snatchers, 30

The Arabic word *"dahw"* means rotundity like that of the ostrich's egg. The above verse was also interpreted to refer to the shaping of the earth in the form of an ostrich egg. Prof. Dr. Suleyman Ateş, former head of Religious Affairs in Turkey, gives the following definition of the word, based on the famous Arabic dictionary *Lisan u'l Arab:* "The word *'dahw'* means to spread out, giving (something) a round shape." The word *"dahw"* had also been defined as a game played with walnuts. Derived from the same stem, the word *"medahi"* referred to round stones. Despite the meaning of rotundity concealed in words derived from the word *"dahw"* there have been translators for whom a spherical earth was difficult to conceive, who had to translate it as "to spread out." The actual shape of the earth does have the shape of an ostrich egg. Thus the shape of the earth is spheroid with depressions at the poles. The exact figure of the earth which had posed a problem throughout history was established by the Quran.

Even the books written a few centuries after the descent of the Quran likened the shape of the earth to a tray. Beliefs according to which the earth rested on the horns of an ox or was supported by a fish reigned over mentalities in the Arabic peninsula and many believed that earthquakes occurred when the fish down below waved its tail. The Prophet had no ocean-going ship to cross the earth from one extremity to the other, that would have supplied him with evidence proving the spheroid shape of the earth, nor had he a spacecraft from which he could have had an overall view of our world that would have provided him a photographic image of it, as he was not equipped with a camera. Our knowledge of the sphericity of the earth, which seems to us as an established fact, was then beyond the comprehension and imagination of the majority. Therefore, the Quran's statement to this effect failed to be grasped. Men believed that the verse referred to the plenitude of the earth, ignoring the sense of rotundity.

Thus, at a time when most of the people believed in the shape of earth's figure as a tray supported by an ox or fish, the Quran had beautifully described its actual shape. The fact that ostriches abounded in the Arabian Peninsula at the time must have permitted those who inquired into this mystery to hold an ostrich egg in their hands and examine it. The geoidal form is a gentle indication of this. The subtlety of the Quran's expressions provides men with evidence.

174- O people! Verily there has come to you an infallible proof from your Lord. We have sent unto you a manifest light.

4-The Women, 174

CHAPTER 23

ROLLING THE NIGHT OVER THE DAY

5- He created the heavens and the earth truthfully. He rolls the night over the day, and rolls the day over the night...

39-The Throngs, 5

The Arabic word for "roll" is *"yukevviru."* The word is used to depict the act of wrapping a turban around someone's head. This word was also used in the sense of overlapping of the night and day and vice versa. The reason for the day's turning into night and the night's turning into day is due to the spheroid form of the earth. In this verse also we observe implied the sphericity of the world.

VIEW OF THE WORLD FROM SPACE ABOVE

During the Prophet's lifetime it was impossible to scientifically determine the correct view. The scientific demonstration of the statements of the Quran was only possible after the lapse of a millennium. Why were these scientific explanations in the Quran-beyond the comprehension of the Prophet's contemporaries, contradicting the hypotheses prevalent at the time and likely to cause harm to their messenger, certainly being of no benefit to him? We see that the Quran's objective is to tell the truth at all costs. The fact that these phenomena could be explained thanks to the advance of science one thousand years later testifies to the universal address of the Quran and its character; it addresses not only its own time, but also the entirety of humanity until the end of the world.

When the astronomers went to space, they bore witness to this statement of the Quran and took photographs. The face of the world facing the sun was day, while the other side was night. The rotation of the world around its own axis made the night and day alternate, and in some parts the transition from day to night took place simultaneously.

The phenomena related to the roundness of the world and the succession of days and nights are the *sine qua non* conditions of our life on earth. Had our world not been of a spherical shape, had night and day not succeeded each other thanks to its rotation, life on the face of the earth exposed to heat would be extinct and in the portion left in the shade vegetation would not thrive. God's omniscience, omnipotence and art, His perfect design of everything, and the miraculous character of the Book are better understood as we contemplate them.

CHAPTER 24

DIAMETERS OF THE EARTH AND SPACE

33- O society of jinns and men, cross the diameters of the heavens and the earth, if you have the ability, then pass beyond them. But you cannot, unless you acquire an authorization.

55-Gracious, 33

The Arabic word for diameter is "*kutr*" of which the plural is "*aktar*," this refers to the fact that the heavens and the earth have a plurality of diameters. The Arabic language has a special plural to express "duality;" the word *aktar* expresses a magnitude superior to one or two. We must be careful in the case of three-dimensional objects; "diameter" exists only in spheroid figures. In the case of a perfect sphere we cannot speak of a plurality of diameters, for, in a perfect sphere, there can be only one diameter. We observe in the verse the use of the plural, which is remarkable.

This verse is particularly important, as it refers to the geoidal structure of the world. Doubts about the spheroid structure of the world were dispelled by the law of gravitation of Newton (1642-1724). Previously it was believed that men, the living beings and the seas beneath the surface of the earth would have fallen down had the world been a sphere. Isaac Newton's law of gravitation convinced men that their belief was false. Objections to the sphericity of the world were henceforth withdrawn, although many people still adhered to their former convictions. If you spoke of "diameters" of the earth, Newton would have corrected you saying: "the diameter of the earth." A sphere can have but one diameter but in the geodesic sphere, which is the actual shape of the world, this is possible.

CONFINES OF SPACE

The mention in the verse of "the diameters of the heavens" is also significant. Until man took cognizance of the primeval explosion and the expanding universe, many scientists believed space to be infinite. Space continuously expands and wherever it expands a new and still larger diameter is formed (this was explained in Ch. 1, 2 & 3). As a matter of fact, scientists have likened space to an inflating balloon in accord with the statement of the verse. Measurements taken at various spots in space would give different diametrical results, while even these measurements taken would change every instant. The use of the plural for the diameter of the heavens is of towering importance, since there is more than just one diameter and because the concept of infinite space is refuted.

The equatorial axes and the diameters in between the equatorial axis will be the longest, while the shortest diameter will be in the polar region. Other diameters will range in between. The diameter measured from the level of the poles to the end point of the atmosphere, the one drawn from the equator to the end point of the atmosphere, and the diameters in between differ also.

We should like to draw your attention to a point. In a good many translations of the Quran there are references to the confines of the earth and the heavens, to its periphery and contours and frontiers, and the word "diameters" is skipped. Indeed, the extremities of the diameter of an area give the contour, the limits and the periphery of that area. We draw the attention of translators to this subtle point.

CHAPTER 25

THE EARTH DOES ROTATE EVEN THOUGH WE ARE NOT CONSCIOUS OF IT

88- When you look at the mountains, you think that they are standing still. But they are moving like clouds. Such is the artistry of God, who disposes of all things in perfect order. He is indeed fully aware of what you do.

27-The Ant, 88

The mountains' features seem to make them the most stationary components of the earth's surface. The idea of the unattainability of mountains led certain primitive mentalities to believe in polytheism and fancy that the mountains were the abode of divinities.

The idea of mountain peaks being beyond man's reach was an illusion, as was also their stationary aspect. The verse refers to this illusion and speaks of the motion of mountains like clouds. If the mountains that had a stationary aspect did move, it would follow that the earth itself also moved. The verse thus dismisses the idea of a fixed world entertained as a consequence of false perception, and informed the public of the time of the movement of mountains, likening them to clouds.

This sign, beyond the grasp of the public contemporary with the Prophet, led people to believe that it was a premonitory sign foretelling the end of the world. Even someone who had no knowledge of the Arabic language could see that this interpretation was groundless and conflicting with the Quran. In the verse it is stated that men believe that the mountains are stationary, but this is an illusion. It is impossible to deduce from the mountains in motion that this is to take place at the end of the world.

WHAT WOULD HAPPEN IF THE EARTH DID ROTATE?

These false assumptions deduced during the first century after the Prophet may be condoned after we read the commentaries of Sheikh Abdul Aziz Bin Baz from Saudi Arabia. As late as the 1970s, he claimed that the earth did not move and that anyone who asserted the contrary was considered to have committed a blasphemy. The Saudi Sheikh spoke as follows: "*Anyone who thinks otherwise would be considered to have gone astray and be called on to repent. If he does repent, so much the better, if not, he will be declared to have uttered a blasphemy and be put to death, his estate being forfeited by the treasury of the Muslim State. If the earth rotated as they asserted, lands, mountains, trees, rivers and seas would turn into an absolute chaos. The Western lands would have changed directions and shifted to the East. And the Eastern lands would shift to the West changing the direction of the Kibla (Mecca), henceforth impossible to determine. As none of these happenings are observed, the assertion that the world is in motion is a false statement for many reasons.*"

We see that the opinions entertained about the stationary character of the earth were so firm that bigoted theologians disregarding the revelations of the Quran could utter that anyone who thought that the earth moved had to be subjected to capital punishment in the twentieth century! The Quran is full of miraculous revelations, but there is no end to the lies concocted in the name of religion. The people who took as their guide such concoctions and merely read the Quran as a textbook without understanding its meaning have done the greatest harm to religion. One must understand the reliability of the Quran and avoid all superstitions.

GALILEO'S ORDEAL

Though historically it is a rare and anecdotal reaction and not shared by many Muslim scholars, I mentioned the bigoted reaction of a scholar who railed against the idea of a rotating earth. The case of Galileo, however, is known all over the world. Galileo was an Italian astronomer and physicist, one of the founders of modern science; he believed that the universe was created by God. His empirical and observational scientific approach enabled him to be a pioneer in many fields of science. His ordeal is well known. His postulation that the earth rotated caused him to undergo terrible and painful experiences. The Church had adopted the views of Aristotle and Ptolemy on the universe and the world. This conception posited that the earth remained fixed while the sun revolved around the moon. The Church adopted this earth-centered view as its official credo. The Church propounded all its views as the reflection of God's will; to oppose them was tantamount to taking a stand against God. We witness once more that one of the main sources of commentaries trying to show that religion and science are mutually exclusive were ignorant dogmatic bigots and the religious establishments under their domination. So has been the case with Islam.

Once man ceases to mix his own ideas with God's, the problem will be solved. Otherwise, man will continue committing the sin of mixing his views with God's revelations. Galileo Galilei, like Copernicus and Kepler, argued that the earth moved and the sun stood in the center. According to their contention, the earth had no central position. The Church was not as tolerant as it had been in the case of Copernicus and Kepler. Galileo's adoption of the Copernican system was refuted by the Church, and under threat of torture from the Inquisition, he was forced to publicly recant his heretical views. This was not the end of the ordeal; he still had to face material and spiritual tortures. He was forced to spend the last eight years of his life under house arrest. The story of the Church and Galilei illustrates best the quarrel between "religion" and science. But the fact remains that the original religion as such was not to blame, but the so-called representatives of fabricated religion were. The Quran warns us against those people who will show up and present themselves as spokesmen of God's religion as well as against the ignominies perpetrated for material gains.

34- O believers, many rabbis and priests devour the substance of men and hinder them from the way of God.

9-Repentance, 34

We must beware of the class of the unenlightened and opportunistic who call themselves representatives of religion. True enlightenment is possible only by guiding ourselves by the precepts of the

Quran. To adopt the Quran as our guide is the remedy against super-stitions and the *sine qua non* of coming face to face with the truth.

MOUNTAINS IN MOTION

The verse we are studying in this chapter may have another sign, as well. The terrestrial crust moves as if floating on the mantle, which is denser. This was the reason why the continents, once a whole, were severed from each other. The ideas posited by German meteorologist and geologist Alfred Wegener in an article published in 1915 made him the first serious proponent of the theory of the continental drift. His theory was not espoused by most geologists of his time. It is, however, accepted now as correct in principle. The continental drift is the concept of continent formation by the fragmentation and move-ment of masses of land on the surface of the earth. The seas and lands are in collision with each other like floating rafts on a lake, sometime overlapping each other. Their speeds vary between 3cm and 15cm per year. Thus, the mountains, that appear stationary to us, are in fact in motion along with the earth, as well as with the continent of which they form a part.

The world we inhabit rotates around its axis and revolves about the sun in its rapid course in space along with the solar system; in addi-tion, we must take into account the world's movement in relation to the moon. We shall include also the gravitational force of other plan-ets. Unconscious of all these phenomena, we sleep tightly, enjoy our meals with relish, and take pleasure in reading and doing sports. A car is considered super when it does not let us feel we are riding in it. Our world travels at an immense speed and follows extremely complex courses unpiloted, without our being consciously affected by them. The verse we analyzed at the beginning of this chapter is an evidence of the incontestable perfection of God's design.

CHAPTER 26

FECUNDATING WINDS

22- And We send the fecundating winds.

15-Hijr, 22

Research conducted on physical phenomena and plants demonstrated the importance of the fecundating property of winds. Winds play a role in the reproduction of plants by transporting small reproductive bodies produced in pollen sacs of the seed plants. The winds have also the character of fecundating the rain clouds, another essential factor for life on earth.

Before rising to the upper layers of the atmosphere, the gaseous suspension of ultramicroscopic particles of a liquid called aerosol, generated by foaming in seas and other waters, gets mixed with the dust that the winds sweep from the lands. These particles combine with water vapor that condenses around these particles. Had it not been for these particles, one hundred per cent water vapor could not form the cloud. The formation of clouds is the consequence of the winds' formation of the water vapor in suspension with the fecundating particles they carry. Had the winds failed to perform this duty there would not have been any rain clouds. As there would be no rain, life could not thrive upon the earth. However, winds have other functions as well. Clouds charged with positive and negative electricity, weighing tons, are swept by winds. Without winds there would be no clouds; even if we assume that they did form, the water would then fall down upon the seas and waters over which they condensed, and human beings, plants and the animal kingdom would be deprived of their benefit.

So the clouds are formed thanks to winds, and it is thanks to winds that rains fall over the land. Life can only thrive upon the earth thanks to rain. We are witnessing again the perfect design of our Creator.

WINDS' WONDERFUL SYSTEM

The Quran stresses the great role of the wind, an essential for our lives; another example of the generosity of our Lord. Indeed, the rain is affected, among other things, by the rotation of the earth, by the topography, by the low and high pressure zones, etc. If our world did not have an inclination of 23.5 degrees, the cooling and the effect of the sun on the North and South poles would not be subject to daily change. The difference of temperature between the equator and the poles is reduced, the consequence being moderately blowing winds. If the topography of the world had been different, the winds blowing from the poles to the equator and from the equator to the poles might turn into ravaging storms.

Mountains, planes and plateaus are designed so as to allow the winds to penetrate every nook and corner, creating warm and cold front systems. The wind, the rain, the mountain, the rotation of the earth and the heat are interconnected. Whoever created one of these elements is also the Author of the rest. This interconnection cannot be refuted. This interrelatedness is another evidence of the oneness of the Creator. All these subtleties, perfections and details are meant to reflect His artistry, wisdom and unlimited power.

When a breeze blows, refreshing the sultry atmosphere we are breathing, let us remember His munificence, as we take delight in having been caressed by it. The wind is mathematics, art, power and science all at the same time. All these phenomena bespeak a perfect design behind them and show that we are not forlorn abandoned figures. The wind, regardless whether it is a gentle breeze, a brisk northern wind or a sultry south wind, is still the one designed by our Creator, governed by physical laws without which man cannot survive.

5-...and the manipulation of the winds are signs for those who understand.

45- Kneeling, 5

CHAPTER 27

CLOUDS AND THE PROCESS OF RAIN

43- Do not you see that God drives the clouds, then joins them together, then piles them on each other, then you see the rain comes forth from between them. And He sends down hail from the sky, where there are mountains of it. And strikes those with it whom He will and diverts it from whomever He wills. The vivid flash of its lightning nearly blinds the sight.

24-The Light, 43

Water is life. The greater portion of water that is the basic need for the living beings on earth is in continuous motion and transformation. The uninterrupted sequence of these successive transformations is referred to as cycling. Water is always present in the air. It goes without saying that this state of water differs from its state in the seas and rivers. The formation of clouds by water in the state of vapor, the transformation of these clouds into rainwater and their falling upon the earth as precipitation are the result of God's impeccable cycling system. More than 1400 years ago, the Quran began to draw our attention to the facts that today can be established only by the help of satellites. Scientists studied types of clouds and established that they were the consequence of well-designed systems and stages. Meteorologists examined the cumulonimbus clouds. The stages they described tallied with the process described in the sura The Light, verse 43.

1- Clouds move thanks to winds: The fact that the wind is the primary cause in the process of the formation of clouds that generates rain is depicted in the sura, The Romans, verse 46 (In the previous chapter, we saw the role played by wind in the formation of clouds).

2- Joining: Then the small clouds combine to form a single large cloud.

3- Piles them on each other: When the small clouds join together, updrafts within the larger cloud increase. The updrafts near the center of the cloud are stronger than those near the edges. These updrafts cause the cloud body to grow vertically, so the cloud is stacked up. This vertical growth causes the cloud body to stretch into cooler regions of the atmosphere where drops of water and hail formulate. When these drops of water and hail become too heavy for the updrafts to support them, they begin to fall from the cloud as rain, hail, etc.

GENIUS OF A MAN?

Meteorologists have acquired what they know about the formation, structure and function of clouds only in recent years by the help of satellites, computers and balloons. It is significant to read about the formation of clouds in the Quran. Today's data are obtained through the use of instruments and satellites that have a panoramic view of clouds from above, otherwise, it would be impossible for men living on the surface of the earth to have an insight into the updraft in the clouds during their formation and the precipitation emerging from this cloud expanding vertically.

In the verse above, the simile of "mountain masses" is an apt one, since the cumulonimbus rain clouds at an altitude of 5-6 km present a formation like a mountain.

While the verse reveals knowledge unavailable at the time of the Prophet, there is no mention whatsoever of the misconceptions of the time. Up until the 1600s the western world was dominated by the meteorological lore of ancient Greece, itself a hotchpotch of correct and wrong data. It was believed that the atmosphere was made up of two different types of vapor, namely the dry and the moist; that thunder was the outcome of the collision of dry clouds with their neighbors, and that the flash of lighting was produced by the kindling of the dry vapor. In the verse in question no such false information has been provided, while a description is made of the flash of lightning, along with the downfall of rain and hailstones, establishing a link between them. The lightning flash in atmospheric electricity is the total observed luminous phenomena accompanying a lightning discharge, which is a series of electric processes by which change is transferred within the atmosphere along a channel of high ion density between electric charge centers of opposite sign. The water droplets within the clouds are a source of electricity. The water droplets falling down as a result of gravitation break down into yet smaller droplets with positively charged electricity while the surrounding atmosphere is negatively charged. The electric charge of droplets increases at each division into smaller units. Along with the emergence of the electrical charge as a consequence of disintegration of water droplets, the ice crystals at the upper portion of the cloud gain positive electricity charge, thus separating from the atmosphere with negative charge and increasing the electrical charge of the cloud. This process results in an electric arc, i.e., a flash of light. The verse draws attention to the connection of the precipitation with the flash of lightning, leaving out the wrong information that attributes this process to the kindling of clouds. Describing the meteorological process that creates rain accurately, while eliminating the false ideas predominant at the time successfully, cannot be explained as pure coincidence or the genius of a man.

12- It is He who shows you the lightning for fear and hope, and raises heavy clouds.

13-The Thunder, 12

CHAPTER 28

DUE MEASURE IN RAIN

11- And He is the One who sends down water in due measure from the sky, to revive dead lands therewith. Similarly you will be raised.

43-Vanity, 11

Rain is one of the gifts of God to man. In the verse above, God says that the rain has its own mathematics and that it is sent according to "due measure." Water on earth is subject to an impeccable process and passes in due order from the state of liquid to the state of gas and solid. It has a marvelous balancing power, as it balances energy while satisfying the vital needs of the living being.

You would not have gotten an answer if you were, a century back, to ask a scientist whose field of interest was rainfall in particular, "Is there a measure in the rainfall; can it be quantified?" Being ignorant of the meteorological phenomena going on in every part of the world, the scientist would not have been in a position to say anything on the issue. The Quran told us 1400 years ago that the rainfall had a certain measure. Research conducted in the last century revealed the process of rainfall, shedding light over the cycling characteristics of water. One of the facts discovered was that the earth's annual rainfall was always of the same amount. The amount per second varied between 16-17 million tons. Thus, the amount of rain falling was above 500 trillion tons a year while an equal amount evaporated. These yearly values remain constant. This constancy was of great significance in establishing the ecological balance of the world. The scientist of a few centuries back could not have estimated the amount of the rainfall in the region where he lived since the precipitation yearly changed according to region. He might have concluded, therefore, that rain is not quantifiable.

CALCULATIONS RELATED TO WATER CYCLE

The rainfall and cycle of water involve complicated calculations. To give you an example, researchers were curious to know the reason for the maximum temperature of the upper portion of the tropical ozone layer which was maximum 28 degrees Celsius, despite the sun's continual warming of the water. Their research produced the following finding: the factor that prevented the overheating of the ozone layer in warmer regions was not merely water vapor, but at the same time the shadow cast by clouds. In the shade, the temperature dropped. The shield prevented the earth from overheating. Water vapor also exerts a greenhouse effect. Along with carbon dioxide, methane and other gases, it creates an invisible insulation layer in the atmosphere. This layer prevents the totality of every radiation coming down on earth under normal conditions from getting lost in the space where cold is reigning. Water vapor forms 60% of the "natural greenhouse effect," making the basic climate of the earth relatively warm. All these things are finely calculated; we can gain an insight into this if we examine the greenhouse clouds revolving around the planet Venus. The dense clouds muffle it, so that only half of the sun's rays reach it. The quantity of 97% carbon dioxide there creates a super greenhouse effect and the temperature rises up to 500 degrees Celsius. This temperature far exceeds the temperature range in which man can live. The water cycle on earth, passing through the states of liquid, cloud and water vapor, is calculated with precision.

In contradistinction with the general properties of water, the clouds do not freeze, even at a temperature of - 30 degrees Celsius. As it is stated in the Quran, there are masses of clouds as large as mountains, but they do not freeze into mountains of ice to fall upon the earth. Had it not been for this precise calculation in the formation of clouds and the rainfall and for the ideal arrangement of the chemical composition of water by its Creator, the system would certainly not function.

When we throw an object of a few kilograms from a balcony, we can follow its descent. If we empty a large pan full of water from the balcony, we can observe the splash on the ground. The fall of tons of water from above, thanks to God's programming, is so arranged that water coming down in drops from above is a blessing rather than a natural disaster. This is the wonderful artistry in the physical rules imposed by God. Such a balancing of acceleration is definable in physical formulas. This definability, this calculation is due to God's creation of rain in "due measure."

RAIN IS LIFE

In the same verse, God speaks of the rain's regenerative power. It is a well-known fact that dry land is revitalized by rain and the vegetation becomes lush once again. The basic element of the animate being is DNA in which the hydrogen bonds keep changing, perpetuating life. This hydrogen is exchanged with the hydrogen that emerges during the ionization of water. A dehydrated living being is like a frozen skeleton even though it may preserve its DNA and genetic code; it cannot reproduce or move. Only when the water comes up and lends the hydrogen from its disintegrated ions can the code be activated. Such characteristics can be observed in living microorganisms like microbes. The more developed living beings cannot recover their vitality when fresh water is supplied, as their tissue surfaces have already deteriorated. Rain is thus the source of regeneration of plants and bacteria. The last sentence of the verse that reads: **"Similarly you will be raised"** evokes the following association in our mind: God sends down rain in predetermined amounts, by which plants and bacteria that are near death are resuscitated. The rising of man from the dead is no problem for God, who knows the measure of all things. God, who devised the system of regeneration of plants and bacteria through a well-calculated amount of rain, will raise man from the dead according to the measures and knowledge in His wisdom. The sprouting of vegetation from the dead soil is something our eyes behold. What we see is the evidence of the facility by which our Creator will re-create His creation whose measure, calculation and formula are known only to Him.

CHAPTER 29

UNDERGROUND WATERS
AND WATER CYCLE

21- Do not you see that God sends down water from the sky and places it into underground springs.

39-The Throngs, 21

The rainfall and its role in our lives as mentioned in the Quran give us correct information. Had we been living in some other periods of history, we could not have grasped it. Now we are in a position to understand this, as the world's water cycle has been made clear by the knowledge provided by contemporary science. If we compare the ancient lore about water with the information contained in the Quran, we realize that the Quran's communications are free from errors, as always.

Let us take up the verse of the Quran that speaks of the formation of underground waters as a consequence of the rainfall (sura 39, verse 21). Was this fact, which is no mystery for us today, as clear in the minds of the ancients as it is in ours? Two specialists, G.Castany and B. Blavoux, give the following account: *"According to Thales, the waters of the ocean that gushed out in the air by the pressure exerted by winds blowing from the depths of continents fell back down, penetrating the earth. Plato shared this view and believed that its return to the ocean was caused by a huge whirlpool. Aristotle contended that the vapor that rose from the earth condensed in the cool recesses of mountains, forming subterranean lakes and spring waters that were fed by these lakes. The first significant discovery of water's perpetual cycle was by Bernard Palissy in 1580. According to him, underground springs were formed by the penetration of rain water into the earth."*

The view adopted during the Middle Ages was Aristotle's. According to this erroneous view, water springs were fed by underground lakes. Remenieras gives the following account: "*The concepts of purely philosophic character about the natural phenomena related to waters had to wait until the Renaissance in order to yield their places to impartial observations. In the Renaissance, Leonardo da Vinci (1452-1519) argued against the assertions of Aristotle. Bernard Palissy in his work 'Discours admirables sur la nature des eaux, des fontaines, de la terre, etc.' gives a clear account of water's perpetual cycle with special reference to feeding of underground springs by rainwater.*"

The knowledge that underground springs were fed by rainwater provided in the Quran was first postulated in the 16th century in Europe against Aristotle's contention. The prominent figures of philosophy like Thales, Plato and Aristotle had made errors in the accounts they gave of water. Muhammad in the desert, who had no other claim than that of being a messenger of God, proved to be correct when he uttered the related statements of the Quran.

203- Say: "I follow only what my Lord reveals to me." These are enlightenments from your Lord, and guidance, and mercy for those who believe.

7-The Purgatory, 203

RAINWATER PURE TO DRINK

68- See you the water which you drink?
69- Do you bring it down from the clouds or do We?
70- If We wish, We can make it salty. You should be thankful.

56-The Inevitable, 68-70

All sorts of details related to the water cycle have been impeccably designed by God. The physical laws and the chemistry of water reflect the fine calculations behind it. The fact that rainwater contains no salt is again a blessing. We saw that the rain was the consequence of evaporation of water. More than 90% of water that evaporates has, in its origin, oceans and seas with salt waters. The rules that govern the evaporation of water are arranged in order that the water is purified and disposed of its salt content and other impurities. The water of oceans and seas is not potable, while rainwater is, thanks to the evaporation process. In the Quran, reference is made to pure water coming from above.

48- "And we send down pure water from the sky"
25-The Distinguisher, 48

The Quran informs us that water was created after the formation of the earth.

31- From it, He produced its own water and pasture.
79-The Snatchers, 31.

At the time of the Quran's descent, the first stages of creation of the earth were a mystery. The fact that the emergence of water on the surface of the earth was a phenomenon that took place after the creation of the earth, as mentioned in the Quran, is a miraculous statement. The earth in the beginning was extremely hot. As it gradually cooled down, heavy metals like iron settled in its center, while granite and oxides remained at the upper layers. As a result of the cooling, an outermost solid layer formed. When the surface temperature fell below 100 degree Celsius, the water in the depths rose to the surface, forming the oceans and seas. This emergence of water is in perfect accord with the account given in the Quran.

PROPERTIES OF WATER

The proportion of water on the earth is of great importance. Had lands extended into an expanse larger than the seas, the difference between night and day temperatures would have been higher and the greater portion of the living space would turn into a desert. The fact that waters form more than 70% of the surface of the earth is the result of an intelligent design. Had the water displayed disintegrative properties like certain acids during chemical reactions or remained unaffected like argon, it could not perform its function in the universe and in our bodies.

Chemical laws have special applications for water, so essential for life. All other substances, whether solid or liquid, contract as they grow cooler. The volume of a substance in solid state is smaller and denser. Water, however, has quite different characteristics. Water, like any other substance, contracts until the temperature drops down to +4 degrees Celsius. Nevertheless, as the temperature continues to fall, it begins expanding, unlike other substances. That is, its volume increases. When it freezes, it expands still further. That is why it floats on the surface instead of sinking. All other substances behave differently; in solid state they sink. Thanks to special chemical relations proper to water, life becomes possible in the seas. Had the density of ice been greater than the density of water, the frozen water in lakes and seas would have sunk. And as there would be no layer of ice on the surface, the freezing process would continue upward. In this way, the depth of the oceans, seas and lakes would be transformed into mountains of ice and when the temperature in the atmosphere became warmer only a thin layer of water would thaw; thereby the aquatic life would come to an end.

MARVELLOUS CHAIN AND WEAKEST LINK

The other chemical properties of water are such that they allow life to perpetuate. Thanks to its chemical properties, plants carry water from the depths of the soil up to the top of large trees (which distance can be measured in meters). If the surface tension of water were low, as in the case of many other liquids, the plants could not absorb water. This would be the end of the vegetation and animal kingdom.

We have so far covered many essential subjects vital for our life on earth. The subjects covered ranged from the precise regulation of the velocity of the atom in the aftermath of the primeval explosion to our remoteness from the sun, from the features of the atmosphere to Van Allen belts, from the surface temperature of the earth to the heat in the depths of the earth; the least change in any one of these creations would be the end of our lives. Our life depends on a chain of phenomena with thousands of links, each one being in perfect order and of extremely complex structure. This chain may break at its weakest link. So, the chain's life entirely depends on that particular link.

Supposing that each of the prerequisites making life possible displayed excellent performance of its function; if a seemingly insignificant event like water's tension were ignored, our life would vanish. All these minutiae are so many evidences of precise calculation by our Creator, Omnipotent and Omniscient.

CHAPTER 30

BARRIER BETWEEN SEAS

19- He has let free the two seas meeting together.
20- Between them there is a barrier which they do not transgress.

55-Gracious, 19-20

A famous French oceanographer, J. Cousteau, gives the following account as a result of his studies in water barriers: "*We studied the assertions by certain researchers about barriers separating seas, and noticed that the Mediterranean Sea had its own salinity and density and housed autochthonous fauna and flora. Then we examined the water of the Atlantic Ocean and discovered features entirely different from those of the Mediterranean Sea. According to our expectations, these two seas that merged in the strait of Gibraltar should present similar characteristics in terms of salinity, density and other properties. The two seas presented different features even though they were adjacent. This greatly puzzled us. An incredible barrier prevented the two seas from coming together. The same sort of a barrier had also been observed in Bab Al-Mandab in the Gulf of Aden connecting with the Red Sea. Subsequent to our observations, further researchers made it clear that the seas which had different characteristics had some barriers.*"

This fact that astounded oceanographers was revealed 14 centuries ago in the Quran. This aspect, not visible to the naked eye and appearing to be in conflict with the properties of water known to man, was first revealed to men in the Arabian peninsula, men who were not at all experienced in any sense with oceanography.

125

THE COLORFUL WORLD IN THE DEPTHS OF THE SEA

The barriers between adjacent seas demonstrate a rich diversity, a result of the perfect planning of God. Wherever we turn our gaze, the complexion of human beings, the infinite diversity of flowers, etc., demonstrate the marvelous diversity of God's creation.

The Quran refers to the waters that do not coalesce. This is because of a physical characteristic called "surface tension." Thus, neighboring seas present different densities, salinity rates and compositions. These differences enable media that permit different species to coexist. Thus, fish, plants and microorganisms living under water present untold varieties. Water, that usually mixes easily, can turn into a wall thanks to God's imposition and operation of physical laws, contributing to this variety. This fact is not affected by strong waves and currents. This property to which the Quran refers is a miraculous statement unknown at the time of the Prophet and presents clear evidence for the man of understanding.

53- He is the One who has set free the two seas; one is sweet and palatable, and the other is salty and bitter. And He made a barrier between them, a partition that is forbidden to be passed.

25-The Distinquisher, 53

CHAPTER 31

DARKNESS AND INTERNAL WAVES IN THE SEAS

40-... or is like the darkness in a deep sea. It is covered by waves, above which are waves, above which clouds. Darkness, one above another. If a man stretches out his hand, he can hardly see it. For any to whom God gives not light, there is no light.

24-The Light, 40

The construction of submarines dates back to the 17th century. A vessel that navigated under water was first contrived in 1620 by C. Drebber. Submarines developed rapidly, and in 1954, nuclear submarines were made. The development of submarines made possible the study of submarine geology and topography, and life in the depths of oceans. Collection of data had been possible thanks to the means developed in recent centuries without which a man could not dive to a depth more than 50 meters.

At a depth of 200 meters from the surface of the sea, darkness reigns. At this depth, then, **"If a man stretches out his hand, he can hardly see it,"** as described in the verse. The bottom of seas and oceans are pitch dark. While broad daylight reigns on the surface, 200 meters below it is again completely dark. At the time of the descent of the Quran, there were neither scientific data nor knowledge based on observation about the darkness reigning in the depth of seas. Just as it told about many aspects of heavenly phenomena comprehensible by man without the help of satellites, the Quran also provided information about submarine life in the depth of seas and oceans hardly accessible to man without submarines and instruments. The Quran - whose range of information is vast enough to cover everything, from the space high above down to the depth of the seas - itself proves its divine origin by the very fact that it is flawless.

WAVES ABOVE WAVES

In general, we have the impression that the wave only breaks on the surface and that the water underneath is calm and still. That is why the expression in the Quran, **"by waves, above which are waves,"** may seem puzzling. These waves were discovered in 1900 and are as described in the Quran. The dark depth of the sea contains these waves topped by the waves on the surface.

In the verse, we also observe the motion of light. The sun's rays are refracted as they strike the clouds and lose some of their luminescence. The rays that reach the surface of the seas diffract as they continue their journey in the spectrum, the first layer holding onto the yellow, while the second holds onto the green; in the last layer, the seventh in fact, the blue disappears. Thus, as the journey goes further downward, light vanishes. The sunlight refracted in the clouds, the light that vanishes in the levels of oceans, completely disappears in the depths of oceans and cannot light the bottom. Not even fish can see their way unless they themselves generate some form of light.

6- Say: "The Quran was sent down by Him, who knows the mystery that is in the heavens and the earth: verily He is Forgiving, Merciful."

25-The Distinguisher, 6

CHAPTER 32

MOUNTAINS AS PEGS

6- Have We not made the earth habitable?
7- And the mountains as pegs?

78-The Event, 6-7

Mountains are often mentioned in the Quran. The simile of pegs seems to be preternatural in the light of geological findings of the last century. The mountains we observe on the surface of the earth rest on immense strata that may be ten to fifteen times as deep as the portion remaining on the surface of the earth. For instance, the highest mountain on earth, whose peak attains an altitude of 9 km from the ground, possesses a substratum that goes about 125 km into the depths of the earth. For a peg to be able to fulfill its function, the length of the portion stuck in the earth is important. The same holds true for the mountain.

There also exist mountains rising from the bottom of seas that also possess substratum. These substrata support the visible portion of the mountains in accordance with the Archimedean principle. These substrata were unknown until a few centuries back, let alone during the time of the Prophet. The simile in the Quran is once again a miraculous statement.

FUNCTION OF MOUNTAINS

In geology textbooks that have not been updated, information is not available about the role the mountains play, the role of stabilizing the crust of the earth. However, there are some publications on this issue.

The book entitled "*Earth*" is one of the many now on the market. Frank Press, author of this book, is the president of the Academy of Sciences, adviser to Jimmy Carter, ex-President of the USA. This author likens the mountains to wedges, the greater part of which remain underneath the surface of the earth. In this book, Dr. Press explains the functions of mountains, drawing special attention to their important role in stabilizing the crust of the earth. This information exactly matches the statement in the Quran:

31- "And We have set on the earth mountains standing firm lest it should shake with them."

21-The Prophets, 31

Actually, the crust of the earth floats on a liquid. This outermost layer of the earth extends 5 km from the surface. The depths of the mountain strata go as far down as 35 km. Thus, the mountains are sort of pegs driven into the earth. Just like the pegs used to stabilize a tent on the ground, so these pegs stabilize the crust of the earth. Mountains are the outcome of collisions between strata of the earth's crust; the result of the encroachment of a given stratum on another one. These strata that go deeper and deeper enable the crust layers to integrate.

Isostasy is defined in the *Webster's Third New Twentieth Century Dictionary* as follows: "Isostasy is the general equilibrium in the earth's crust, maintained by a yielding flow of rock material beneath the surface under gravitate stress, and by the approximate equality in mass of each unit column of the earth from the surface to a depth of about 100 km." At a time when mountains were viewed as mere prominences, the Quran's reference to mountains' strata invisible to the eye and their stabilization role leaves us in awe.

CHAPTER 33

FAULTS ON THE EARTH'S SURFACE

12- By the fractured earth.

86-The Knocker, 12

In the verse preceding the above verse (The Knocker, verse 11), the returning property of the sky was stressed; this refers to phenomena unknown to men 1400 years ago (Chapter 20 of the present book). In the above verse there are also factual implications that the public during the Prophet's time did not know. As faults had not yet been discovered, the verse was believed to refer to the opening of the earth for the sprouting of vegetation.

In the post-Second World War years, scientists intensified submarine research activity with a view to having access to precious metals and minerals. During this research work, they came across something quite unexpected; the bottom of the seas were covered with fissures that came to be called "faults" or "cracks." If we draw an analogy between the period that has elapsed since the second world war until today with the period that has elapsed from the time of the descent of the Quran 1400 years ago, when there was reference to this information in the Quran, we can better appreciate the value of this reference.

EVERYTHING IS INTERCONNECTED

The Quran now draws our attention to the sky, now to the earth, displaying the hidden mysteries and inciting us to inquire into them. As is the case with the sky, so it is with the depths of the earth-endless mysteries waiting to be unraveled. The "fractured earth" referred to

131

in the verse is of towering importance from the point of view of establishing a connection between the magma under the ground and the surface. These cracks also play a decisive role in the formation of the submarine topography.

Information about the faults is also important as it provides us with detailed knowledge about earthquakes. Big earthquakes occur along the fault lines on the crust. Differentiated movements in the huge masses of substrata form a strain along the fault line. The rocks on each side of the cracks try to resist it before the crust gives way.

In any single earthquake, the amount of slip, in other words the relative displacement of the two fault surfaces, may be a few inches, it is so even in big earthquakes. Studies have been carried out on faults to map out the regions likely to suffer greater damages, the requirements for the construction of edifices to resist the tremor.

The greatest fault upon the earth is the one that stretches from Greenland's offshore to Antarctica. The second largest one stretches along the Pacific Ocean along the Western shore of North and South America. The third important fault lies in the depths of the Asian continent under the Himalayas and follows the South Asian direction. Along with these greater ones there are shorter ones as well.

The Quran directs our attention to places where earthquakes can be expected to take place. If we give up our custom of reciting the Quran merely for the souls of those who have departed, and take it as a guide for our life, we can reach the truth hidden in it.

89- We have sent down to you a Book explaining all things, a guide, a mercy and glad tidings for those who submit.
16-The Honeybee, 89

CHAPTER 34

EARTHQUAKES' MESSAGE
AND HEAVY BURDENS

1- When the earth is severely quaked.
2- And the earth throws out its heavy burdens.
3- And man enquires, "What has come over it?"
4- On that day, it will tell its information.

99-The Earthquake, 1-4

The Arabic word "*zilzal*" means "earthquake." The above verses are quoted from the sura The Earthquake. These verses are believed to refer justifiably to the earthquake expected to occur in the end of the world; however, we should take due notice of its wider sense, depicting earthquakes in general. The fourth verse announces that men will be informed on that day. A terrible disaster like an earthquake associates in one's mind destruction in the first place causing material damage and bodily injury, leading to a general terror and panic. This announcement must have astounded the public.

To establish a link between earthquakes and knowledge of certain facts seemed inconceivable to people up until the last century. Today we have a great many data in our possession regarding the ground beneath our feet, thanks to earthquakes. The shortest radius we could draw from where we might be to the center of the earth is longer than 6000 km, a distance we can never cover. Yes, an earthquake provides information about that portion of the earth inaccessible to us. (During the earthquake to take place at the end of the world, it is possible that men will be further enlightened on subjects beyond His prediction. We certainly do not assert that the verse's meaning is limited to our interpretation.)

BURDENS OF THE EARTH

The second verse of the sura Earthquake is interesting in that it refers to the burdens of the earth. Years have gone by and men have failed to understand what those burdens might be. The widely accepted interpretation was that the sura referred to the earthquake that was going to take place at the end of the world when the dead would be resurrected and treasures hidden underground would rise to the surface. No one could have guessed that the ground beneath was formed of dense and heavy matter that would rise to the surface. References to earthquakes in the Quran contribute to our better appreciation of them. Let us not forget that people believed at the time that the earth rested on the horns of an ox or on a fish whose tail, when it moved, produced earthquakes (The commentary of Ibn Kethir is an example). The fact that the Quran made no reference to such false beliefs is another indication of its miraculous character.

The more we know about the contents of the Quran and about the universe, the more we appreciate God's artistry and the perfection of his religion.

9- Say: "Are those who know equal to those who do not know? Only men of understanding take heed."

39-The Throngs, 9

CHAPTER 35

FORMATION OF PETROLEUM

4- He brings out the pasture
5- Then turns it into a blackish floodwater.

87-The Most High, 4-5

Petroleum is primarily the outcome of a long process during which herbage like algae and fern in the interstices of rocks is exposed to the chemical effects of various bacteria. Today the origin of petroleum is believed to be organic material. Pastures created before man was created were destined to turn in time to petroleum within the framework of the ecological balance of the world. Oily organic residues decomposed beneath the floor of the seas for millions of years. The underlying oily substance eventually was transformed into petroleum.

Petroleum presents the properties of "floodwater." Petroleum, more often than not, moves away from where it was originally formed. It does not have a settling property. Petroleum behaves like flood liquid, traveling long distances and collecting at spots where it comes across hard rocks without pores. Petroleum beds have been discovered in places where they were found as deposits, hindered from continuing their course.

In brief, petroleum, as described in the verses, is

1. made of organic matter,
2. blackish and
3. moves like floodwater.

PETROLEUM'S PLACE IN OUR LIFE

Until the mid-nineteenth century, crude petroleum was collected at places where it had leaked to the surface. Because it mixed with water where animals quenched their thirst and with wells drilled for drinking water, it was considered to be a nuisance. In the 1850s Ferris, and Kier who succeeded him, initiated studies that led to its use as fuel for lamps. Edwin L. Drake discovered petroleum beds at a depth of 21 meters, on August 27, 1859. As petroleum was more reliable than whale fishing and much cheaper to be consumed as lamp oil there was a ready market; and the petroleum era was thus ushered in.

God had devised the composition of this substance in such a way that it serves different purposes in many aspects of our life. Some of the best known derivatives of petroleum are fuel oil, petrol, and paraffin oil. Derivatives less known find their usage in the manufacture of candles and wax, perfumes and cosmetics, even in substances used in cheese production wherein it prevents the cheese's decomposition. Still other petrol oils are used in the following products: insecticides, acetone used in nail polish, artificial rubber, plastic material, chemicals used in the production of detergents and certain drugs containing petroleum derivatives. Last but not least, many textile products also contain petroleum in their composition.

The story, whose beginnings go back to the decomposition of pasture, continues with the petroleum beds in the depths of the soil, with the production of detergents, t-shirts and nail polish. In verses 4 and 5 of the sura The Most High, there are allusions to petroleum. The three verses that precede it mention that God said that everything was given in due order and proportion.

1- **Glorify the name of your Lord, The Most High**
2- **Who creates and proportions**
3- **Who determines in due order and guides.**

87-The Most High, 1-3

CHAPTER 36

RESPIRATION AND PHOTOSYNTHESIS

18- And the dawn as it breathes.

81-The Rolling, 18

The verb to breathe is a term originally used to describe the process in which many living organisms take in oxygen from their surroundings and give out carbon dioxide. But what has respiration to do with the dawn? What brings together these two seemingly incongruous subjects? Does something new happen in the daylight different from the night? These questions were bound to remain unanswered until the time the process of photosynthesis came to light, the synthesis of simple carbon hydrates like glucose and starch from carbon dioxide and water, with the liberation of oxygen, using the energy of light, in green plants chlorophyll being the energy transformer. Nutriments of high-energy content formed as a result of this process, called photosynthesis, are stored in tissues while oxygen is given out. Briefly stated, photosynthesis is a metabolism process in contradistinction with respiration. During respiration, carbon hydrates mix with oxygen, breaking down into the component elements of water and carbon dioxide, the end products of the reactions during respiration are the primary substances of photosynthesis.

This phenomenon takes place only during the day. Photosynthesis is dependent on the energy of light and cannot be realized in the dark. When the "dawn breaks" as described in the verse, light shines and oxygen, the *sine qua non* of respiration, begins to be given out by plants. This makes clear the reason of juxtaposition of words "breathe" and "dawn" in the verse.

WHAT WOULD HAVE HAPPENED HAD THERE BEEN NO PHOTOSYNTHESIS?

Energy is absolutely necessary for living organisms. This energy, which contributes to the functioning of our muscles and heart, and plays an important role in the chemical reactions of our body, is supplied by animal products and vegetables. The primary source of the energy contained in nutriments is the sun. At night, the sun's rays do not reach us. The "dawn" is the time these rays begin to reach the earth. The plants that receive those rays transform this light energy into chemical energy through the process of photosynthesis. Regeneration and growth of plant tissues depend on this energy. While the plant continues to grow using this energy, it stores some of it in the form of chemical energy. A man or an animal that consumes this plant receives the energy it contains. This perpetuates the chemical reactions in their bodies and stores energy in their tissues. Consequently, the energy we derive from animal products and plants is the energy coming from the sun through the plants, forming the initial stage of nourishment. Had there been no process that enriched the oxygen in the air, the oxygen available in the atmosphere would have been exhausted by now. Thanks to this process that begins at dawn can we breathe. At the time of the descent of the Quran, people knew nothing about photosynthesis or transformation of oxygen and carbon dioxide in the atmosphere, or again, about the role played by the sun's rays in the realization of this process. The establishment of such a connection between the dawn and respiration in this verse astounds us once again.

Energy is absolutely necessary for all biochemical processes fundamental to living organisms. The energy is the result of the breaking down into elements of nutriments stored in the cells. When they come into contact with oxygen during this process, the chemical energy stored in molecules of the nutriment is released. This is a reaction similar to the phenomenon that takes place when a piece of wood kindled gives out heat and light. So the act of respiration must not be considered exclusively as an exchange of oxygen and carbon dioxide, but as a more complex process that forms the basic energy source of plants and animals.

Had God not created the various requirements for photosynthesis, such as, for instance, the chlorophyll necessary for the plants' realization of photosynthesis, not a single organism would survive. Like many phenomena in the universe, photosynthesis, the transformation of oxygen and carbon dioxide necessary for respiration, is a part of the great and perfect design.

Knowledge of photosynthesis is of fairly recent origin. Scientists have conducted major research projects; among others, those of the team headed by Melvin Calvin, an American chemical engineer, are of great import. This team was awarded the Nobel Prize for chemistry in 1961.

The photosynthesis that enables us to breathe and supply oxygen can be epitomized as follows:

Light energy (coming from the sun) + Carbon dioxide (coming from the air) + Water = Chemical energy + Oxygen.

The chemical formula is:

Light + $6CO_2$ + $6H_2O$ = $C_6H_{12}O_6$ (Glucose) + $6O_2$

CHAPTER 37

DIFFICULTY OF ASCENDING TO THE SKY

125- ...And whomever He wills to send astray, He makes his bosom narrow and strained as if he was ascending into the sky.

6-The Cattle, 125

A person subject to spells of dejection and who feels strained is likened to a person who is ascending to the sky. We know today that during ascension, atmospheric pressure gradually decreases, rising blood pressure causing strain on the functioning of heart and veins topped by lack of oxygen, which in turn influences the lungs, making one feel constricted. If one persists going even higher, there comes a moment when the individual loses his life.

There were no airships or aircraft at the time of the Prophet. Torricelli was the person who in 1643 invented the mercury thermometer with which he demonstrated that the atmosphere exerted a pressure. To speak of a decrease of pressure at the time was out of the question. Nor was there reliable information about circulation of the blood or lungs. One can guess that men climbed heights and had difficulty breathing as they went higher and higher. In the verse, however, ascension is toward the sky. A person experiencing difficulty of respiration on top of the mountain he has climbed may attribute this difficulty not to the lack of sufficient oxygen at the high altitude to which he has climbed. The verse speaks of a process that takes place as one rises to the sky. The question is not of the experience one has on the top of a hill. Ascension to skies has a much wider connotation.

OPTIMUM PRESSURE AND OXYGEN
FOR PERPETUATION OF LIFE

The oxygen and pressure ratio being ideal, a man's bodily functions run across no difficulty from sea level up to a height of 3000 meters. At altitudes ranging from 3000 to 5000 meters, elevated blood pressure and difficulty breathing are experienced. At an altitude of 7500 meters, the tissues are badly in need of oxygen. Above this height, a person experiences a blackout; the blood circulation, the respiration and the nervous system begin to falter. Changes in atmospheric pressure affect the circulation, increasing the pressure of the blood running through the veins and arteries. The balance of gases in the vacuums of the body and the distribution of gases in the blood and tissues (in particular of the nitrogen) is upset. The mechanical effect of a sudden rise and fall in blood pressure results in the rupture of blood vessels. Effects of the changes in gas volumes may be grouped as follows: eardrum ruptures, inflammation of the middle ear, sinusitis due to change in the volume of air in the sinuses, toothaches (dental carries), difficulty passing gas, and colic...

Thanks to the ideal proportion of oxygen, we can comfortably breathe and our circulation functions properly. Prof. Michael Denton says that if the density of the air had been a little higher, the air resistance would reach great proportions and it would be impossible to design a respiratory system to supply enough oxygen for a breathing organism. Between the possible atmospheric pressures and the possible oxygen proportions, looking for an optimum digital value for life, the bracket we come across is a highly limited one. The fulfillment of so many requirements for survival within this narrow bracket certainly points to perfect design.

The perfection of God's creation becomes once more manifest in the course of our study of the atmospheric pressure, in harmony with the oxygen content of the air, suiting our biological makeup.

CHAPTER 38

MAN AND POLLUTION

41- Corruption has appeared on land and sea because of what the hands of people have earned, He thus lets them taste the consequences of their works that they may return.

30-The Romans, 41

Man has been paying the cost of damages he has inflicted on his surroundings and nature throughout centuries. Passion for more money, sloth and irresponsibility have made man blind to the fact that he is part of his natural environment and that the damage he causes it will unavoidably affect him. The development of environmental consciousness in man, who has suffered from damages of his own doing, is a recent event. Environmental awareness only received special emphasis in the world after 1970.

In a century and place where environmental awareness cannot be said to have existed, the reference made in the Quran to this fact, that is to the corruption caused in the land and the sea on account of that which men's hands have wrought, is a lesson of great scope. We translate the Arabic word "*bahr*" as "sea" (However, it may also designate large lake, reservoir, inland sea, waterway, etc.). We are advised that we are not allowed to dispose as we like of nature's endowments since otherwise we shall have to pay for it. We are also informed that the damage caused by man to his own environment will also affect the land and the sea beyond his own limits. Therefore nobody is allowed to say, "I am on my own. No one can meddle with what I do." Nature is our common heritage and it is everybody's duty to contribute to the checking of this transgression.

DAMAGE CAUSED TO THE ENVIRONMENT

It is correct to say that the industrial revolution in the 19th century highly contributed to the growth of pollution. It is, however, not correct to say that this was the beginning of pollution of the environment. This process had been going on since ancient times. What is new, however, is the development of ecology and the ecological consciousness. To begin with, the burning down of forests is a happenstance that has been going on for ages. Forest fire was the principal cause of such diseases as man often suffered in the past, like antrakosis. These pyromaniacs had certainly no inkling of what they were perpetrating with their own hands.

During the Middle Ages, environmental pollution seems to have been an important problem. In the England of 1345, people who tossed feces out of their windows were fined two shillings. In the 12th century, Philippe Auguste of France was the first king to ordain the collection of abominable waste littering the streets of the city. The public who disposed of their waste by channeling it into waterways polluted the springs they drank from. The first law on pollution that we know about was passed in 1388 by the British parliament; this law prohibited the throwing of waste into the streets and waterways. Transgressors were to be reported by the people residing in the precincts to the private secretary to the king. Only after it reached extraordinary proportions was the pollution made subject of the law.

The situation became even graver during the industrialization period in the 19th century. Metallurgy and iron and steel works polluted the land, the water and the air. This is reflected in the novels of Charles Dickens and writings of Friedrich Engels that describe the pollution in London. In 1930, sixty-three people died of pollution in the Mosa Valley in Belgium. The situation in London, in 1952, was even more serious. Four thousand died of upper respiratory tract diseases because of man's ravages of nature.

The situation at present is hardly any rosier. There may not be such mass mortality, but according to the World Health Organization, more than one billion people are under threat from pollution. It is impossible to evaluate the degree of damage the public has suffered from throwing garbage and waste to the sea. This habit is still going on. Sea pollution that threatens the marine fauna and flora, and the settlement in their tissues of noxious substances, is thought to be the cause of many illnesses, including cancer. Carbon dioxide emissions from cars and factories also contribute to the so-called "greenhouse" effect, and it is feared that drastic changes in global climate are causing catastrophic disasters.

We see that environmental pollution is one of the greatest dangers for humankind. This reference to pollution in the Quran at a time when there was no environmental awareness is remarkably interesting. The Quran was not penned like books that are products of the human mind under the influence of social and sociological realities in due consideration of the current issues. It is sent by God, Lord of all times and beings. Knowledge unavailable at the time of its descent, problems of the past and of the future are all present in the Quran. Man is the author of his own destruction. The verse serves as a warning to redress his wrongdoings. The more we expend effort to counteract our past shortcomings, the better we can protect ourselves against catastrophes. Ecology must be our common concern.

CHAPTER 39

SEX IN PLANTS

53- And has sent down water from the sky. With it have We produced diverse pairs of plants.

20-Ta-He, 53

3- ...And fruit of every kind He made in pairs two and two.

13-The Thunder, 3

During the time of the Prophet, biology was not a developed science and the system of reproduction of plants was not known. Differentiation of sex in plants was to be a later discovery. The concept of the production of diverse pairs of plants as stated in the Quran 1400 years ago is very meaningful.

Most species of plants exhibit features of sex, namely, the production of specialized sex cells or gametes and the fusion of these cells in pairs, called fertilization. In flowering plants, the gametes are produced within the flowers. In the female portion, the egg of the plant forms a bulge: this is the ovum with its small and round seeds. Sperm is produced within the pollen tubes and then is carried by wind or insects or other agents from the pollen-producing organs of the flower to the stigma of the pistil. Inside the pistil are ovules, within each of which a female sex cell (egg) is produced. The fertilized egg develops into the embryo of the seed, and the ovule eventually becomes the mature seed. The pollen grain with its tube and contents is the male gametophytes of a flowering plant, and the central tissue (embryo sac) of the ovule with its egg constitutes the female gametophytes of a flowering plant.

PERFECT HARMONY

Plants are of almost infinite variety, their range stretching from the tiniest of plants to the gigantic Californian redwood (Mammoth tree) reaching a height of 90 meters. In the sexual reproduction of plants, male and female organs are differentiated. They have an extremely complex and perfect microscopic world. Thousands and thousands of female and male organs fit each other as if encoded. Had this harmony been a little bit less perfect, none of these plants could have perpetuated their species, since everything depended on these male and female reproductive organs. The least defect in any of them would mean the end of that particular species. These organs must exist in perfect condition within the same species of plant within the same time bracket. This impeccable order shows once again the perfection of the Creator's design, which leaves no room whatsoever for coincidences. A complex code designed to unlock quadrillions of safes cannot possibly be the result of fortuitousness. The case of plants' sexual reproduction is even more complicated, and the sexuality in plants and reproduction are but one of the many aspects of the creation of plants. Every plant in its impeccable form is an ornament of our world, a part of our ecological system, a miracle of creation.

CHAPTER 40

SOIL THAT VIBRATES AND SWELLS AS IT COMES TO LIFE

5- ...You see the earth barren and lifeless, but when We pour down water on it, it vibrates, it swells and puts forth every kind of beautiful growth in pairs.

22-The Pilgrimage, 5

It is general knowledge that there is no life without air and water. Does it ever occur to anyone that soil also is a prerequisite to life? The soil is in continuous development. Throughout thousands of years, especially by the effect of water, it has undergone transformation by erosion of the Lithosphere. As the rate of this erosion is 0.01 mm per year in hard rocks, this transformation is imperceptible (This rate rises up to 20 mm in warmer regions). In this transition process, the earth rises from the inorganic world of minerals to an organic sphere. In a fertile section of earth 1 m^3 there are some 30 million bacteria.

The above verse refers to reactions that occur in series after rainfall. The vibrating and swelling of soil were at first believed to be literary expressions. But Robert Brown's discovery of the earth's shaking referred to as "Brownian movement" was another proof of the Quran's miraculous insight. Three stages are mentioned in the Quran, namely:

1) Earth's vibrating
2) Earth's swelling and
3) Earth's products in pairs.

1) In the first stage, particles in the soil begin moving upon the fall of rainwater. Raindrops falling on the earth at random move in every direction. The particles are ionized. They are positively ionized as there is a fall in the electrical charge and negatively ionized as there is a rise in the electrical charge. With the arrival of water the ionized molecules begin vibrating. Robert Brown, who discovered this phenomenon in 1828, called this movement: "Brownian movement."

2) The second point refers to the growth in size of the earth's particles as they absorb water. Soil particles are composed of joint layers. Between any two layers, there are spaces that allow water particles and dissolved ions to enter. When water and the nourishing elements dissolve in it, they diffuse between layers, resulting in the swelling of the size of the soil particles. The soil's property of holding water prevents its penetration any deeper, and thus provides for organisms and plants to live.

3) The third stage refers to the germination of seeds. As the verse points out, the fertilization process has started. The soil that seemed dead comes to life with water, giving in turn life to vegetation that begins to sprout.

There are many references to the creation of plants. Parallels are drawn between the creation and restoration to life of plants and the resurrection raising from the dead. The period when a plant begins to sprout is likened to youth, and the period when the plant ripens to adolescence, and then to maturity. Just like a man gets weaker and frailer as he grows older and wrinkles appear on his skin, so do plants dry and lose their luster. When they die, they mix with the soil, just like the corpse of a man. As plants grow again, so will man rise from the dead. God, who causes plants to die every year and regenerates them, so will He raise men from the dead.

33- One sign for them is the dead land. We revive it and produce from it grains which they eat.

36-Ya-Seen, 33

CHAPTER 41

FEMALE HONEYBEE, BUILDER OF HER OWN CELL

68- And your Lord revealed the female honeybee; build homes in mountains, and trees, and in the hives people built for you.

16-The Honeybee, 68

In narrating the doings of the honeybee, the Quran uses the feminine gender. In Arabic, verbs are conjugated according to gender. The use in the Quran of the feminine gender in conjugation shows that the acts were performed by the female bee. To translate the honeybee in question with the addition of the adjective "female" before the honeybee would be natural. (It should be noted however that the orthography of both the feminine and the masculine is the same for honeybee.) The working of the female honeybee is described in the Quran as follows:

1- Building of hive (verse 68)
2- Collecting of nectar, new material for honey production (verse 69)
3- Making honey (verse 69)

All the above three functions are performed by female bees. The unique function of the male, more robust with big eyes, is to fertilize the young queen female bee. The male bees that fulfill this function are expelled from the hive by their females at the end of the summer and, as they are used to being looked after by their females, they then die of starvation.

At the time of the descent of the Quran, men did not know the details of the distribution of work among the bees living in a hive; they did not know that those actively working in the hive were females. They did not know that the function of producing honey and collecting nectar from fruits belonged to female bees. Therefore, it is interesting, indeed, that in listing the duties of bees, the Quran used the mode of conjugation in the Arabic intended for the female gender.

MATHEMATICIAN BEES

The functions performed by the female honeybee leave us in wonder. The design of the cells in which she will live call for the erudition of a mathematician. Honeybees produce their honeycombs in the form of hexagons. (Bee fossils show that this was also the case millions of years ago.) Mathematicians inquiring into the reason why this hexagon remained constant and why there were no rectangles, heptagons, octagons, etc. found out that the optimum use of the entire space of unit could be no other than a hexagon, which also accounted for the production of cells using the available material in the most economical fashion. Had the cells been of a different shape, i.e., triangular or quadrilateral, there would be no vacuum, as well. But less material is required to build hexagonal cells than that required for triangular or quadrilateral cells. In many other shapes there would be unutilized space left. Thus the hexagonal cell is capable of storing the greater amount of honey with less wax.

This structure is the result of the combined work of thousands of bees, each contributing to the entire geometrical opus. Mathematicians have proven that no larger space could be arranged with a given amount of wax to fit the geometrical design. The worker bees show how they can realize it in the most economical fashion with what they have.

A French entomologist by the name of Antoine Ferchault posited a geometrical problem referred to as the "Bee Problem." He stated that "a cell of regular hexagonal cross section is closed by three equal and equally inclined rhombuses. Calculate the smaller angle of the rhombus when the total surface area of the cell is least possible." Three leading mathematicians, a German, a Swiss and a Brit, tried to solve this problem, and all of them found the following result: 70

degrees 32 minutes. This exactly fits the angle of cells constructed by the female bees. Even the wisest of men could not suggest an improvement on the female bees' technique of building.

The worker bees' points of departure in the production process of these cells differ. As the work proceeds, the cells converge toward a central point. The angles of cells at the point where they meet are perfect. It is clear that the construction of this design, the distances between the beginning and the end points and the precise calculation of the positions of their fellow workers display unbelievable exactitude.

The most renowned mathematicians demonstrated the bees' unerring calculation measured as 70 degrees 32 minutes. However, were we to suggest that these men of science take a ruler in hand and make a hexagon with perfectly fitting angles, and then add to the instructions given to these three professors, asking that the calculation used to form the hexagons be regular and flawless, they would fail in the task. We see that the bees are not only great theoreticians but also skillful practitioners. In the theoretical field, this calculation is incredibly exact, while their dexterity in applying it is unbelievable accurate.

How do these bees, whose lifetime is very short, achieve all these calculations and construction work? To call this ingenuity mere "instinct" does not explain anything. The Quran states that the bee received revelations according to which God's design and programming were put into execution. Within the span of the honeybee's lifetime, the cleverest of men could not learn even to count, let alone be the author of such a perfect design. We cannot account for the erudition of bees, certainly not as pure luck. The Creator who created the bee made her with all her potentialities, having solved for her all these mathematical problems. The same Creator sees to it that the bee works for ends that also serve mankind in general. In the second part of this book MMLC 15 where the mathematical miracles will be dealt with, we will examine the mathematical code of the suras and verses where "honeybee" is mentioned. God, who endowed the bee with mathematical characteristics, presented further mathematical miracles in the suras and verses in which "honeybee" is mentioned.

CHAPTER 42

THE FEMALE HONEYBEE'S ABDOMEN AND THE HEALING POWER OF HONEY

69- Then eat from all the fruits and flit about the spacious paths of your Lord. There issues from within her abdomens a drink of varying colors, wherein is healing for the people. Verily in this is a sign for those who understand.

16-The Honeybee, 69

The honeybee has a body that varies in length between 1cm and 3cm, and that is divided into three parts: head, thorax and abdomen. The verse quoted above stresses that in the individual female bee there are "abdomens," which in Arabic is "*butuniha*," the "ha" referring to a singular female bee. If the plural of the word "abdomen" was meant to refer to the female bees, then the plural female pronoun "*hunna*" would be attached to the verb "*butuniha*." This makes clear the segmented abdomen of the bee. Inside the abdomen there are two stomachs or crops. When collecting the nectar from flowers, nectar is stored in this honey stomach for transport back to the hive. At the rear of the honey stomach is a valve that prevents stored nectar from passing on into the rear portion of the digestive system, except for the small amount needed by the bee to sustain life. The hind portion of the bee's body is the abdomen that is made up of segments in the form of rings. The abdomen of the bee functions as a chemistry laboratory to produce honey.

The colors of honey vary as stated in the Quran. They change according to the climate, season and weather conditions and the sources where nectar is obtained. The color of honey ranges from dark brown to green, among which the light yellow is preferred. In the honey industry, modern countries with developed techniques use a colorimeter to establish the exact description of honey's color.

THE HONEY DANCES OF BEES

At the beginning of the verse, reference is made to the collection of nectar. The female bees not only produce honey, but also assume the duty of collecting the raw material from flowers to be eventually transformed into honey. During this process of seeking the nectar, incredible phenomena occur.

The bee that has located the spot where there is nectar to be collected returns to the hive to inform her sisters about the location of flowers. The scout bees returning to the hive perform circular dances or tail-wagging movements on the comb. These dances indicate not only that the scouts have found nectar or pollen and that the other workers should go out and seek it, but they are actually performing an amazing charade that conveys precise information to their sisters about the direction and the distance of the location of a newfound source.

Sometimes a normal adult must attend a dance course for six weeks while a bee, whose lifetime is but six weeks, is able to perform a dance for communication purposes. The bee's calculation on her way back to the hive is also of great interest. The bee makes her calculation according to the position of the sun. The sun changes its locality one degree per four minutes. The bee that has spotted the location of her food also calculates her return journey as directly and correctly as possible in relation to the sun. She performs this without any error. All these calculations and harmonious coexistence within the hive cannot possibly be explained by pure coincidence or after a six-week-long training. So, all these are innate in her as an endowment of the Creator.

THE HEALING POWER OF HONEY

The verse speaks of the nutritive property of honey, a product of female bees. The regenerative property of honey is confirmed by medical authorities. In addition to its rich vitamin content, among its components are also such minerals such as calcium, potassium, magnesium, sodium, phosphorus as well as such metals as copper, iodine, iron, zinc, and hormones.

Thanks to the easy convertibility of its sugar content, it is easily assimilated. Honey facilitates the functioning of the brain, thanks to its other sugars. It contributes to the production of blood, to its cleansing and proper circulation. Honey provides for the requirement necessary for proper functioning of our physiology and also it is used externally in cosmetics and dermatology.

The fact that honey had healing properties was nothing new for communities all over the world. Therefore, I am not claiming that this was not a generally acknowledged fact at the time of the descent of the Quran. However there were also such superstitious beliefs as the healing effect of a camel's urine, which was later falsely attributed to the Prophet in hadith books. The Quran never justifies any of such false ideas offered as elixirs. Had the Quran been a product of human imagination, it might also have contained at least a residue of such false beliefs.

The distribution of work of bees in a hive and the multiple tasks performed by bees is too complicated to explain within the scope of this book. The ventilation of the hive, regulating humidity and temperature, keeping a perfect hygienic medium in the hive; guarding the hive, discarding the unwanted foreign matter, dead bees, etc., secreting wax, propolis, all are amazing tasks. How can a bee, whose lifetime is but six weeks, know and perform such grandiose artistry? Without an intelligent Creator the fortuity of all these data is certainly unimaginable. Every inquirer into the doings of a bee - to whose properties there are references in the Quran - will observe the sublime artistry of God in the entity of an insect.

4- Also in your creation and spreading of the animals are signs for people of assured faith.

45-Kneeling, 4

CHAPTER 43

FORMATION OF MILK

66- And surely in the livestock there is a lesson for you, We give you to drink of that which is in their bellies from the midst of digested food and blood, pure milk palatable for the drinkers.

16-The Honeybee, 66

We often see goats, sheep and cows eat grass, and yet it rarely occurs to any of us to establish a link between this process and the milk and the dairy products we consume. God lets them feed on this grass, its ultimate transformation to be milk, one of the basic nutriments. William Harvey discovered the circulation of blood almost a millennium after the Prophet's decease. At the time of the Prophet, the fact that the blood carried the nutriments absorbed from digested food into its constituents to mammary glands for production of milk was not known. The new material transformed from pasture into assimilated food and blood becomes a nutritious food.

The Quran not only draws attention to truths unknown at the time, but also displays facts to derive lessons from. The blood collects and transports the substances formed by digested food to organs; among others, to mammary glands. This process is initiated by blood coming into contact with the contents of intestines, on their walls. Before continuing its journey, carried by blood, part of the digested food is absorbed by the intestines. This information is the result of modern research in biology, chemistry and in the physiology of digestion.

THE RICHEST OF PRODUCTS EASY TO OBTAIN

Milk is the first food of the newborn mammal. It is a fluid secreted by the mammary glands of mammalians as food for their young in the period immediately after birth. From the young of whales to human infants, all mammals feed on their mother's milk. The young animals and the babies obtain their supply of excellent nourishment without any toil. Milk is the best product for infants. No other nourishment can replace what is provided by it. We can identify thousands of nutritious food items in the world. Had the universe been the outcome of happy coincidences and had there been no ingeniously designed creation, there would have been no particular reason for the mother's milk to be the best and most carefully selected nutriment. This perfect order designed for every mammal, including man, is a proof of the Creator's inimitable forethought. Materials digested to become blood turn into milk in the mother's breast and are offered to the newborn by its Creator. Whether ratiocinated or mathematically calculated, it is impossible to assert that this is the outcome of fortuitous events which have nothing to do with a designed purpose. The infant practices sucking its finger in the womb to be prepared for drinking milk as soon as it is delivered. The fact that mother's milk comes exactly in the amount of the baby's need without spurting is also carefully planned.

The milk we first taste from our mother's breast will continue throughout our lives to be consumed by us to meet the requirements of a healthy constitution. Milk is a whitish liquid consisting of small globules of fat suspended in a watery solution containing proteins, lactose sugar and minerals like calcium, casein and phosphorous, plus vitamins. Cheese, butter and yogurt are all made with milk, the basic nutriment of man. The benefits that our body derives from its contents, like minerals and vitamins are more than the present book can contain. When we consume it, we should remember always its Creator.

18- Then which of the favors of your Lord will you deny?
55-Gracious, 18

CHAPTER 44

COMMUNICATION BETWEEN BIRDS

16- And Solomon was David's heir. He said: "O my people! We have been taught the speech of birds..."

27-The Ant, 16

In the above verse, it is said that the Prophet Solomon was taught the speech of birds in addition to the endowments that God's grace had adorned him with. The Quran refers to the communication between birds and to the fact that the twittering and singing of birds has particular meanings. Birds, like human beings, do communicate. This undeniable communication is certainly not as developed as it is in man.

Research conducted by zoologists has established that sounds emitted by animals are meaningful and not haphazard. Birds, ants, dolphins, etc., have systems of communication.

MEANINGS IN SOUNDS EMITTED BY BIRDS

As the Quran speaks of the language of birds, let us take a look at research conducted on birds. Brazilian and American ornithologists have studied the hummingbird (one of the tiniest birds in the world) and published their findings in the British journal Nature. The author of the article, Maria Luisa Da Silva, says that the vocabulary of the hummingbird is not innate but develops afterward. In other words, the hummingbird learns to speak as human beings do.

Studies on crows have demonstrated that they emit a variety of sounds, namely, to call the colony of crows to come together, to express alarm, and to communicate a state of distress. Ornithologists, who have recorded these sounds using a sonograph, are still engaged in deciphering the meanings behind them. Bernd Heinrich, among these scientists who speak of the difficulty in decoding the sonograms, associates this research work with the work of the inhabitants of other planets visiting our earth and trying to decipher eating, playing, making love and activities like catching fish using a sonograph. What we are trying to do is to imagine ourselves in their place. Bernd Heinrich speaks of the difficulty encountered in deciphering the language of animals in general, as different species have different ways of communication, each calling for a different approach.

There is a body language, expressed by the changes in your body position and movements, that show what you are feeling or thinking. Nodding means "yes," hailing is a sign of calling to someone in order to greet him or try to attract his attention. Although the sounds emitted by birds are a means of communication, they also have, in general, a body language. Their body language is easier to decipher. For instance, a bird that emits a sound by touching its beak with his tongue means "I am a friend, I have no intention to harm you." Theresa Jordan gives a whole list of signs, demonstrating thereby that even the body language necessitates a glossary.

The physiology of birds is as interesting as their language, the long distances they cover without swerving from their destination are something to marvel at. Ornithologists studying birds will see God's perfect artistry revealed in these creatures too.

38- All the creatures on earth, and all the birds that fly with wings are communities like you. We did not leave anything out of this Book. Then they will all be gathered before their Lord.

6-The Cattle, 38

CHAPTER 45

FEMALE ANT AND COMMUNICATION BETWEEN ANIMALS

18- When they came to a valley of ants. One of the female ants said: "O you ants, get into your habitations..."

27-The Ant, 18

The 16th verse of the sura The Ant informed us of the language of birds. In the continuation of the same sura, it is understood that Solomon had also been taught the language of ants and in verse 18 the communication between ants is represented by an example. Research on ants has in fact demonstrated that the ants had a very complicated social organization that enabled them to communicate with each other.

In their tiny heads, the ants have some 500,000 nerve cells. They are equipped with extremely sensitive antennae and bodies that secrete many chemical substances, of which they benefit in order to realize their communication. The pheromone secreted by their endocrine glands is one such substance. They use this secretion to communicate with one another. Ants perform certain things in a much more orderly fashion than human beings do; this secretion enables them to gather, share things, defend and feed themselves. Different species of ants have different endocrine glands. For instance, the alarm and attack commands are given by the dufour glands, while the sternal glands are used during exodus in colonies and in chasing their prey. Every ant uses these secretions as human beings use their language.

Apart from the liquids of glands, the ants communicate also by sounds. For instance, ants whose colonies are nested in the bark of trees strike the ground with their bodies. Carpenter ants beat drums to this end. The members of the colony communicate with each other and direct themselves to their destination without any misunderstanding. Giving the alarm, eating, cleaning, gathering together, exchanging food and recognition are the main headings of communication. The Quran draws attention to ants' giving the alarm, which is one of the main points that research work has established.

FEMALE ANTS

In the verse, the ant in question is female. Just like in the case of bees, this use of feminine gender is significant. Colonies of ants show similarity with the hive of bees. The only function of male ants is to have sexual relations when they are mature. Male ants die soon after they copulate. All the work is performed by barren female ants in colonies. As in the case of the beehive, the colony is a world where reign the mother and sisters.

If we consider that it was the ant who guards and collects food that announced Solomon's advancing army, then it must have been the female worker ant. If we consider that ant to be the most privileged and elite member of the caste, then the announcer must have been the queen ant, which is, of course, again a female.

It is estimated that there are 10 million ants per man. Magnitude and the vastness of numerical concepts are no problem for God. This shows again God's power of creation. There are ants that eat leaves, cutting them with the mastery of a tailor; there are harvester ants that live in the desert, etc. All these are proof of the great wisdom and artistry of God.

11- Such is the creation of God, show me now what those beside Him have created. Indeed, the transgressors are far astray.

31-Luqmaan, 11

COMMUNICATION BETWEEN DOLPHINS AND OTHER ANIMALS

In the Quran special consideration is given to the communication between birds and ants. This fact may lead the inquirers to study other animals. For instance, studies on elephants have demonstrated evidence of elephants communicating with one another from very long distances.

Dolphins' communication also has been among the points of interest among researchers. Because of their ability to communicate with one another through a range of distinct sounds, dolphins have become the object of serious scientific and experimental studies. Whistling, screeching and clicking enable them to establish communication. They send sound waves with a kind of sonar. This system enables them to recognize objects in dark waters and measure distances. Their sound frequencies range between 0.25kHz and 200kHz. The higher frequencies are used to spot locations and the lower ones are used for communication and orientation. To detect the communication signs of dolphins, experiments have been conducted by immersing microphones in the sea, and putting artificial obstacles in front of dolphins. After these experiments, scientists have concluded that dolphins talk to each other, although the meanings of the different sounds they emit have so far not been deciphered. (See the experiments conducted by Dr Dreher, Dr Evans and Dr. John C. Lilly).

In all the specimens of creation the perfection and impeccability of God's work have been manifest. Those eyes that can perceive and those hearts ready to receive can witness all these.

46- Have they not roamed the earth so that their hearts may thus understand and their ears may thus hear? Indeed, blindness is not the blindness of the eyes, but the blindness of the hearts inside their breasts.

22-The Pilgrimage, 46

CHAPTER 46

MAN CREATED FROM DUST AND WATER

12- We created the human being from a quintessence of clay.

23-The Believers, 12

7- Who made all things He created excellent, and He started the creation of the human being from clay.

32-The Prostration, 7

20- Among His signs is that He created you from dust...

30-The Romans, 20

54- And it is He who created from water a human being, then has He established relationship of lineage and marriage. Your Lord is Omnipotent.

25-The Distinguisher, 54

According to the Quran, man is created from dust and water. Sometimes the Quran stresses these elements separately and sometimes in combination. There have been an infinite number of speculations about man's creation out of clay (the combination made of dust and water). After the developments in biology and chemistry, analytical studies of clay and the human body were carried out. The result showed that the constituents of clay and those of the human body fit exactly. Let us enumerate these constituents: iron, calcium, oxygen, sodium, potassium, magnesium, hydrogen, chlorine, iodine, manganese, lead, phosphorous, carbon, zinc, sulfur, and nitrogen. The artistry of God was to combine this inanimate matter to create man.

All these constituents are obtainable at reasonable prices. The cost of all these elements is not any higher than a hundred dollars according to the New York Stock Exchange. Yes, a hundred dollars exactly is the basic price of man. God created man out of a combination of elements that costs almost nothing. The mystery does not lie in the material out of which man is made, but in the Creator...

2- Praise be to God, Lord of the worlds.

1-The Prologue, 2

QUINTESSENCE OF CLAY

As it is explained in the sura The Believers, Verse 12, man was creat ed from a quintessence. God combined the elements contained in clay as a result of fine calculations. These elements are harmoniously and proportionately distributed in the body at birth; the body is programmed to make use of them in due proportion and to dispose of any surplus. The human body contains about 2kg calcium. If there is a decrease in this amount, the very act of biting into an apple may cause our teeth to break. Our body needs 120gr of potassium. A decrease of it may cause muscle cramps, fatigue, intestinal troubles, and palpitations. We need only about 2gr to 3gr of zinc. Any lowering in these values may cause loss of memory, impotence, decrease of the capability to act and weakening of the senses of smell and taste. Insufficiency of selenium may bring about the weakening of muscles, hardening of arteries and heart muscles...

All these data show that God, while making use of clay as raw material for man, combined its constituents in ideal proportions. The Quran is exact in its statements. Creating a living being such as man from such ordinary matter is one of the manifestations of the omniscience of God. Careful combination in due proportion of all the constituents of the human body demonstrates God's matchless design. The creation of man, a masterpiece, out of a matter of simple aspect like clay, shows again the greatness of God.

WATER BECOMES ALIVE

30- ...and from water We made all living things. Will they not believe even then?

21-The Prophets, 30

45- God created every moving creature from water...

24-The Light, 45

In the 54th verse of the sura The Distinguisher, it is said that human beings are created from water, and in the suras The Prophets and The Light it is said that all living beings are created from water. Water is the basic biological element of living matter. Cells are made of water in proportions varying between 60% to 80%. A cell whose basic element is water is a living thing. Without water there is no life.

Water is composed of two hydrogen and one oxygen atoms. Water, whose chemical constituents have been arranged perfectly, is made of atoms devoid of organic life and 99% vacuum. How is it that living beings and animals are created from something of which 99% is void? How is it that an entity made of an inorganic and inanimate matter comes to life?

24- He is God, the Creator, the Maker, the Designer; to Him belong the most beautiful names. Whatever is in the heavens and the earth glorifies Him. He is the Almighty, the Wise.

59-Exodus, 24

CHAPTER 47

SEMEN IS A COMPOUND

2- Verily, We created the human from a drop of a liquid mixture in order to try him. Thus We made him a hearer and a seer.

76-The Human, 2

Analyses in detail of organs and substances in the human body could be made with the invention and development of the microscope. These analyses showed that semen is composed of spermatozoa in their nutrient plasma, secretions from the prostate, seminal vesicles and various other glands. Citric acid, prostaglandin, flavins, ascorbic acid, fructose, phosphorylcoline, cholesterol, phospholipids, fibrinolysin, zinc, acid phosphatase, and sperm are among the various constituents of the semen.

Our body is one of the best, the most beautiful and the most complicated of works. Thanks to it, we are able to see and hear, to perpetuate our lineage; thanks to the skills of this body we can design and build machines, computers, bridges and airplanes and do paintings, carve statues and compose music. Our body is the product of one of the initial stages of creation, that entailed the creation of all the constituents of the semen. This was to be followed by the physiochemical processes involved in the union of the male and female gametes to form the zygote, the fertilized ovum before cleavage.

The explanation of only the sperm cord or the prostate gland would take hundreds of pages. Our Creator refers in His book to a "liquid mixture." Our analysis of this mixture and its constituents contributes to our increasing wonder at the presence of the miraculous creation of our body.

Our odyssey, that began with the creation of this liquid compound, led us to acquire such skills as seeing, hearing and other processes of extreme complexity. No man within his senses can attribute his or her perfect creation to the skills of a drop of a mixture and coincidences. The Creator who is Omniscient, Omnipotent, who is exalted and beyond all praise, is the Author of these things as stated in the Quran.

CREATION FROM A DROP

36- Does man think that he will be left uncontrolled?
37- Was he not a drop of semen emitted?

75-The Resurrection, 36-37

The Quran says that God who created man watches over him. In verse 37 it is stated that he is created from "a drop of semen." Here again we are in the presence of a scientific fact inaccessible at the time of the Prophet. In this verse, the Arabic words "*maney*" (semen) and "*nutfah*" (drop) are differentiated. "*Nutfah*" means what is left of a liquid in a bucket whose contents have been emptied. Thus the expression refers to a portion and not to all the semen. The semen contains in a single ejaculation, along with its other constituents, sperm numbering between 100 million and 200 million. One out of hundreds of millions of sperm fertilizes the egg. In other words, the zygote, product of the union of two gametes, is but the result of a small part of the semen. The sperm or the spermatozoon, the male gamete, typically consisting of a head containing the nucleus, a middle piece containing a mitochondrion and a comparatively long tail whose structure is similar to that of a flagellum. Hundreds of millions of sperm, leaving the male's organ, head for the ovum waving their tails. The distance they cover in the woman's organ of reproduction involves a considerably long journey, if measured in microns the length of a sperm (a micron is equal to one millionth of a meter). To cover such a distance means to swim long distances, kilometers in fact. Many of the sperm die on the way and only a few succeed in reaching the target. Of the multitude of sperm surrounding the egg, only one is allowed to penetrate, barring the way to all others. Half of the genetic data of this sperm is contained in a head of 5 microns. The other genetic code is waiting in the mother's womb. All these are the result of many concurring details. God displays his artistry in every instance.

CHAPTER 48

CREATION FROM A QUINTESSENCE AND CHILD'S SEX

8- Then made his offspring from the quintessence of the nature of a despised fluid.

32-The Prostration, 8

In the 46th chapter, our attention was drawn to the fact that man was created from a quintessence of clay. The Arabic meaning of the word, "quintessence" is "*sulala.*" Just as man is created from a "quintessence" of the earth, he is also created from a "quintessence" of semen. While the word "drop" signifies just a small amount of semen, the word "quintessence" draws attention to the essence of semen.

Sperm constitute only a part of the semen, in fact they are the basic element of it. The particular sperm that fertilizes the egg is but a tiny member of hundreds of millions of sperm in semen; it is also the swimmer that reaches the finish, having overtaken all the others.

Each of us is the winner sperm's product. Every human being coming to the world has behind him hundreds of millions in this swimming race. We, who are reading these lines, have come out victorious, since we are far ahead of those we have left behind. Each of us has carried the day. And we are the quintessence!

57- It is We who created you, so why do you not affirm the truth?
58- Do you then see the semen that you emit?
59- Is it you who create it or are We the creator?

56-The Inevitable, 57-59

DETERMINATION OF THE CHILD'S SEX

45- That He did create in pairs, male and female;
46- From a drop of semen which emitted.

53-The Star, 45-46

Even today there are still people and families on the husband's side who blame mothers for giving birth to girls rather than to boys. That it is the mother who decides on the sex of her child is a lingering prejudice among the ignorant. Although well-informed scientific circles were exempt from such misconceptions, even they had until quite recently the impression that the child's sex was the joint product of equal contribution by the mother's egg and the father's sperm. The fact that it is the sperm that determines the child's sex has only recently been established. In a fabricated hadith falsely attributed to the Prophet, we read: *"Male's water is white. Woman's water is yellow. If the two come together and the man's water overcomes the woman's, a male child is born, if, on the other hand, it is the woman's water that dominates, the child is a girl."* One can see that during and centuries after the time of the Prophet the factor that determined the sex of the child was not known.

The implication in the Quran of the formation of sex is astounding, as it indicates that it is a drop of semen that determines it. The 46 chromosomes that human cells contain form the genetic code of a human being. Two of these determine the child's sex. Male chromosomes are defined as XY and the female ones as XX. The chromosomes are split during ovulation into two each, containing an X chromosome. Some sperms contain X and some Y chromosome. If an X chromosome unites with an X chromosome in the woman's egg, the sex of the child to be born will be female, while a Y chromosome in man uniting with an X chromosome in woman means the offspring will be of the male sex. We see that whether the future child will be a boy or a girl is entirely dependent on the arrival of an X or Y chromosome from the sperm. Biological research continues. The discovery in the1990s of the SRY protein in the Y chromosome, and the conclusions derived from it, have enriched the available data on the issue.

This information that the Quran implied more than 1400 years ago was not known until quite recently. We can mention, for example, the story of Henry the VIII, who divorced Catherine his queen for having given him a girl child. This fact, alluded to in the Quran, had also an ironical touch. Women have been blamed for centuries for having been responsible in the determination of the sex of the child they were going to give birth to. The discoveries of science have explained this miraculous event, while ruling out the grounds which put the blame on the woman.

SECURE PLACE

20- Have We not created you from an unassuming fluid?
21- The which We placed in a secure place.

77-The Emissaries, 20-21

The uterus is described as a secure place. Being placed in the center of the pelvic cavity, it is well protected. Man's organ is not favored with such an endowment. The uterus is a cavity whose walls are made of muscles and have the shape of a pear. In an adult woman the length of it is 8cm, the width measures 5cm and the height 2.5cm. The uterus, relatively small in size, dilates considerably during the last phase of pregnancy. The weight of it is 50gr while it attains about 1000 gr at the end of pregnancy. The child it holds within it can even exceed 5000 grams. This means that the child is 100 times heavier than the uterus itself.

It is the only organ that can grow so rapidly and is given to rapid development. With its tightly wedged thick muscles, it protects the fetus, rapidly growing in size, against all kinds of external impacts and adverse conditions. The fetus, exposed to all sorts of dangers, owes its survival to the solid structure of the uterus, its ideal place. The Quran's drawing our attention to the solidity and durability of the womb calls for our studying it more deeply is a proof of the God whose grace protects the fetus against all ill intentions.

1- In the name of God, Gracious, Merciful.

1-The Prologue, 1

CHAPTER 49

HANGING ON THE WALL OF UTERUS

13- Then We placed him as a drop in a firmly established lodging
14- Then We developed the drop into a hanging...

23-The Believers, 13-14

"*Alaq*" is the Arabic word referring to something that is hanging on a place. Embryology did not exist as a science at the time of the Prophet. Neither was there special terminology yet. The Quran described the stages using the words current at the time. According to this description, the zygote then hangs on the wall of the uterus. The Quran brings clarification to something unknown at the time. To render the word "*alaq*" with the signification 'embryo' may not exactly reflect its original meaning, and would moreover fail to convey the spirit of it. To translate it as "a clot of blood" deviates from the literal meaning of the word. This rendering has often been adopted, giving it the attribute of a secondary meaning of the word. The reason was the failure of exegetists to conceive the true meaning of the word.

In 1641, Harvey's statement, according to which the origin of every living thing was an egg, and saying that the embryo underwent transformations, passing through stages of development, was one of the major contributions to the advancement of science. In the 17th century, when man already had the microscope at his disposal, the respective roles of the egg and of the sperm were topics of discussion. Bonnet (1720-1793) speculated that female eggs consisted of a countless number of smaller eggs, one inside the other, and generalized on the "preformation theory," which maintains that a child arises from an

170

adult in miniature contained within the egg, and he applied this theory to all animals. This hypothesis found many adherents in the 18th century.

Men, some thousand years prior to the 18th century, had been acquainted with the Quran. What was said in it about the reproduction of the human organism was rendered in a clear expression that was to take man centuries to confirm. Keith Moore, anatomy professor in the Toronto University of Canada, says that the information contained in the Quran about embryology cannot be accounted for by the data available in the 7th century. He goes further and says that, even a century back, this was hardly known. Only today are we in a position to understand what the verses of the Quran meant, thanks to the development of modern embryology.

In history, the only book that exactly describes the development of the human being within the womb is the Quran. Let us once again tackle the subject of hanging to the uterus wall. Only after the invention of the microscope was man able to bring this fact to light as a result of developments in the fields of physiology, anatomy and embryology.

PROOFS FROM THE STAGES OF THE EMBRYO

6- These are the signs of God which We rehearse to you in truth. Then in which word other than God and His signs do they believe?

45-Kneeling, 6

The sperm that encounters its other half in the fallopian tube continues its way from there toward the uterus. The embryo, in its journey, does not cling on to the fallopian tube. The embryo proceeds on, and when it reaches the uterus hangs onto a spot where the blood vessels are dense. The stage of "*alaq*" referred in the Quran has started.

How is it that this powerless cell devoid of all intelligence eventually finds for itself a shelter in the uterus, the ideal place for it? How is it that the embryo that arrives at the uterus hangs on its wall and is able to receive all the nourishment necessary for its development, like a leech? (One of the meanings of the word "*alaq*" is "leech.") All these things are carefully planned by God's ingenious artistry. Those who are blind to this fact and refuse to see in this God's doing, interpreting it as pure coincidence or the embryo's genius, will be in a ridiculous situation.

The process of the embryo hanging on the uterus wall is the result of a complicated system. To penetrate the acid layer of the uterine wall, the embryo secretes an enzyme (hyaluronidase) that catalyzes the uterine tissue and allows the penetration of the embryo, which settles in it like a plant. Henceforth, it will supply its need for food and oxygen from this very point. The hyaluronidase secreted by the embryo catalyzes the breakdown of the hyaluronic acid. Furthermore, the embryo releases some chemicals to protect itself from the mother's immune system, which would otherwise treat the embryo as a foreign invader to be destroyed.

The embryo's discovery of the place where it is going to hang is a marvel. The embryonic cells have so many activities to perform that a scientist who studies them can easily come to the conclusion that they are entities of high intelligence.

1. Read in the name of your Lord who created
2. He created man from a hanging.

96-The Hanging, 1-2

CHAPTER 50

CHEWED LUMP OF FLESH

14- Then We developed the drop into a hanging, then developed the hanging into a chewed lump of flesh.

23-The Believers, 14

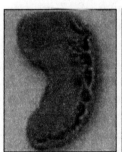 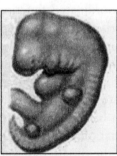

A plastic model of the embryo made by Keith Moore

The Quran continues displaying its miracles in its description of "alaq" succeeded by the "mudga" (chewed lump of flesh) stage. As a matter of fact, the embryo in the uterus has the appearance of a chewed lump of flesh, a tiny piece of flesh. Sura 22-The Pilgrimage, verse 5, speaks **"of chewed lump of flesh, partly formed and partly unformed,"** which is a good description of the aspect of the fetus. The aspect presented to our sight is of an indented figure whose head, feet and internal organs have begun to develop (partly formed, partly unformed).

Prof. Keith L. Moore says that he had a model made in plastic in the shape of an embryo and bit on it, leaving the marks of his teeth; this seemed to be an exact reproduction of an embryo, and explained the indentation referred to in the Quran.

ADVENTURE OF THE CHEWED LUMP OF FLESH

A single cell undergoes many stages in forming the various organs and tissues of the body. A chewed lump of flesh at one stage, it is transformed into organs, muscles, skeleton, brain, eyes and ears, until in time man finally emerges. To review all the stages of this development renders our awe still greater at the presence of God's artistry.

There is a time when the lump turns into a heart, a heart that beats 100,000 times a day without our being aware of it and without any conscious contribution on our part. Blood that comes to the heart and leaves it does not get mixed together. Blood is distributed in the body in perfect proportions. The ventricles and atriums of the heart are wonders of creation. The organized movement of blood within the arteries and veins presents matchless complexity and would take pages to describe.

The day comes when this "chewed lump of flesh" is transformed into a liver, the organ that assumes more than 400 functions. This tiny lump becomes muscles to help us in our numerous movements like eating, running, walking, sitting and laughing. The muscles function within the framework of an extremely complex net of coordination. Merely smiling requires the coordinated functioning of 17 muscles. Our brains, hands, feet, intestines, kidneys, respiratory systems and the blood circulating in our veins and arteries owe their origins to this tiny lump of flesh, once a drop of liquid. The story of our creation would take up a whole encyclopedia. The Quran invites us to study these phenomena and meditate upon them. The prayer and ritual enjoined to man in the Quran have been a topic of long discussion. The verses that refer to ratiocination and meditation, which, although superior in number to those of the rituals, have received less attention.

6- O human beings! What has seduced you from your Lord, Most Beneficent?
7- The One who created you, designed you in due proportion, and disposed you aright.
8- In whatever design He chose, He constructed you.

82-The Shattering, 6-8

CHAPTER 51

BONE FORMATION AND CLOTHING OF BONES WITH FLESH

14- ...then created the chewed lump of flesh (mudga) into bones, then covered the bones with flesh (lahm)...

23-The Believers, 14

259- Look further at the bones, how We construct them and then cover with flesh (lahm).

2-The Cow, 259

The embryo is a boneless lump. Its cartilage tissue is transformed into bones in due time, as stated in the Quran, followed by their being clothed in muscular flesh. The Arabic word *"lahm"* means the muscular flesh. This process was unknown 1400 years ago. It was believed that the bones and muscles developed simultaneously. Advanced microscopes and micro cameras introduced into the uterus corroborated once again the truth expressed in the Quran.

PERFECT STRUCTURE OF THE SKELETON

The verse quoted from the sura The Cow draws our attention to the skeleton and invites us to examine it closely. While reading this verse, we will try to meditate upon the miraculous formations within our bodies. Our skeletons, marvels of engineering, are formed of 206 bones of varying sizes. They are towers made of bones connected with each other by joints and ligaments, enabling us to jump, run, bend, sit, etc. To turn the page of a book necessitates the concurrent action of our shoulder, elbow, wrist and fingers, without our being aware of the fact that it is the skeleton that performs this act.

The skeletal system is made up of structures composed of bones or cartilage or a combination of the two, which provide a framework for the vertebrate body and serve as attachment for muscles. Every part of this system independently performs the duty with which it has been charged. Where the movement is deemed to involve danger, the joints are fixed, like in the skull and pelvis, while in the hips or shoulders they are mobile. Cervical vertebrae permit the head to revolve around its axis up to 180 degrees. Thus, one does not have to turn his body to look around. The lungs and heart are protected by ribs to ensure their proper and safe functioning without being exposed to any hazard. The skeletal system supports the body like the columns and beams of a building. However, it is to be wondered at that while in modern buildings the frame forms 60-70% of the building's weight, the human skeleton forms but 15% of the body weight. The structural frame is highly resistant. For instance the thighbone (the femur) in vertical position can carry a weight of one ton. Solidity and elasticity coexist.

The skeleton has a lubricating system, the details of which the present book can hardly touch. Every joint in our bodies is regularly lubricated with special oily substances. Verse 259 of the sura The Cow, **"Look further at the bones,"** directs our attention to these data that form but a small portion of man's marvelous makeup.

2- Verily, We created the human from a drop of liquid mixture in order to try him. Thus We made him a hearer and a seer.

76-The Human, 2

How marvelous it is to think that a day will come when a mixture called semen will be able to hear, see, laugh, weep, think, understand; and artistic works may be created by him endowed with aesthetic feelings. What a great gift for a man!

While the Quran says that there will be a day when a drop of a mixture will be able to hear and see, maybe it implies the fact that seeing is to succeed hearing. In many verses we frequently come across "hearing and seeing." In all these verses hearing comes first and seeing second. By the 23rd week of pregnancy the development of the ear is completed while the retina is still undeveloped even in the 25th week. The fact that the verse mentions hearing first and the organ of vision afterward may be an allusion to this fact.

8- God knows what every female bears, and how much the womb falls short or exceeds. Everything He does is perfectly measured.

13-The Thunder, 8

CHAPTER 52

CREATION IN THREE DARKNESSES

6- ...He creates you, in the wombs of your mothers, in stages, one after the other, in three darkness.

39-The Throngs, 6

The fetus in the mother's womb is a fragile thing. If it were not protected well, heat, cold, temperature variations, impacts or even the mother's sudden movement might kill it or cause it irreparable damage. The three zones within the mother's womb protect the fetus against all sorts of dangers. These are:

1- The abdominal wall,
2- The uterine wall, and
3- The amniotic sac.

With the level of knowledge at the time, this information could not have been available. The fetus continues to develop in the dark of these three regions. The amniotic sac contains a fluid that fills the amnion to protect the embryo from desiccation and shock. This substance is a kind of cushion that absorbs shocks, balances exerted pressures, prevents the amniotic membrane from adhering to the embryo and enables the fetus to change position in the uterus. If the fetus could not easily move in the said fluid, it would remain idle as a mass of flesh and would likely suffer injuries leading to various complications. Equal distribution of heat enables the fetus to be at a constant temperature: 31°C. We observe that our Creator has designed everything perfectly in its minutest detail, satisfying all the requirements of our body and protecting it against the dangers lurking in the outside world.

FROM ONE STAGE TO ANOTHER

It was also said that verse pointed to the fact that during the stages of creation we passed through three different phases of development. According to this view the three veils of darkness refer to:

1- The fallopian tubes: Either of the paired oviducts that extend from ovary to uterus for conduction of the ovum in mammals. The sperm, having fertilized the egg, proceeds on along the fallopian tubes. The zygote during this journey begins to divide and reproduce itself.

2- The uterine wall: The stage during which the embryo hangs on the wall.

3- Amniotic sac: The sac fills with a fluid that surrounds the fetus. The next step of evolution calls for a longer period of development.

A glance at the outward aspect presents a uniformity of sight. But were we to dwindle to the size of a tiny cell and explore the environment, we would see how different these chambers were. The first dark space is reminiscent of a monumental tunnel with respect to the cell. The second compartment is a dark forest where no light penetrates, and the third compartment reflects the dark depths of the sea.

There are three interconnected layers or three spaces through which the fetus passes. God knows whether the reference is to one or to the other. And there are three stages through which the embryo evolves.

The three stages in question are:

1- The pre-embryonic stage: This stage is called the "first trimester." As the cells multiply, they get organized in three layers; this process takes two weeks.

2- The embryonic stage: Basic organs begin to emerge from the cell layers. This stage is referred to as the "second trimester" extending from the second week to the eighth week.

3- The fetus stage: The face, hands and feet appear and the human figure is formed. This is the "third trimester" that extends from the 8th week until birth.

Our shaping up takes place in stages, in each of which new evidences emerge. Data relative to embryology have been acquired only in the recent past. Neither before the descent of the Quran, nor in the course of the millennium succeeding it can you find such information available. The Quran indicated the composition of the semen, from a drop of which man was created. The Quran coined names that describe the development stages of the embryo; namely hanging to the wall of the uterus (*alaq*), succeeded by the chewed lump of flesh (*mudga*). Thus the Quran uses terminology based on the positions the fetus assumes. There was no source before the Quran which asserted that the muscles were made after the formation of bones.

To assert a scientific fact, a scientific background is a must. It is on such a foundation that other data can rest, which, in turn, calls for advanced microscopes and micro cameras. At the descent of the Quran, there was no such scientific background or such instruments. Nobody of sound mind can come forward and say that the information in the Quran was a result of fortunate coincidences.

4- We created the human being in the best design
5- Then turned him into the lowliest of the lowly.

95-The Fig, 4-5

35- Were they created of nothing or were they themselves the creators?

52-The Mount, 35

CHAPTER 53

IDENTITY ON FINGER TIPS

3- Does the human being think that We cannot assemble his bones?
4- Surely, We are able to reconstruct even his fingertips.

75-The Resurrection, 3-4

Fingerprints did not mean much to the people at the Prophet's time. An Englishman by the name of Genn Ginsen, in 1856, found out that the pattern of lines at the tip of a person's finger was something unique to the individual. Until 1856, men knew nothing about this characteristic of fingertips. The discovery of the fact that the pattern of lines on fingertips was a sort of identity card is often used by the police to help find criminals. The pattern lines of the fingertips differ even in identical twins. This identity card cannot be forged; it affixes a unique signature to whatever it touches. One cannot imitate or deny it. We carry it about us till the end of our days. Epidermal burns or injuries or aging distort our bodies in one way or another, yet cannot change this fact.

These patterns of lines are traced within the womb when the fetus completes its three months' period. Research is currently being carried out to see whether these lines may be used to detect genetic defects in our body. To the best of our knowledge so far, nothing positive has been discovered on this issue. It is, however, likely that something new may emerge any day.

At the time of the descent of the Quran, fingertips had nothing special about them. God, who will cause man to come back to life on the Day of Judgment, stresses the importance of fingertips.

181

DATA CONCEALED ON FINGERTIPS

One of the basic indications of this verse may refer to the patterns of lines on man's fingertips. There may be other indications, according to which all the characteristics of our body are encoded on our fingertips. It could be implied that during our re-creation all the particularities and features of our body will be restored, so it may be that what lies on our fingertips, apparently of little significance, will be sufficient for this process. The reason why fingertips are given as example is the general acceptance that they are simple things of not much worth. Nevertheless, even the seemingly insignificant tip of a finger is a data bank, thanks to which the entire body may be re-fashioned. DNA is one of the most important discoveries in human history. The discovery of DNA put an end to the idea that the human cell had a simple structure with its contents. As the cell came to be analyzed more and more, the complexity of its makeup was better understood. Even one piece of DNA includes a cipher formed of a series of more than three billion codes. From the color of our hair to our little finger, everything is contained in this code. A printout of data related to DNA would form the contents of about 1000 volumes of one million pages. What is more, DNA has the capacity to duplicate all these data within 20 to 80 minutes. In the lore contained in the 1000 volumes of one single DNA, one can find all the characteristics of the body. The DNA of a simple cell on the fingertip will give one all the necessary information. Our Creator can easily have recourse to this lore to re-create man. It would be as easy for Him to do so as if He were creating him for the first time.

> 78- And he makes comparisons for Us and forgets his own creation. He says "Who can resurrect the bones after they are rotten?"
> 79- Say "He who created them the first time. He has knowledge of every creation."
>
> *36-Ya-Seen, 78-79*

CHAPTER 54

LANGUAGE AND MAN

30- When your Lord said to the angels: "I will place a successor on earth." They said: "Will you place one there who will commit disorder and shed blood, while we praise You, and extol Your holiness." He said: "I know what you do not know."
31- And He taught Adam all the names. Then presented them to the angels, saying: "Tell me the names of these if you are truthful."
32- They said: "Glory to you, we have no knowledge except what You have taught us. You are Knowing, Wise."
33- "O Adam, give them their names." When he told them their names, He said: "Did I not tell you that I know the secrets of the heavens and the earth? I know whatever you reveal and whatever you conceal."

2-The Cow, 30-33

So far we have dwelt on subject matters related to such natural sciences as physics, chemistry, biology, medicine and geology as miraculously developed in the Quran. In this chapter and in the next three chapters, we will embark on important philosophical considerations coming within the compass of the Quran.

In the verses quoted above the subjects treated are the creation of man by God and His placement of him on earth. Angels who fail to conceive the reason for man's creation - a potential for committing disorder and shedding blood - bring up the problem of evil and ask God for a justification. God says that He knows things that they do

183

not know and that there is wisdom in everything He creates. Whereupon God emphasizes the superiority of man in that he is taught how to use language.

In this chapter we are going to tackle the importance of man's use of language. The superiority of man as a being depends on his capacity to use a language. The philosophy of language developed in the 20th century and the vast studies carried on the issue asserts that without language we could not exist as persons as such. Once, Bertrand Russell in the 1920s (he was in his 40s then and had already produced most of the works which had given him prominence) acknowledged that he considered language as a means at the disposal of man, that he could handle without giving it special attention. Bryan Maggee claimed that this held true not only for philosophers, but also for novelists, poets and playwrights. Self-consciousness in the use of language developed, especially in the twentieth century, and became one of the philosophical characteristics of the age.

This development is not limited to a superficial interest in words but also includes in its scope beliefs related to basic issues. The abstract thought made possible by language has proven to be the most important factor in conceptualizing all the aspects of reality in which we had not participated directly, and in handling it as well as in our communication with our environment. The general consensus is that this is the major characteristic that differentiates us from animals. Thus, learning a language enables us to become ourselves. The importance of language had not been conceived as so great, both as regards mankind in general and the individual in particular.

The Quran, 1400 years ago, stressed this importance. Those who take an interest in philosophy should know that most of the new ideas are based on the depository of past acquisitions. Wherever there are hot debates, wherever ideas clash, new concepts arise, be they correct or irrelevant. During the Prophet's time, there seems not to have been significant philosophical discourse. The Quran's reference to the relevance of language at such a time - which people would only realize long afterwards - is an interesting statement indeed. At the time and place of the descent of the Quran, there were neither concerns about language nor about its philosophical profundity.

CONTRIBUTION OF WITTGENSTEIN

Using and understanding a language is the distinctive characteristic of man that separates him from other living beings. This forms the essence of our inner existence. The questions raised by Ludwig Wittgenstein played a great role in conceiving the importance of language in the history of philosophy. Wittgenstein asked questions which at first sight would seem platitudes, just like in the case of Newton inquiring into the reason of the planets' not changing their courses and of the falling of stones thrown in the air back on the ground. Wittgenstein had his precursors, like Locke and Leibniz, as well as Frege and Russell. However, it was Wittgenstein who first brought the issue of "language" into focus in the history of philosophy.

In *Tractatus*, a work belonging to his first phase, he tried to construct an ideal definition of language that gave a picture of the world. According to him, a sentence that said something (a proposition) had to be "a picture of reality." Wittgenstein thinks that if we analyze what is said, we can reduce it to words that are but names of things and the connection established between the words of a sentence would represent the connections between things in the world. In this way, the sentence may draw the picture of the world.

Wittgenstein believed he had solved all the philosophical problems. Nevertheless, later on as he advanced in years, he began feeling out of step with *Tractatus*. In his second period, he began to conceive of language as a kind of tool. In this period he claimed that language was a social phenomenon and activity. The commonality between Wittgenstein's former view and the latter is that the language skill occupies the center of his concern and that it is transformed into the philosophy of language. Wittgenstein is one of the rare philosophers who managed to gather around him a large number of disciples, despite his two contradictory periods. Wittgenstein saw, during his second period, that language had more meaning than he had originally thought. In our opinion, the merits of a language and the targets that it conveys exceed his belief, even at this period. I shall dwell on this point longer in a book devoted to this subject. These studies are important since they direct our attention to the importance of language, a special gift of God to mankind.

HOW DOES THE BABY BEGIN TO SPEAK?

Frege's and Russell's studies of the philosophy of mathematics led to the emergence of the philosophy of language. Noam Chomsky's statements about language had a considerable impact in the 50s. To be able to handle something as complex and difficult as language cannot be explained just with the hypothesis that the baby learns it only after he is born without any *a priori* tendency. Formerly, it was believed that a language consisted of a series of habits, skills and aptitudes and was acquired by exercises, repetitions, generalizations and associations. The undeniable fact is that the majority of the public receive no systematic education. In other words, the parents, in general, do not teach their children about pre-established linguistic principles. This becomes all the more apparent if one considers that the great majority of the world's masses lack a proper education. Yet, this does not rule out the fact that babies do learn how to speak in their tender age.

I agree with Noam Chomsky. The baby must be fully equipped and ready to learn how to speak as soon as it wants to communicate with its environment. As our eyesight is made ready to perceive the world at large, so is our mind prepared to use its innate capacity to acquire what is being spoken around it. As the eye begins to see, wherever there is light enough, so are the ear and the mind exposed to hear the language spoken, in an environment ready to acquire it. As Humboldt says, we acquire as a baby the skill to use finite means in infinite ways. Even intellectually restricted children do the same.

The following example demonstrates the innateness of this aptitude: The mind can be visualized as a function at first, when the empirical data are entered as input; one has the linguistic output, just like the number 5 is obtained when the square root of the number 25 is sought. The mind is even ready to learn how to speak like a calculator. When it meets a language, it acquires it and makes all sorts of operations.

3- He has created the human beings.
4- He has taught him speech.

55-Gracious, 3-4

Language is an innate gift of God to Adam and his offspring. If we go back to the days of our babyhood and inquire into the ways by which we acquired the faculty of speech and built a vocabulary, would we not be in a difficulty to account for the process? How is it then that we learn how to speak without any conscious contribution on our part?

WHAT WOULD HAPPEN IF THERE HAD BEEN NO SUCH THING AS LANGUAGE?

To appreciate the value of language, we must look for an answer to the question "What would happen if there had been no language?" Had there been no such thing as language, there would have been no states, cities, villages or even families. In a milieu deprived of all social institutions, no production would ever take place. Consequently, there would be no textile products, cars, glassware, pencils, note-books, etc.

Our mere conception of the importance of language is made possible by linguistic expression. An article on the importance of language is the result of our use of it. Language is not an invention of human beings. Language requires as premise a will and an orientation. Given the fact that the importance of language finds its expression in language, would man be in a position to create a language when the very concept of it was absent? Language is a social phenomenon, and where there is no language, there is no society.

The development of language is certainly possible. But this is possible only when one has the rudiments of a language. A language can develop just like a plant that sprouts. The absence of a language would mean the absence of seeds, the consequence of which would be the absence of vegetation. Just consider (for a while) the coinage of a word to mean a particular concept. On the assumption that men were deprived of a "language," the fancied word would be doomed to sink into oblivion. The invention of writing was a subordinate process. Where there is no concept of a language, accumulation and transmission of information would be impossible. Given the fact that the importance of language cannot be conceived without it, the socialization of occasionally uttered unintelligible words or sounds emitted cannot be made into a coherent common means of communication.

Language is a means calling for consensus of a community. In a milieu deprived of social consciousness, the invention of a language based on consensus is unimaginable.

The newborn is the most helpless creature among the creatures of the earth. It is dependent on its parents for survival. In the absence of a common language there would be no communication, and, therefore, no family. The paternity of the child could not be established. Only the mother could be identified. Where knowledge does not exist, it is difficult to establish any connection between the sexual act and the birth, notwithstanding the period of nine months that elapses before the child is born. Even this connection is made possible by the use of language. The establishing of the family unit and the restriction of sexual relations to couples in humans require the use of language. In such a milieu, the child can only recognize its mother. It would not be easy for a mother to feed her child all by herself. Man cannot be compared with other living beings. Most of the living creatures begin to walk, to fly and seek food a very short time after they are born. The majority of the species of animals are programmed to protect themselves. The long lasting maintenance of the human baby - the weakest of all living beings - is secured thanks to the culture and the communication the language provides. The faculty of thinking through the use of words replaces the innate programming of other living beings.

Had men been deprived of speech from the beginning of their days, they could hardly have survived. The Quran's statement that the first human being was taught to speak is very important in this respect. Man is born equipped with the mental capacity, with an ear ready to receive what he hears, and a mouth and tongue to express his intentions. Coincidences cannot account for the perfect and complex creation of our ear, mouth and tongue. To all these, however, has to be added the endowment by our Creator of the potential *a priori* faculty of speech. A more detailed study of this issue will be tackled in a further work.

37- Then Adam received from his Lord words...
2-The Cow, 37

CHAPTER 55

SIGNS WITHIN OURSELVES

53- We will show Our signs to them in the horizons, and within themselves, until it becomes clear to them that it is the truth. Is it not sufficient that your Lord witnesses all things?

41-Elucidated, 53

The Quran uses "*nafs*" (self) to express consciousness, the quintessence of our personality. "*Nafs*" is integrated with our physical body; the author of all good and bad acts is our "*nafs*."

The fact that the atoms of our physical body - of which 99% is vacuum - deprived of all consciousness, perform such conscious acts as seeing, hearing, and thinking, cannot be explained materialistically will form the subject matter of another book I am intending to write, in which this issue will be tackled within a larger framework, stretching from the philosophy of mind to the quantum theory wherein many scientific branches will find room. With this in mind, I refrain from taking up this issue in this present work.

The point I should like to dwell upon now is the verse's allusion to signs in ourselves. There are *a priori* categories that the mind is constitutionally endowed with, concepts or ideas that are not derived from experience. The subject I speak of in this chapter is not based on findings obtained by satellites, telescopes, submarines or on the recent developments in physics, chemistry or biology. Here we find ourselves surrounded by the available data of a rich philosophical background. The tribe to which the Prophet belonged dealt in trade and animal husbandry. The Prophet himself was not brought up in a milieu like Plato's Academy or in an environment where the colorful and lively schools of philosophy like Cartesianism flourished. Therefore, the fact that the Quran made a distinction between the outward signs and the signs immanent in man's soul is noteworthy.

ONTOLOGICAL ARGUMENT

The basic message transmitted by all the religions revealed by God is the fact that He is a Perfect Being. This becomes all the more apparent when we witness all the entities created by God. In the ontological argument, attainment of God is achieved not through exterior means, but from the idea of "Perfection" or "Perfect Being" inherent in each of us.

Farabi and Avicenna were among the first philosophers to refer to the initial arguments of ontology. Farabi analyzes the ontological argument together with the cosmological argument. According to them, God must be self-existent (Necessary-Being); assuming that He does not exist would be a contradiction in terms. All other creatures are possible creatures; both their existence and nonexistence can be a topic of discussion. If the possible entities are not resolved in the Necessary-Being, there would be a contradiction in terms. Given the fact that Farabi's conclusion is a combination of ontological and cosmological arguments, many thinkers believed to have found traces of this for the first time in the works of Avicenna.

Nevertheless, this argument is, more often than not, associated with Descartes. To avoid committing error, he sets out in his philosophical quest by considering all past knowledge as if it were nonexistent. He begins with the statement that many of the preconceived opinions he has accepted since childhood have turned out to be unreliable; so it is necessary once in a lifetime to demolish everything and start again right from the foundations. There follows a systematic critique of previous beliefs. Anything based on the senses is potentially suspect, since I have found by experience that the senses sometimes deceive and it is prudent never to trust completely those who have deceived us even once.

Elsewhere Descartes expresses this "*cogito argument*" in the famous phrase, "*cogito ergo sum*" (I think, therefore I am). He derives from this argument that he exists incontestably and that thinking can never be confuted. Later he realizes that knowing is more perfect than

190

doubting and explains how this idea of perfection leads him to the most perfect, to the idea of a supremely Perfect Being.

He reasons that the representational content (or objective reality) of this idea is so great that it cannot have originated from inside his own (imperfect) mind, but must have been planted in him by an actual Perfect Being - God. Things outside him like the sky, the earth, the light and the heat and a thousand other things, all these things contained nothing that would surpass him. If they were unreal he might have concluded that he had acquired them from the void. However, this could not hold true of a Perfect Being. He could not have acquired it from nothingness.

Descartes concluded the existence of God after having examined the evidence inherent in the self. He said that this conclusion was not an invention of his imagination, and that to add or subtract anything to or from it was beyond him. He had to accept the fact that he had come to the world with this *a priori* sign. Like the initials that an artist imprints on his work, God had implanted this idea as He created him.

While Leibniz contends that Descartes' views need to be supplemented, he formulates an ontological argument bearing similarities to Avicenna.

KANT'S TIME AND SPACE CATEGORIES

The Quran speaks of signs in the "self." So far, I have gone over "the idea of the existence of God" innate in us, as propounded by Descartes and other thinkers like him. I believe that the verse that refers to signs in the "self" meant much more. I am of the opinion that the "self" considered an *a priori* entity and all the characteristics innate in us come within the scope of this verse.

According to Kant's matchless discovery that made him what he is, time and space are innate in us before all experience and encounters with the outside world. A little child, who has no notion of distance, moves away from things he dislikes and approaches things that seem pleasant to him. Therefore, man knows whether such things are within or outside his reach as an *a priori* intuition. In other words, the idea of "space" is already there in his mind without having previously experienced it. The same thing holds true for the "time" factor. The child has the sense of "before" and "after," prior to other perceptions. Had it not been so, all our perceptions would become chaotic, disordered, in disarray. To go into the details of other evidence related to the innateness of the idea of time and space would necessitate longer discussions. Kant referred to those innate characteristics while analyzing our contacts with the outside world. He said nothing about the fact that these were evidence of God's existence.

We live in a unique place as the "self." We can liken the space in which we live to an extremely complex gate. The "self," along with the *a priori* categories such as time and space we possess from birth, is the only key to this gate. We open this gate, which is of a complex structure, with the key (viz. our "self"). Whoever it was who created this universe, time and space is also the author of the "self."

Our capacity of learning how to speak is also innate in us, as we saw in the previous chapter. The innateness of this capacity is also an evidence of our perfect creation along with the time and space categories implanted in us. Not only our physical being but also our mental makeup is made to fit the outside world.

It is our belief that anybody taking up arms against *a priori* knowledge is doomed to perish!

ENCODED

30- Therefore you shall devote yourselves to monotheism, the creational instinct placed into the people by God. There is no alternation of God's creation; this is the right religion, but most people do not know.

30-The Romans, 30

What have been encoded in us as *a priori* data when we were created, conforming to the precepts of the religion revealed by God, are evidence of the perfect creation of God. If we consider the contents of the verse (41-The Elucidated, 53) that speaks of signs in the "self" as being in conformity with the Creation, the matter may be understood better. Many people encounter difficulty in understanding Descartes' expression of "innate ideas." To have a better insight into Descartes' arguments, we need to concentrate very attentively on the structure of the mind. It might be better to conceive of this as the conformity of our creation with the precepts of religion, since it can be understood easily. Most of us seek answers to the questions, "From where do I come?," "What is the purpose of my existence?," "Where am I heading?" The reason for our asking such questions is that we are created in such a way as to feel the necessity of asking them. There are many people - people who have inhibited their own impulses - who evade asking such questions and avoid meditating upon them. Our Creator's inducing us to pose such questions, His creating us disposed to have faith in religion, are indications of a religion that He would reveal. For there is nothing that can provide an answer to such questions outside religion. One of the evidences of the existence of religion is our having been made in a way to be in need of believing in it.

God who makes us thirsty has also created water to quench thirst. God who makes us hungry has also created the food we need. Getting thirsty and hungry are different from the existence of water and food in the outside world. We might feel the need for something that did not exist in the world, rather than water, viz. the molecules whose constituents are hydrogen and oxygen. But the fact is that our body is made to want what it is programmed in it. To be immortal is the thing we desire most, more than our need for water and a meal. Survival is more important than all desires and passions. God made us in such a way as to wish for an afterworld. This need we feel is an evidence of the Hereafter.

Our creation includes in its scope all His evidence, of the evidence of religion and of the Hereafter. I would like to draw your attention to the expression in the above verse: **"There is no alternation of God's creation; this is the right religion."** This postulate is coeval with man's creation. The person who can decipher the meaning of these signs believes in God, His religion and the Hereafter. The last sentence of the verse, in which it is said that the majority of people do not know this, is very meaningful. As a matter of fact, many people fail to appreciate these signs innate in them, thereby denying themselves.

CHAPTER 56

TELEOLOGICAL CAUSALITY

> 45- Have you not seen how your Lord lengthens out the shadow? He could have kept it motionless had He liked. Then We made the sun a proof for it.
>
> *25-The Distinguisher, 45*

In the above verse, there are important signs related to causality. Persons who study philosophy should know that discussions about causality necessitate a philosophical background. At the time of the descent of the Quran, there was not a single treatise that dealt with philosophy or causality in the region in question. It is noteworthy that the Quran emphasizes an issue of extreme importance, causality, in a region where ignorance prevailed among the Bedouins. Most philosophical commentaries considered important were improvements on philosophies inherited from the past. Whereas the statements of the Quran, not based on any heritage, are evidence of its authority.

God says that the shadow He created was not the necessary consequence of the sun, but was created because God willed it so. In the verse, the causality between the shadow and the sun is acknowledged, but the said causality is created on purpose. The pattern laid down by the Quran differs from the one offered by skeptics like Hume, who is skeptical about causality, and from the viewpoints that try to explain the universe based on the determinism of causal principles that have come into existence by pure coincidence.

Causality is one of the basic tenets of science. It is the relation between two events or states of affairs in which one brings about the other or produces it. That is, it connects everything existing in the universe. It stops our world from turning into chaos by establishing relationships between cause and effect. Had there been no relation between cause and effect, understanding our world would have become even more complex than a dream. Sciences like physics and chemistry take causality for granted. The manufacture of airplanes, satellites and televisions is the result of reliability of the cause and effect relationship. David Hume was skeptical about causality, but like all men, he could not help basing himself on the principles of causality. For nobody can go on living while denying causality. For instance, had Hume not taken into his head to write, he could not have produced the *Treatise of Human Nature* because writing was the cause to produce a book! Gazali's inquiry into causality was not meant to deny it. His opposition resulted from the attempts at replacing it with God's will. The famous example he gave about the burning of cotton purported to postulate causality as a created system, to which we refer as teleological causality.

These may seem absurd to those who are not familiar with the deliberations that the issue of causality has given rise to in philosophy. The reason why I am trying to give such explanations is the place occupied in the history of philosophy by extremists' opinions that deny "causality." Natural sciences have already gone beyond such contentions, while certain philosophers remain irresolute.

The Quran acknowledges causality. Causal relationships, referred to in many a verse by the attribute of "*sunnettulah*" (God's system), are valid throughout the universe. As we shall be seeing in the coming chapters, the Quran points to the mathematical order reigning in the universe. This means the functioning of the cause and effect relationship in a mathematical order. The statements of scientists who translate the principles of causality by having recourse to physical and chemical formulas in the universe and those of the Quran are in perfect conformity.

Although the Quran acknowledges causality, it defines its purpose as a teleological argument. Although, in causal relationships, the cause precedes the effect, the latter's design precedes the cause. The causality chain, as expounded in the Quran, functions within God's knowledge and means, and cannot be creative. While it acknowledges causality, the Quran is against the idealization of causality. The existence of shadow is not a necessary consequence of the sun. The Creator of the sun has foreseen the shadow's existence as a consequence of the creation of the sun. What the Quran propounds is the universal model based on "created causality."

PROTEIN'S PROBABILITY AND TELEOLOGICAL CAUSALITY

Probability calculations provide us with objective data of a mathematical nature that let us see whether the alternative of intelligent design or the one of coincidence is more credible. In particular, the fact that Hume's criticism of the analogical version of the "argument from design" was generally accepted in philosophy circles has been one of the reasons for the rise to prominence of the probabilistic version of the "argument from design." The structure of proteins makes the application of probability calculations possible. Every living cell is made up of proteins. Both as far as the enzymes and as far as their other functions are concerned, proteins are the basic units that run the activities of cells. In the comparison between cells and a factory, the proteins correspond to the factory's machinery. Proteins are made up of a succession of amino acids. In a living organism, a protein is made up of 20 amino acids. The fact that these 20 amino acids should be placed in a certain order, and that the proteins should have a three-dimensional shape, are absolute requisites for a protein. There is a very great difference between the proteinoids, which are formed by a coincidental succession of amino acids, and the proteins, which have a special function within a cell. Amino acids come in two kinds, left-handed amino acids and right-handed amino acids. While proteinoids, which are a result of a coincidental union of amino acids, are made up of both kinds of amino acids, proteins include only left-handed amino acids. What is more important, proteins have to be set up in a certain order if they are to be able to carry out specific duties. The probability that amino acids will turn into proteins just because they have been subjected to energy is the same as the probability that a stack of bricks, which have been blown up in the air with dynamite, will fall back down and form a house.

In living organisms, alongside relatively short proteins like ferrodexin (found in clostridium pasteurianum), which is made up of a succession of 55 amino acids, there are also long proteins like twitchin (found in caenorhabditin elegans), which is made up of a succession of 6049 amino acids. As an example for our probability calculations, let us consider the medium sized serum albumin protein, which can be found in the human body and which is made up of 584 amino acids. The probability that the amino acids in this protein would be

196

made up only of the left-handed kind, can be calculated in the following way:

The probability that an amino acid should be of the left-handed kind: $1/2$

The probability that two amino acids should be of the left-handed kind: $1/2 \times 1/2$

The probability that three amino acids should be of the left-handed kind: $1/2 \times 1/2 \times 1/2$

The probability that 584 amino acids should be of the left-handed kind: $(1/2)^{584}$

In addition to this, all amino acids have to form a peptide bond, which is necessary for tying up with the other amino acids in the protein chain. There are also many other kinds of chemical bonds that can be formed in a natural environment, among amino acids; the probability of a peptide bond forming is roughly equal to the probability of other kinds of bonds forming. Within the serum albumin, made up of 584 amino acids, 583 peptide bonds are required. The probability of these forming is as follows:

The probability that two amino acids should bond with a peptide bond: $1/2$

The probability that three amino acids should bond with peptide bonds: $1/2 \times 1/2$

The probability that four amino acids should bond with peptide bonds: $1/2 \times 1/2 \times 1/2$

The probability that 584 amino acids should bond with peptide bonds: $(1/2)^{583}$

The probability that the amino acids of a single protein should be all left-handed and that they should be connected with peptide bonds is:

$$(1/2)^{584} \times (1/2)^{583} = (1/2)^{1167} = (1/10)^{351}$$

We realise that this probability is a practical impossibility from a mathematical point of view, by means of the following reasoning. If we add the 10^{80} protons and neutrons (total of all protons and neutrons in the universe) to the all photons and electrons in the universe, we obtain a number smaller than 10^{90}. The life span of the universe, 15 billion years x 365 days x 24 hours x 60 minutes x 60 seconds = 473.040.000.000.000.000, expresses the time that has elapsed since the creation of the universe. We could say approximately that this number is equal to 10^{18}. If we multiply the two numbers, the number we get is 10^{90} x $10^{18} = 10^{108}$. This number expresses the number of attempts made, if all the protons, neutrons, electrons and photons in the universe had each made an attempt, every single second of the existence of the universe. If we assume that attempts made in a second by each of these are with the highest chemical speed 10^{12} (one trillion), it makes 10^{108} x $10^{12} = 10^{120}$; but even the probability of two simple events like the formation of a protein with 584 amino acids with only left-handed amino acids and the formation of its peptide bonds is 1 in 10^{351}. This shows us that even if all the protons, neutrons, electrons and photons in the universe had turned into one of 20 amino acids in living creatures and that even if they had made 10^{12} attempts in each second since the creation of the universe, it would not have been enough even to ensure that the amino acids of a single protein like the serum albumin should be left-handed and that they should be connected with peptide bonds.

This conclusion is indeed very interesting. Following the discoveries of Copernicus, the earth lost its central position in the universe; however, even mobilising the entire matter in the universe could not ensure the coincidental creation of a single protein, which exist in thousands in living organisms that we can see only by means of a microscope.

It is vitally important that the succession of the amino acids in proteins be in the correct order. We can show the probability calculation for the serum albumin protein in the following way:

The probability that an amino acid should be in the correct position: 1/20

The probability that two amino acids should be in the correct position: 1/20 x 1/20

The probability that three amino acids should be in the correct position: 1/20 x 1/20 x 1/20

The probability that 584 amino acids should be in the correct position: $(1/20)^{584} = (1/10)^{759}$

If we multiply this number with the 1 in 10^{351}, which we have already calculated, we get the probability that a given protein should be made up only of left-handed amino acids and that it should form peptide bonds and that the succession of amino acids should be in the correct order. This corresponds to a probability of 1 in $10^{351} \times 10^{759} = 10^{1110}$, which practically means that it is impossible (Generally in mathematics all probabilities less than 1 in 10^{50} are considered impossible). It could be said that only a certain part of the succession of amino acids in proteins is active and that changes in the amino acids outside this part could be tolerated. This would mean that the actual probability was higher than we calculated; but, on the other hand, if we include the probabilities also of things like the necessity that the protein should happen to be in the correct position within the cell and also that it should exist in the required quantity, then the probabilities decrease.

Those who deny that the causes were created target-oriented have succumbed to mathematics. This calculation of probability was made on the assumption that amino acids are the ones that are used in the living organism, that the three-dimensional folding of the protein has been realized and that after the formation of the protein the functions have been frozen. Supposing that all these stages had been added to the probability- what was impossible would be even more impossible. However, the figure mentioned indicates this impossibility for those who are versed in mathematics. This serum albumin protein whose formation cannot be coincidental is being produced in the millions by our body.

According to the "blind coincidentalist" materialist view, serum albumin is a fortuitous formation. According to the believer, this protein is a target-oriented creation. This example about the formation of the protein can be stretched to cover many things, from the functions in our body to those in other animals and plants, from the phenomena occurring in our world to space. In all these domains the principles of causality function within a teleological framework.

WHAT CAN BE THE CAUSE OF THIS CAUSALITY?

The absence of causality would rule out all mental functions. Whether a universe would be possible without causality is a different matter, but the fact is, we could not understand the world. Our getting hungry is a cause. Our opening the door of the refrigerator with a view to getting the food in it is a cause; so is our reaching for food. The fact that the meal we have before us is subject to gravity and the fact that what we swallow goes down to our stomach are causes and all these causes are simultaneously the effects of prior causes. The principles of causality govern us in understanding all that is created in the world. Our study of the universe, that contributes to our understanding of God's magnificent artistry and the omniscience of God, is also based on causality. We understand the principles of causality thanks to our mental capacity, God's gift. We reason based on causality. Our ratiocination is based on causality. Had the causal relationships been simpler, many of us might not have given the creation its due. Had the creation been more complex than it actually is, and had we been unable to solve the mysteries of causality, we could not be in a position to understand the universe. In the existence of the universe, the cause and effect relationship is a consequence of God's perfect design.

The great blunder of atheists is their attribution of the effect merely to the cause, since they are convinced that the causes in the principles of causality owe their existence to coincidences. The irrelevance of coincidences is shown in the simple instance of a protein. If one concludes that in the cause and effect relationship, the cause is not a fortuitous act, one can derive from this that all effects are but God's doing. The materialist atheism that considers causality not to be a created process, but the cause's own making, idolizes matter and the causality principles immanent in it. Once the idea of coincidence is ruled out, all the creatures in the universe automatically become the consequence of an Infinite Knowledge and Infinite Power. Assumptions of coincidental formations in the concept of time in which the stages of creation take place have prevented atheists from conceiving of the Creator. Once the concept of coincidence is dealt with, all knowledge is promoted to the Eternal Existence. Those who assert that an object or knowledge is the product of coincidences establish a connection to a process in time. Once coincidences are ruled out, the existent becomes the outcome of the wisdom of the Eternal Being. This leads to the understanding of the universe as the result of a process, the product (within the principles of causality) of a process, the work of the Eternal Being.

CHAPTER 57

ERROR OF THE UNILINEAR PROGRESSIVE CONCEPT OF HISTORY

82- Do they not travel through the earth and see what was the end of those before them? They were greater in number than these and superior in strength and in the traces in the land: Yet all that they accomplished was of no profit to them.

40-The Believer, 82

There are verses in the Quran that speak of certain communities in the past who had reached a level of civilization higher than the community in which the Prophet lived. These communities had been the authors of works far superior to those produced by the latter.

Especially at the beginning of the 19th century, the "historical point of view" occupied an important place. Hegel (1770-1831) spoke of reality as a historical process that could be understood by the categories of historical explanation. His giving meaning to history, understanding and evaluating it were remarkable indeed. But Hegel interpreted history as a linear and evolutionary system that involved continuous and unilinear development. His approach was progressionist. His interpretation of history may be acclaimed, but a viewpoint that conceives every historical period superior to the one preceding it is untenable.

The Quran, an infallible book, proves once again that it is in the right. It acknowledges that past civilizations sometimes produced superior works and proved to be more powerful, thus refuting the linear concept of history. Linear development may have taken place in a given period of history. As a matter of fact, the advancement of science, whose origins went back to the 16th century, have followed a positive trend up until the 21st century. However, to generalize this progressive advancement to cover all of history and every domain would be a great mistake. While formulating his thesis, Hegel seems to have been bewitched by the advancement of sciences from the 16th century up until his own times.

There are more disastrous effects of this concept of history than the uninitiated may conceive. A glaring example is communism. Marx' materialistic interpretation of Hegel led to massacres in which millions of people succumbed and gave rise to both cold and hot wars. As a matter of fact, the share of this Hegelian concept of history in Marx's ideology is great. While Hegel evaluated history through metaphysics, Marx preferred to view history materialistically, calling his school "Historical Materialism."

HISTORICAL VIEW OF COMMUNISM

Marx had a progressionist-linear-historical view (Marx's emphases on the means of production and economics had had a great impact). This conception contended that a given community had to pass through stages, namely through feudalism, capitalism and socialism, before reaching communism. According to this conception, each of these stages would mark a higher degree of development than the previous one. Thus, the communist stage would be superior even to the modern one. The communists assumed that communism would be supreme bliss and the ultimate perfection in history. Moreover, this was a "scientifically established" view! Those who were against it were considered unscientific. The eventual collapse of communism discredited the Marxist conception of a scientific interpretation of history. According to them, history's progressive course could not be forestalled, so that communism was the ultimate stage.

Yet most of the school textbooks of today are under the influence of that concept of history whose fundamental logic is that of linear progress. There are no scientific data to justify the opinions that assert that man's ancestors were primitive hairy creatures as described in the books on anthropology. Engels himself, founder of modern communism along with Karl Marx, acknowledged this. On the assumption that men are fortuitous, he claims that the historical stages must be accepted. Describing the primitives as deprived of language, not even knowing how to kindle a fire, similar to hairy monkeys, would be an illusory account devoid of all scientific justification. There is no corroborative evidence to justify that men were first hunter-gatherers before they came to be acquainted with farming. The idea, which took for granted the fact that history was of a linear and progressionist makeup, led necessarily to the adoption of the new conviction that man's initial stage had been hunting and gathering, the simplest means of supplying food. The distinct periods of the past qualified as Stone Age, Bronze Age, etc., are also devoid of all scientific evidence. Whenever such classifications are made, there come moments when gadgets are unearthed, which, in principle should not be dating from the age to which they are supposed to belong. Yet, writers of textbooks are loath to make any corrections therein.

PYRAMIDS, MARTIANS AND ACUPUNCTURE

According to the progressionist linear history conception, every one of the stages that human history has gone through is superior to the preceding one. This erroneous conception is inculcated into the brains of the majority of mankind. The supporters of this conception of history were nonplussed in the face of the superior characteristics of pyramids. The question has cropped up, inquiring into the mystery of the designers of pyramids, whether their authors might not have been Martians! The great Cheops pyramid at Giza, whose volume is about $2.515.000 m^3$, is 147m high, the base measuring 230m. This structure required the quarrying of six million stones, their transportation, amassment and laying in a fashion likely to challenge long centuries to come. The power coupled with skill of the Egyptians leaves us astounded. Mentalities shaped according to the erroneous conception of history fail somehow to conclude that architecture in ancient Egypt was at a very advanced stage. For those familiar with the Quranic verses, there is nothing to wonder at in this, since the Quran mentions of works of superior quality that were accomplished long ago.

9- Do they not travel through the earth and see what was the end of those before them? They were superior to them in strength, furrowed the earth and dwelt in it more than they...
30-The Romans, 9

Acupuncture, practiced in China for more than 4,500 years, shows that at a given spot on the earth, people were in possession of anatomic knowledge more precise than we can believe. Acupuncture was the result of a thorough knowledge of the nervous system of the human body and of the distribution of electricity in the body. Someone convinced of history's linear; evolutionist and developmentalist structure cannot come forth claiming that it appears that the Chinese were more versed in the anatomy of the human body than the following generations. Otherwise this would lead people to attribute the discovery of such facts to the Martians, like certain writers! To try to understand history and give it meaning is certainly commendable. But to dare interpret all the periods of history in every geographical corner of the earth within a unilinear and progressionist concept of history is a great error frequently committed.

This understanding of history has been the source of views that denied the personalities of individuals. These views that idealize the "state" led the right-minded to fascism and leftist persons to communism. The cause of a great many disasters, this viewpoint favored the oppression of the individual by the state, refused to see the state at the service of its nationals as a superstructure created by man, and preferred to consider man as a servant of the state, in which he had an insignificant presence. For those who are not familiar with the philosophy of history, these considerations may seem overstatements. If we look closer at the process initiated by Hegel, we may observe that it played a role, on the one hand, in the emergence of Hitler, and at the same time, of Marx. According to this view, the direction of history cannot be diverted. According to this mentality, whether laudable or execrable, the acts people indulge in have no effect on the retrogressive or progressive courses in history. It is the "state" that plays the historical role, and the course of history cannot change its direction. The human element is absent here as well. The Quran contends that human acts have their consequences in the future development of communities and that many communities have perished because of the evil doings of their members. This view of life is one that saves man from being swept by the storms that have raged in history.

It is true that at certain periods of history mankind has marked significant progress by following a unilinear and progressive course. But it is simply wrong to generalize this movement to cover the entire past. To view a period of two or three millennia from a similar angle would be incorrect. To call a given century before Christ the "Stone Age," thus generalizing it to cover the entirety of humanity would be improper. Great divergences between communities at a given age, lack of proper communication, and reasons that thwarted the political and cultural development of societies the world over made a simultaneous development of peoples around the earth impossible. Let us assume that one thousand years hence, archaeological excavations conducted with a view to having an insight into our level of civilization will give different results according to whether these excavations are made in New York or in a remote corner of Africa. While the one that generalizes his findings will conclude that there had been a progression in the history of mankind, the other, having recourse to the same method of ratiocination, will conclude that there had been retrogression.

Another error generally committed is the assumption that products of different domains like communications, arts, medicine, engineering, architecture, morals, farming are put hotchpotch in the same basket. The idea of progression in a given field must not be stretched to include other areas as well. Therefore, while history advances in certain fields, it may recede in others.

The correct thing to do would be to adopt an analytical approach and pick up every single product separately and evaluate it accordingly, thus getting rid of the generalizations and facile deductions of the unilinear progressive and evolutionist concepts of history.

POSITIVISM AND RELIGION

Religion has been the field exposed to misconceptions to which the unilinear progressive conception of history led. Auguste Comte (1798-1857) was the prominent representative of this movement. Comte divided history into separate phases. He was confident that mankind would go through three phases before ending up in the system of philosophy to which he gave the name of positivism. In his historical study of the progress of the human mind, he discerned three phases: the theological, the metaphysical and the positive. Comte contended that the origins of the theological phase went as far back as fetishism, and that it was followed by polytheism, ending up with monotheism.

In the ultimate phase, qualified "positive," he stated that science had taken the place of religion. He made use of this argument to condemn all religious orders and philosophical systems prior to his own positive system. While the other systems are "a series of primitive historical phases," his own system was "the most perfect ultimate phase." In the whirlwind of his passion, he dared set up a positivistic religion. This pseudo-Christianity would have a large clerical organization with positivistic temples and positivistic clergy.

Comte's efforts to show the monotheistic religions as but an interim phase in the series of historical periods are devoid of all scientific evidence and findings. Quite the reverse had been the case, since the Ebla tablets of ancient history discovered in 1975 bore monotheistic traces. Comte's views, utterly devoid of all tangible and convincing evidence, are taken for granted in many school textbooks. In every stage of history there has existed the idea of one God. Monotheism was opposed by the idolaters of the moon or the sun, or communists or positivists at different periods of history. All other beliefs have become calendar pages of history to be torn off, while the belief in one God abides forever.

Those who fail to make a historical classification of religions having archeological findings have suggested the following train of thought: "Let us find the most primitive community on earth, for the oldest religion should be theirs, since it must have preserved its traditions." Some of the supporters of this line of thought, devoid of all scientific foundation, took the tribe that worshipped natural phenomena as the most primitive of the communities on earth, and its religion, the most ancient. Those who considered the pygmies of monotheistic outlook contended that the primeval religion was monotheistic (Such a line of thought led naturally to different conclusions).

This theory on religion, whose proponents have been Andrew Lang and P.W. Schmidt, has been very interesting. According to this theory, most of the religions of the world are but corrupted versions of monotheism. According to Schmidt, idolization of powers of nature is irrelevant, since in order that the powers of nature may be made into gods, one should already have the notion of "God." According to this view, the reason for the corruption of monotheistic religions and the emergence of polytheism is man's transforming, in time, of metaphors into identifications. The line of thought ran something like this. "God is Creator, He is like my mother." "God is the source of everything, He is like the earth." These metaphors have in time replaced the original conceptualization that came to be identified with a concrete image. Schmidt contended that one of the evidences of the fact that polytheistic religions' origins lay in monotheism was the fact that the idea of a primeval and all powerful divinity still survived. The common characteristics of the Eble tablets, Egyptian mythology, and monotheistic religions of differing configurations support the idea that they originated from a single source, but underwent corruption for various reasons.

The logical reasoning of Schmidt is more convincing. As a matter of fact, there is hardly anything in Comte deducible or defensible on the grounds of consistency to support the theory of a positivistic phase being the ultimate phase of human evolution. Anyway, based merely on written evidence, it is impossible to arrive at an identification of the primeval religion. But as I have pointed out, both the Ebla tablets dating from 3000 B.C. and the evidence provided by the historical times prove that the faith in one God has always existed. These tablets, in which the names Adam, Eve, Noah, Abraham, Ishmael, Michael, David are mentioned as they figure in the Quran, and the Old and New Testaments, prove that monotheistic religions always existed.

47- Each community has a messenger ...

10-Jonah, 47

CHAPTER 58

MIRACLES BASED ON ARCHAEOLOGY AND THE PEOPLE OF SABA

109- ...Do they not travel through the earth and see what was the end of those before them?

12-Joseph, 109

So far our attention has been focused on the miraculous revelations of the Quran and our effort has been to try to work out correlations with natural phenomena. The four preceding chapters were reserved for philosophical issues expounded in the Quran that had had no dialectic background at the time of its descent. The said four chapters must be classified in a separate category. The present and the next three chapters will deal with archaeological findings and their relevance to the ancient communities. Archaeological data differ from the natural sciences in many respects and deriving erroneous conclusions from them is all the more likely. In due consideration of these findings, those tribes that have disappeared must be examined accordingly.

The accounts given in the Quran about ancient peoples are not mere stories. They are mostly parables illustrating a moral or spiritual lesson.

128- Did they not learn from the many generations that We destroyed before them, in whose haunts they move? Verily, these are signs for those who possess intelligence.

20-Ta-He, 128

THE PEOPLE OF SHEBA AND
THE FLOOD FROM THE DAM

15- There was a sign for the people of Sheba in their habitations: two gardens, one on the right and the other on the left. "Eat from your Lord's provisions and be thankful to Him. Good land and a forgiving Lord."
16- But they turned away and We sent against them the flood from the dam. And We converted their two gardens into gardens of bitter fruit, and tamarisks and a few sparse cedar-trees.

34-Sheba, 15-16

Some of the accounts we come across in the Quran also exist in the Old and the New Testaments. As the flood that followed the burst of the dam referred to in the Quran dates from after Christ, it is not mentioned in the Old and the New Testaments.

The "flood from the dam" is also referred to as the "*arim flood*," "*arim*" meaning "dam" in Arabic. Mawdudi, a contemporary Pakistani scholar, made the following comment: "*The word 'arim' used in the expression 'seyl-ul Arim' derived from the word 'arimen' meaning 'dam' is used in Southern Arabia. This word was frequently seen during the excavations at Yemen. For instance, in a tablet dictated by Abraha, the ruler of Yemen of Ethiopian origin, after the restoration of the great Marib Dam dated 542-543 A.D. the said word was often used. So the expression 'seyl ul arim' means the flood disaster in the wake of the burst dam.*" The capital of Sheba was Marib. The people of Sheba had become prosperous thanks to this dam. Pliny describes this region as a green spot covered by lush vegetation. The height of the dam at Marib was 16m and its width 60m, while the length measured 620m. The area irrigated was 9600 hectares, of which 5300 hectares were in the southern plain and 4300 hectares in the northern plain (See Cavit Yalçın, *The Perish of Nations*).

The "two gardens" referred to in the Quran were these sumptuous gardens in the said valleys. Thanks to this dam and the irrigation system, this region was renowned as the best spot in Yemen, well irrigated and fertile. The Frenchman J. Holévy and the Austrian Glaser proved the existence of the Marib dam. In documents written in the Himer dialect, it was said that the said dam had made the land fertile.

The year of its destruction is believed to be 542 A.D. In the wake of its destruction the *"arim flood"* occurred and ravaged the entire area.

Archaeologist Werner Keller also corroborates the account as reported in the Quran: *"The fact that such a dam existed and that its destruction ravaged the city demonstrates that the account given in the Quran about the destruction of the gardens is a true account."*

As we read of the disaster that the people of Sheba faced, one cannot help feeling that this was the consequence of the ingratitude of the people for the gifts with which they had been endowed. We must acknowledge the fact that the Creator of all the beauties is God, Whom we must extol and give thanks and try to avoid the fate of the people of Sheba.

17- That is how We requited them for their ingratitude. And never do We give requital except to those who are ungrateful.

34-Sheba, 17

CHAPTER 59

THE AAD PEOPLE AND THE CITY OF ERAM

6- Have you not seen what your Lord did to the Aad.
7- Of Eram with lofty pillars,
8- The like of which were not produced in the land.

89-The Dawn, 6-8

There are many passages where the Aad people are mentioned in the Quran. The Prophet Hud was sent to the Aad people to warn them against attributing a partner to God. The Aad people, however, turned a deaf ear on the Prophet's warning and continued their practice. The Aad community lived in the city of Eram, a city built on beautiful tall pillars, which was destroyed by a storm.

At the beginning of the 1990s the leading papers in the world covered the story of a discovery of towering importance under such headings as "Discovery of a Sumptuous Arabian City," "Legendary Arabian City Unearthed." What made this archaeological finding more significant was the mention of its name in the Quran. This discovery confounded those who had insisted that the existence of the Aad community was only legendary.

The city in question was discovered by an amateur archaeologist, Nicholas Clapp. Based on written evidence, he set off to unearth the lost city. After long efforts he managed to persuade NASA to have satellite photographs taken of the region in question ; these photographs resulted in the eventual discovery.

As the ruins came to be unearthed, it was concluded that the site corresponded to the city of the Aad people mentioned in the Quran. Among the unearthed ruins were the tall pillars described in the Quran. Dr. Zarins claims that what made this city referred to as Eram

211

different from others of its time was these pillars described in the Quran. The other accounts related to this event exactly tallied with the archaeological findings.

DESTRUCTION OF AAD

6- And the Aad were destroyed by a furious, roaring storm...
69-Incontestable, 6

24- So when they saw it as a cloud advancing towards their valley, they said: "This cloud will give us rain." No, it is what you were trying to hasten! The wind that carries the grievous punishment.
46-The Dunes, 24

When the Aad people saw the cloud that was to bring punishment to them, they thought it was a rain cloud. The sandstorm was seen from afar as a rain cloud. The destruction of the Aad people is often referred to in the Quranic verses. The city in question was unearthed following an excavation that went deep down into the ground. The description in the Quran is in accord with the evidence of the burial of the city of the Aad people under dunes of sand.

21- Remember the brother of Aad. When he warned his people at the dunes, but there have been warners before him and after him. "You shall not worship any except God. I fear for you the retribution of a great day."
46-The Dunes, 21

"*Ahqaf*" is the plural of "*hiqf*" (dune of sand). Some commentators mention the name as a proper noun. But this does not change its signification in any way. Historical data and archaeological findings clearly refer to the Aad people and the city Eram with tall pillars mentioned in the Quran. The unearthing of the city is a recent affair. The Quran says that there have been instances in the past from which we have to derive lessons and archaeology as a science provides us evidences to prove the truth revealed in the Quran.

15- As for Aad, they behaved arrogantly on earth, against all truth, and said, "Who is more powerful than we?" Did they not see that God who created them is more powerful than they? Yet they refused to believe Our signs.

16- So We sent upon them a furious wind for several miserable days to afflict them with a humiliating retribution in this life. But the retribution of the Hereafter is more humiliating, and there will be no help for them.

41-Elucidated, 15-16

CHAPTER 60

MYSTERY BEHIND THE NAME HAAMAAN

36- Pharaoh said: "O Haamaan! Build me a high tower that
I may attain the ways and means."

40-The Believer, 36

38- Pharaoh said: "O Chiefs! No god do I know for you
but myself. So, O Haamaan! Fire some clay to build a tower
for me that I may mount up to the God of Moses. I believe
that he is a liar."

28-The History, 38

Haamaan's name is quoted several times in the Quran as promoter
and supporter of Pharaoh, who, claiming to vie with God, and taking
a stand against Moses, had ordered Haamaan to erect a high tower so
that he might reach the God to whom Moses referred.

Prof. Maurice Bucaille, in his *Moise et L'Egypte*, speaks of the use of
the name Haamaan mentioned in the Quran, alluding to the objections raised in history to the use of this name, and gives an account of
the corroboration of the account given in the Quran after the deciphering of the hieroglyph.

The name Haamaan is also mentioned in the Old Testament as the
chief minister or vizier of King Ahasuerus. After the failure of his
attempt to cut off all the Jews in the Persian Empire, he was hanged
on the gallows which he had erected for Mordecai. The name
Haamaan is mentioned five times in the Quran. People with prejudice
looking for errors in the Quran claimed that the Quran had made
errors while copying the Old Testament and brought forth the name
of Haamaan as evidence.

HEAD OF THE QUARRY WORKERS

Jean Francois Champollion (1790-1832), a French Egyptologist and a pioneer in the study of ancient Egypt, is best known for his success on the Rosetta Stone in 1822. The stone in question was found near Rosetta on the western mouth of the Nile by one of Napoléon's officers in 1799. Its text, a decree commemorating the accession of Ptolemy V, is written in two languages and three scripts: hieroglyphs forming Egyptian parts of the inscription were deciphered by Jean-Francois Champollion, and this led to the interpretation of many other early records of Egyptian civilization. In the Hof Museum of Vienna one can read of Haamaan's close relations to the Pharaoh. (See: Walter Wreszinski, Aegyptische Inschriften aus dem K.K. Hof Museum in Wien, 1906, J.C. Hinriesche Buchhandlung.) The name "Haamaan" is recorded as the head of the quarry workers, which is in accordance with the sura The Narrations verse 38. (See: Herman Renke, *Die Aegyptischen Personnennamen, Vierzeischnis der Namen*, published by J. J. Augustin in Glückstadt, Band I, 1935.)

Maurice Bucaille gave the name "Haamaan" to a French Egyptologist, telling him that he had seen it quoted in an Arab manuscript dating from the 7th century. (He did not, however, tell him that the Manuscript in question was the Quran, so as not to prejudice the Egyptologist's reaction to this). He suggested to Maurice Bucaille that he refer to the "*Dictionary of Personal Names of the New Kingdom by Ranke.*" Bucaille eventually found the name in the German hieroglyph transliteration list as being the head of the quarry workers. Another discovery was the engraving of the name Haamaan on a monument in Vienna. The bracket appended to the name Haamaan indicates his special position in relation to the Pharaoh. (The Egyptians used to write the words linked together unless it was to indicate a special situation.)

So, objections raised against the contents of the Quran are brought to naught in every instance. Whenever probing becomes necessary about a particular point, the Quran displays further miracles. The Quran's quoting the name Haamaan cannot be coincidental. No source other than revelation could possibly have included the name so appropriately in the Quran.

CHAPTER 61

ANCIENT EGYPT AND THE PHARAOH'S BODY

104- Moses said: "O Pharaoh (Firawun)! I am a messenger from the Lord of the worlds"

7-The Purgatory, 104

72- They said: "We lost the cup of the king (malik) ..."

12-Joseph, 72

Studies conducted on data acquired about Pharaoh thanks to the deciphered hieroglyph script and Egyptological explorations corroborate that what is said about the parables of Moses, and the accounts related to Egypt and the Pharaoh in the Quran, are exact when compared with tangible historical data.

The Quran referred to the Egyptian ruler at the time of Joseph as *"malik"* (ruler, king) but for the ruler coeval with Moses the Quran uses the word *"Firawun"* (Pharaoh). Pharaoh was the Hebrew form of the Egyptian *"Per-ao"* (the great house) signifying the royal palace, an epithet applied in the new kingdom and after as a title of respect, to the king himself. Never before had it been used in this sense.

To quote the Encyclopedia Britannica: Pharaoh was referred to in narrative as "his majesty" or "the good god" or "the sovereign" as a circumlocution of respect. In accordance with the concept of divine kingship, his person was sacrosanct and his insignia - diadem, crowns, scepters, states - had magic properties. Fire gushed from the mouth of the serpent on his crown to exterminate his enemies; in the battlefield

216

his power was such that he could wipe out his enemies regardless of their multitude. He was said to be omnipotent and omniscient, the one who had the overall control in his hands and was the cause of prosperity. The main source of information is the information that the deciphering of the hieroglyphs made available.

However, one should keep in mind that this script had been sunk in oblivion since the 3rd century B.C., to be revived long after. The hieroglyph script that had been forgotten about 1000 years prior to the descent of the Quran was discovered and deciphered after more than a millennium.

The Quran relates the events that happened between the Pharaoh and Moses, giving details additional to those found in the Old Testament. What is said about serpents and the prevalence of magic at the time, and Pharaoh's statement of his divine attribute, tallies with the information about the Pharaoh revealed from the deciphered hieroglyph tablets.

IPUWER PAPYRUS

10: 3-6 Lower Egypt is devastated. The court came to a standstill. Whatever was stored, wheat, rye, geese and fish, perished.
10: 6-3 Crops wasted everywhere
2: 5-6 Disasters and blood everywhere
2:10 Blood flows in rivers
3: 2 Gold and lapis lazuli, silver and malachite, carnelian and bronze decorate the necks of slaves
Ipuwer Papyrus-Leidon 344

130- We punished the people of Pharaoh with drought, and shortage of crops, that they might take heed.
7-The Purgatory, 130

133- So We sent on them; the flood, the locusts, the lice, the frogs and the blood. How many different signs! But they still remained arrogant, for they were a people full of sin.
7-The Purgatory, 133

57- So We expelled them from gardens, springs.

58- Treasures and every kind of honorable position.

59- Thus it was made the children of Israel inheritors of such things.

26-The Poets, 57-59

The accounts given by the Quran about the punishment inflicted upon the Pharaoh and his followers, like drought and other disasters, and the accounts of the Ipuwer Papyrus are perfectly in tune with each other. As an evidence of the offense committed by the dynasty of the Pharaoh in its denial of Moses' prophethood, the Quran says that blood was foreseen (the same thing holds true for the proliferation of the locusts, the lice, etc.). In the Ipuwer Papyrus it is said that blood ran in riverbeds, everywhere was smeared with blood. (Studies conducted to this day seem to explain the red coloration of rivers by the existence of protozoa, zooplanktons, sea and fresh water planktons or dinoflagellates. All these organisms would deplete the oxygen in water, giving rise to rapid growth of toxic substances, killing the living organisms and rendering the stream water undrinkable.)

Researchers have devised a course of events that might have taken place in relation to the disasters described in the Quran. According to this fictive account, "The fish in the Nile perished as a consequence of the intoxication of the river, leaving the Egyptians deprived of sustenance. Frogs, whose eggs multiplied in the meantime, invaded the surroundings before they themselves succumbed to poisoning. Decomposition of fish and frogs coupled with the poisonous water of the Nile polluted the fertile land around. Annihilation of the frogs caused the pests like locusts and grain moths to proliferate:" All these are but the product of imagination, surely. We do not know exactly how things happened since we have no available data in hand to make valid deductions. Yet, this account may give us an idea of them.

The Ipuwer Papyrus records the curse of blood, drought and disasters to which the Pharaoh's dynasty fell victim, and the situation of the slaves, who later were to inherit the former's possessions almost literally as described in the Quran.

PHARAOH'S BODY SIGN UNKNOWN BY MAJORITY

90- We took the children of Israel across the sea. Pharaoh and his army followed them aggressively and sinfully. When drowning became a reality for him, he said, "I believe that there is no god except the One in whom the children of Israel believe. I am of those who submit."

91- "Ah now! For you have rebelled in the past, and you did mischief."

92- "Today, We will save your body, so that you may become a sign to those who come after you. But verily, many people are heedless of Our signs."

10-Jonah, 90-92

When he understood he was going to die, the Pharaoh was converted. This so-called conversion is looked at askance by God, who says that his body shall be saved as a sign for the coming generations. At the time of the Prophet, and for quite some time afterward, we could not guess that a science called museology would be developed to harbor objects of historical value, amongst others mummified bodies of the Pharaohs. The Quran's reference to this and to the people heedless of God's signs are points deserving attention. The signs of God are many and the majority of people are unaware of this.

At the time of the revelation of the Quran, mummified bodies of all the Pharaohs lay concealed in the Valley of Kings along the banks of the Nile. Their discovery took place in the 19th century. The Pharaoh mentioned in the Quran may have been any of them, it happens to be among those preserved in the Cairo Museum, open to public visitation. To the period in which Moses is believed to belong, Rameses II and his son Merneptah correspond. Merneptah's body bears the traces of fatal blows. It is reported that these marks may have been caused during his drowning or after the recovery of his body, that had washed ashore; the Egyptians mummified him like all the other Pharaohs. The evidence available does not permit us to derive a convincing conclusion about the details of his death. However, no conflicting relationship could be established between the death of this Pharaoh and the account given in the Quran.

The discovery of the Pharaoh's body took place after an interval of 3000 years (1881-1898). Considering that the Quran had predicted that Pharaoh's body would constitute a sign, one supposes that it should have been found. Indeed it was found. When and how? Well, after a time gap of 3000 years. What happened though was as the Quran predicted. **"...But verily, many people are heedless of Our signs."**

CHAPTER 62

SIGNS IN THE OLD TESTAMENT

146- The people of the Book know this as they know their own sons; but some of them conceal the truth, knowingly.

2-The Cow, 146

In this chapter, we shall be studying the implications in the Old Testament made to the Prophet, to the region where he lived and to the message he brought. The greater part of our book has so far treated such subject matters as physics, chemistry, geology and biology. Also we have tackled, in a separate category, philosophical speculations, and in another separate category archaeological issues. Now we shall be dealing with those parts of the Old and New Testaments that are of special relevance for our present study. Questions that have found answers in the natural sciences, based on observation, were followed by ratiocination in the chapters on philosophy and were followed by historical data calling for detailed analyses in the chapters on archaeology. Now we are to tackle the veracity of information contained in the Bible. According to the Quran, Jews falsified their scriptures by changing the context and meaning of words. This misled the commentators in their interpretations of the signs heralding the advent of the Prophet:

46- Some among the Jews distort the words out of context and say with a twist of their tongues...

4-The Women, 46

41- They change the words from their right places and say "If you are given this, accept it, but if you are given anything different, beware."

5-The Feast, 41

The fact that Jewish rabbis have tried to misinterpret the signs related to Islam dates from the time of the Prophet. There is reference to this in the verse quoted at the head of the present chapter.

ALL PROPHETS HAVE PROFESSED ISLAM

The Quran accepts that all the prophets descending from Adam are Muslim (submitter). The word "*Islam*" has also the connotation of "peace." The Jewish word "*Shalom*" and the Arabic word "*Salam*" stem from the same root.

> *As for the prophet who prophesies peace (shalom), when the word of that prophet comes to pass, then it will be known that the Lord has truly sent the prophet.*
>
> *Jeremiah 28, 9*

The word "peace" in this translation has the same root as the word "Islam." The two prophets, Christ and Muhammad, who came after Moses, announced 1) that there was one God; 2) to worship only one God; 3) To believe in all messengers of God; 4) that man was to believe in the Day of Judgment; 5) that man should lead an honest life, 6) that man should not kill his kind or commit theft, and 7) that man should protect the needy and the orphans, etc. According to the expressions used in the Old Testament, the proof of prophethood was whether the message brought was one of peace (Islam) and whether his word turned out to be true. Thanks to the message brought by Muhammad, billions of people have believed in what he said and have loved God and believed in the Omniscience and Omnipotence of God and that the truth of the revelations in the Book transmitted by him came to be demonstrated by the ensuing historical events and developments in science. Nowhere in the Old Testament can we come across a statement to the effect that Moses is the last prophet. Someone who believes in the Bible can easily deduce from its contents the evidence of Muhammad's prophethood. Moreover, the Old Testament's criterion for the recognition of a prophet was his coming with the prophecy of peace, i.e., Islam in its etymological sense, which word came to be integrated with the name of Muhammad.

6- For thus says the Lord of Hosts: "Yet, once more, in a little while, I will shake the heavens and the earth and the sea and the dry land.
7- And I will shake all nations so that the treasures (himada) of all nations shall come in, and I will fill this house with glory, says the Lord of Hosts.
8- The silver is mine, and the gold is mine, declares the Lord of Hosts.
9- The latter glory of this house shall be greater than the former, says the Lord of Hosts. And in this place I will give peace (shalom), declares the Lord of Hosts"

Haggai 2, 6-9

The Hebrew word "*himada*" mentioned under verse 7 of Haggai stems from the same root as H-M-D in the Arabic language which is the root of the name "Muhammad," carrying more or less the same meaning. Thus the name of the Prophet or the meaning of his name is mentioned with reference to a glorious event that was to take place in the future. What can be a more glorious event than the advent of Muhammad -who came after the Old Testament- and whose message announced God's existence to billions? Remember that the word "*shalom*" (peace) in verse 9 comes from the same root as the word Islam.

A PROPHET LIKE MOSES

18- I will raise up for them a prophet like you from among their brothers. And I will put my words in his mouth, and he shall speak to them all that I command him.
19- And whoever will not listen to My words that he shall speak in My name, I myself will require it of him.

Deuteronomy 18, 18-19

In Deuteronomy the coming of a new prophet is predicted. Christians claim that reference is here made to Jesus Christ. However, Muhammad, in many respects, was more like Moses and had many more common traits with him than with Christ. It may be that both Jesus Christ and Muhammad were meant. Only God knows the exact reference.

On the other hand, being of Jewish descent, it is quite possible that Jesus Christ was meant, although Arabs and Jews had common ancestors. Michael Hammer, from the University of Arizona, Tucson, in collaboration with some colleagues from the University of Israel, examined 18 divisions in the Y chromosomes of 1371 persons who came from 29 different communities. Among these were European Jews, Latinos, people from North Africa, Kurds, Iranians, Yemenis and Ethiopians, Palestinians, Lebanese, Syrians, Israeli Durzis, Saudis and 16 non-semitic groups. The studies conducted have shown that Jews from different origins and Arabs descended from a common stock. This is in accordance with the belief that Abraham is the common ancestor of Jews and Arabs.

If we may be allowed to go back to Deuteronomy, it is easy to establish the many traits Moses had in common with Muhammad, rather than with Jesus Christ. Moses, like Muhammad, established a realm. The Christians' realm was realized after Christ's death.

Knowing that prophets transmit messages bearing common traits, it is difficult to decide whether this prediction refers to Christ or Muhammad.

ORIGIN OF THE PROPHET

1- This is the blessing with which Moses, the man of God, blessed the people of Israel before his death.
2- He said: "The Lord came from Sinai and dawned from Seir upon us; he shone forth from Mount Paran; he came from the ten thousands of holy ones with flaming fire at his right hand."

Deuteronomy 33, 1-2

Moses' prayer just before his death is interesting. The place referred to as Sinai is where Moses had emerged; the second place, Seir is the place where Jesus came from; while the third place is the Paran Mountains and it is the place where Muhammad came from. Thus, in the Biblical statement quoted above, allusions are made to the monotheistic religions which had an outstanding influence on humanity. Here we also see the corroboration of the prophets to come, viz. Jesus and Muhammad; just as the Quran corroborated Moses and Jesus as prophets, so had the Old Testament done this. The prediction in Deuteronomy that the Prophet would come among the ten thousands of holy ones is a remarkable indication because while Muhammad was living, he had ten thousands of followers.

THE CHOSEN SERVANT FROM AMONG THE PEOPLE OF KEDAR WILL BREAK THE IDOLS

Accounts related to future events in Isaiah make allusions to Muhammad as Prophet. Accounts related to the future in the Old Testament (Isaiah, 42) are in perfect conformity with Muhammad's ways, in that he broke the idols (8), that he established justice upon earth during his lifetime (3 and 4), that he received the message from Gabriel, the Holy Spirit (1), had ideal ethical values (2-3), shed light over the souls of men who had been blinded (6 and 7), carried over new messages he had received to mankind (10), and was a descendant of a community that had descended from the line of Kedar (11).

1- Behold my servant, whom I uphold, my chosen, in whom my soul delights; I have put my Spirit upon him; he will bring forth justice to the nations.
2- He will not cry aloud or lift up his voice, or make it heard in the street.
3- A bruised breed he will not break, and a faintly burning wick he will not quench; he will faithfully bring forth justice.
4- He will not grow faint or be discouraged till he has established justice in the earth; and the coastlands wait for his law.
5- Thus says God, the Lord who created the heavens and stretched them out, who spread out the earth and what comes from it, who gives breath to the people on it and spirit to those who walk in it:
6- I am the Lord; I have called you in righteousness; I will take you by the hand and keep you; I will give you as a covenant for the people, a light for the nations.
7- To open the eyes that are blind, to bring out the prisoners from the dungeon, from the prison those who sit in darkness.
8- I am the Lord; that is my name; my glory I give to no other; nor my praise to carved idols.
9- Behold, the former things have come to pass, and new things

225

I now declare; before they spring forth I tell you of them.
10- Sing to the Lord a new song, his praise from the end of the
earth, you who go down to the sea and all that fills it, the coast-
lands and their inhabitants.
11- Let the desert and its cities lift up their voice, the villages
that Kedar inhabits; let the habitants of Sela sing for joy, let
them shout from the top of the mountains.

Isaiah 42, 1-11

A careful perusal of these verses may suggest to their reader that allusions to Muhammad are plain. What is still remarkable is that these statements would turn out to come true. This prediction was not made for the time of Isaiah but for later, as mentioned in verse 9. It is interesting to note that in the 17th verse of Isaiah it is said that idolaters would be put to shame, an event that had come true by the revelation of the Quran.

70- O people of the Book! Why do you reject the signs of God of which you are witnesses?
71- O people of the Book! Why do you clothe the truth with falsehood, and conceal the truth, knowingly?

3-The Family of Imran, 70-71

CHAPTER 63

SIGNS IN THE NEW TESTAMENT

15- O people of the Book! Our messenger has come to you to proclaim for you many things you have concealed in the Book, while passing over much. A light and a perspicacious Book has come to you.

5-The Feast, 15

The Quran claims that the Jews and Christians have used every endeavor to hide or suppress many data. Some of these are related to the tidings of the arrival of Muhammad. In this section of our book we shall dwell on passages that have likely been suppressed.

The three monotheistic religions have addressed mankind, bringing almost the same message, with a few reservations that are particularly related to rituals. That God is one and man should adore only one God, the Omnipotent and Omniscient, are common to all the three religions. The Day of Judgment is another common feature. Protection of human life and of the right of possession, sharing one's riches with the poor, seeking peace and justice, praise of God on every occasion, giving thanks to God and praying are some other points shared by these three religions. As time went by, the clergy and their ignorant followers corrupted the original tenets of the creed. The Quran makes allusions to these men who corrupted the originality of the religion in the garb of religious devotees (See: 2-The Cow, 75; 5-The Feast, 13; 9- Repentance, 31-34). This issue is outside the scope of the present work and will be the subject matter of another publication. To misconstrue meanings, to idolize and deify prophets or religious men, and to make interpolations in the scriptures have been the salient points of this trend. Once the bigots of all the three religions are disposed of, mankind will understand better that the messages of all of them are the same. This is, however, beyond the scope of the present book.

The Torah, the first Book of the three monotheistic religions, predicts the advent of Jesus and Muhammad. The gospels bear witness to Moses and make allusions to Muhammad, while the Quran, being the last Book sent, confirms both Books that preceded it. The miraculous predictions in the Quran are valid evidence that confirm the other Books. (However, we must take due note of the fact that the Old Testament and the New Testament may have been affected by interpolations in the course of time, although many of their fundamental messages remain the same.)

I intend to examine the indication related to the advent of Muhammad. What many Christians are apprehensive about is the discrediting of the concept of the Trinity and the belief that Jesus is merely a Prophet. If one accedes to the fact that the gospels predicted the advent of Muhammad, the extolment of Jesus to the point of deification will automatically cease. The signs in the gospels heralding the advent of Muhammad have been hushed up. The church will continue to stick to its age-old creeds in order to be able to wield its ongoing authority and maintain its very existence. We must remember that Jesus spoke Aramaic. The oldest versions of the gospels are in ancient Greek and Latin. Some interpolations may have taken place during the translation into those languages.

PARACLETE

61- And when Jesus of Mary said, "O children of Israel! I am God's messenger to you, confirming the Torah before me and giving glad tidings of a messenger to come after me whose name is praised (ahmad)."

61-The Column, 6

The Quran says that Christ gave glad tidings of the advent of Muhammad. Those who failed to directly recognize such an expression in the Gospels - based on the Quran's statement that the believers in the Bible had concealed their religion - thought that the Christians had obliterated the relevant verses in the gospels. This may

228

have been true for some of the verses. Some researchers have concluded that some of the meanings have been misconstrued and that the said tidings in the Quran still existed in the Gospels.

The Quran mentions the adjective "*ahmad*" (meaning being more praised). As a matter of fact the names Ahmad and Muhammad stem from the same root. Some are of the idea that "Ahmad" was a proper noun. In our opinion, its literal sense should prevail here. For the name Muhammad is mentioned in four different places in the Quran: (See, 3-The Family of Imran, 144; 33-The Parties, 40; 47-Muhammad, 2; 48-Victory, 29). This is our opinion. However, nothing would change if "Ahmad" were to be taken for a proper name. Both have some meaning and are derived from the same root, viz. H-M-D.

Let us take a look at the prediction of the Prophet in the Gospel according to John. Jesus' last words, exchanged with his disciples before he was arrested and taken away at the conclusion of the Last Supper, are recorded only in the Gospel according to John. The other three Gospels do not mention them (ascribed respectively to Matthew, Mark, and Luke). How should we explain, then, the absence of his conversations with his disciples in the three other gospels? Can it be that they existed once in the other gospels, but were omitted afterward?

15- If you love me, you will keep my commandments.
16- And I will ask the Father, and he will give you another
Helper (Paraclete) to be with you forever.
John 14, 15-16

26- But the Helper (Paraclete), the Holy Spirit whom the
Father will send in my name, he will teach you all things and
bring to your remembrance all that I have said to you.
John 14, 26

7- Nevertheless, I tell you the truth; it is to your advantage that
I go away, for if I don't go away, the Helper (Paraclete) will
not come to you. But if I go, I will send him to you.
8- And when he comes, he will convince the world concerning
sin and righteousness and judgment.
John 16, 7-8
13- When the Spirit of truth comes, he will guide you into all
the truth, for he will not speak on his own authority, but what-

*ever he hears he will speak, and he will declare to you the things
that are to come.*

*14- He will glorify me, for he will take what is mine and
declare it to you.*

John 16, 13-14

Christians claim that by "*Paraclete*" is meant Gabriel. On the other
hand, Prof. Maurice Bucaille, who censures the interpretation of the
word "*Paraclete*" mentioned in the gospels as the Holy Spirit (Gabriel),
gives the following account based on the etymology of this Greek word,
pointing to its meaning: "*The teaching of mankind referred to here is in
no way restricted to the inspiration provided by the Holy Spirit (Gabriel).
Due to its intrinsic meaning in the Greek that denotes spreading of knowledge, it has a concrete connotation. The Greek verbs 'akouo' and 'laleo'
refer to concrete acts which can only be related to a being endowed with the
sense of hearing and speech. Therefore, attribution of such acts to Gabriel
is preposterous. The logical conclusion is that the reference in John's Gospel
must be to a man endowed with the sense of hearing and talking, like Jesus
Christ. The Greek text categorically requires these faculties. It follows from
this that Jesus Christ had predicted that God would send after him another man who would bear God's commandments and messages, to be transmitted to mankind like the mission of a prophet. The words in some of the
present texts referring to the Holy Spirit are interpolated. The objective was
to alter the meaning of a text in which the advent of a new prophet was
predicted.*"

THE PROPHET

*19. Now this is the testimony of John, when the Jews sent priests
and Levies from Jerusalem to ask him, "Who are you?"*

*20. He confessed, and did not deny, but confessed "I am not the
Christ."*

*21. And they asked him "What then? Are you Elijah?" He said,
"I am not." "Are you the Prophet?" And he answered: "No."*

John 1, 19-21

Three questions are asked to John the Baptist to which he gives negative answers:

1) Are you Christ? 2) Are you Elijah? 3) Are you the Prophet?

In the Gospel according to John, John the Baptist explicitly states that he is not Elijah. Three different people are mentioned: 1) Jesus; 2) Elijah; 3) The Prophet. We know that John the Baptist was contemporary to Jesus. The Gospel says that Elijah had come and suffered in man's hands (Matthew, 17, 12).

Who was "the Prophet" then? Men had been waiting for the advent of the Prophet mentioned in the Old Testament (Deuteronomy18, 18; we have already examined this in the previous chapter). It is clear, then, that "the Prophet" is a person other than Jesus. Who was, then, "the Prophet" who had not come yet during the time of Jesus and carried the messages of God to the people? We think that there is no other person than Muhammad who fulfilled this mission after Jesus.

HOW TO RECOGNIZE FALSE PROPHETS?

15- Beware of false prophets, who come to you in sheep's clothing, but inwardly they are ravenous wolves.
16- You will recognize them by their fruits. Are grapes gathered from thornbushes or figs from thistles?
17- So every healthy tree bears good fruit, but the diseased tree bears bad fruit.
18- A healthy tree cannot bear bad fruit, nor can a diseased tree bear good fruit.
19- Every tree that does not bear good fruit is cut down and thrown into the fire.
20- Thus you will recognize them by their fruits.
Matthew 7, 15-20

Nowhere in any of the gospels does it say that no other Prophet will come. The following criterion is given in the gospel: Examine the fruit and distinguish between the one who speaks the truth and the one who is a liar. If no other prophet had been predicted to come after Jesus Christ, he might have said: Whoever comes after me claiming to be a prophet, he is a liar. The method that Jesus suggested to distinguish between the true and the false prophets is a sufficient proof of the advent of a prophet after Jesus. This fact should constitute an acceptable evidence for Christians. Someone who came after

231

Jesus, who believed in one God, who put his trust in God, who loved Him and was instrumental in establishing societies that had gotten rid of their idols, could not be any person other than Muhammad.

Despite all these signs in the Old Testament and the New Testament, rabbis and the Christian clergy have vied with one another to hush them up; the viewpoints of the Catholic and Orthodox churches, the Pope in Rome and the archbishops, whose names are not mentioned in any one of the Gospels, seem to be more authoritative than the Scriptures for the majority of the Christian population.

MEETING AT A COMMON POINT

Neither in the Old Testament nor in the New Testament is there anything to suggest the validity of the dogma of the Trinity. The idea of the trinity is a forced argument. The authority of the Church has overruled the authority of the gospels. The Trinity has become the *sine qua non* of Christianity. Had the dogma of Trinity been so important, shouldn't it be explained over and over again by God's messengers and prophets in the Old Testament, or at least in the gospels of the New Testament? Christians confirm the Old Testament as an authority. How is it that the Holy Spirit (Gabriel), indicated to be one of the three, is not mentioned as such in the Old Testament? Why is there no mention in the Old Testament of the advent of the Son of God or the transfiguration of God? If this were so important why do we not encounter it anywhere in the Old Testament, which is the revelation of God?

The problem of God the Father and God the Son was the consequence of an interpretation made by the Church. God in the contemporary Gospels is referred to as the "Father" of all men and his believers, his sons. The words "Father" and "Son" are but similes, as an impartial reader may readily see:

So that you may be the sons of your Father who is in the heaven.
Matthew 5, 45.

Our guess is that an expression that the persons referred to in the Aramaic language as the God and Lord of all people was rendered into Greek as "Father" and the expression that referred to "a cherished servant" was rendered as "Son." The source of this distorted translation must have been the men clothed in religious garb. As we have no Aramaic version in hand, we cannot prove this argument. However, the way these words are used in the Gospels supports our point of view. The religious authority that silenced all arguments against it during the Nicene Ecumenical Council laid down the concept of the Trinity. Before concluding, I would like to quote two more verses from the Quran.

31- They take their anchorites, their priests and the Christ, son of Mary, as Lords instead of God. Yet they were all commanded to worship only one God. There is no god except He. Glory to Him, from having the partners they associate.

9-Repentance, 31

46- Do not argue with the people of the Book, except in the nicest manner -unless they transgress- and say, "We believe what has been sent down to us, and we believe what has been sent down to you. Our God and your God is one and the same. And to Him we submit."

29-The Spider, 46

CHAPTER 64

VICTORIOUS ROMANS AND THE LOWEST SPOT ON THE EARTH

2- The Romans have been defeated.
3- In the lowest part of the earth. But after defeat they will soon be victorious.
4- Between three or nine years. God's is the imperative first and last. On that day the believers will rejoice.

30-The Romans, 2-4

At the time of the descent of the Quran, the Romans were practicing Christianity while the Persians were Zoroastrians. The Muslim population was grieved to hear that it was the Persians who had won the war against the Romans since Christians were monotheists. The victory of the Zoroastrians against the believers baffled the Muslims. The Quran predicted that the Romans (Byzantium) would soon become victorious and that the believers would rejoice. The expression "*beda seneen*" in verse 4 refers to the numbers ranging from three to nine.

The number of followers of Muhammad continued to increase. Had this statement of the Quran proved to be wrong, the confidence of the followers in Muhammad would have been shaken and the number of apostates would have grown. For a person not firmly convinced that the Quran was the revelation of God, such a prediction would be fatal for the system. If such a prediction were to prove false, it would have lost more of its authority than it would have gained had it turned out to be true. But it was God who revealed the Quran. So there was no risk. Thus the confidence of the followers increased even more.

SUCH DARING

Yes, self-confidence, daring and categorical prediction! This is either a proof of wisdom or the foolhardiness of the ignorant. The result indicates which was which. Those who doubt that this was not a revelation from God may conclude that it was guesswork, without considering the consequences that would put everything in danger. Something difficult was being heralded. A nation that had lost its cause was promised a triumph in a subsequent conflict.

Had this prediction turned out to be false, the believers might have lost faith and given trump cards to the hands of the opponents of the faithful. None of the accusations by unbelievers of Muhammad- attributing to him insanity, necromancy and opportunism- came to be true as they failed to belie his words. The unbelievers were badly in need of such accusations. It was certainly more difficult to attack the Prophet and his followers with daggers drawn. If the people who attributed partners to God were able to come forth with such evidence, they would prefer to use it rather than wage wars. So all the predictions of the Quran came true and no objections could ever be raised by the unbelievers.

Nevertheless, there have always been and will be people who turn a blind eye and a deaf ear to the revelations of the Quran. This did not prevent the Quran from eventually becoming the sovereign power of the region under the domination of the Prophet during his lifetime.

FROM DESPAIR TO VICTORY

Students of Byzantine (Roman) history should know that the Byzantine Empire suffered one of its gravest defeats in the 7th century at the time of the descent of the Quran. Although the Byzantines solved their problems in the coming years, during that time period, one of the main reasons for their serious downturn was the problem that the Persians generated.

Historical sources approve the Quranic information. It was thought that, since the Byzantines had suffered such a defeat, they could no longer recover. Records speak of Heraclius's collecting and melting in a crucible all the gold and silver of the churches to meet the expenses of the army. The Persians had already occupied

Mesopotamia, Cilicia, Syria, Palestine, Egypt and Armenia, all places that had once been under the domination of the Byzantines. In such a time of despair, the Quran predicted that the Byzantines would triumph within three to nine years. Historical records add that because of this statement the Prophet and his followers were held in derision, as there was little hope of the realization of this prediction coming true.

The Quran was to confirm this like all others. Byzantium won a victory over the Persians somewhere near the ruins of Nineveh in 627 AD, about nine years after the revelation of the prophecy. The Persians signed a treaty, according to which they turned over the territories they had occupied.

CHAPTER 65

THE LOWEST SPOT OF
THE EARTH

3- In the lowest part of the earth...

30-The Romans, 3

Verse 3 of the sura The Romans speaks of the defeat of the Romans at the lowest part of the earth. The Arabic expression *"edna al ard"* (the lowest part of the earth) has been translated by some commentators as "land close by." We think that this rendering does not express the essential meaning of the verse, that such a rendering may be taken as a secondary meaning. The translators were at a loss to understand the exact meaning of *"edna al ard"* and thought it best to give it the secondary meaning. We hope that after our remarks they will revise their work.

The region where the Byzantines suffered defeat was the Dead Sea, a place that is approximately 400 meters below the sea level, viz. the lowest spot of the earth, the highest being the Himalayas. A miracle of the Quran was its prediction of the war that was to be won by the Romans, a fact that at the time could hardly have been expected; another miracle was its foreknowledge about the place being the lowest spot on earth; something that could only be verified with the measuring techniques we gained in the last century.

YOU WILL CONQUER MECCA

27- Truly God fulfilled His messenger's vision. You will enter the Restricted Mosque in security, if God wills. You will cut your hair or shorten it, you will not have any fear. Since He knew what you did not know, He has preceded this with an immediate victory.

48-Victory, 27

237

Another prophecy similar to the victory of the Romans was the realization of the premonitory dream of Muhammad in which he saw himself entering the Restricted Mosque (the mosque which surrounded the Kaaba of Mecca, the place of pilgrimage). Just to remind you, the Prophet and his followers had been expelled from Mecca and the Meccans were superior both in military power and equipment.

Many prophets died before they could establish sovereignty in the land in which they spread their religion. Had there been no such tidings, Muhammad could not possibly have foreseen that the day would come when he would be in a position to conquer Mecca.

All Quranic verses reflect poise, confidence and self-reliance. There is nothing in them to suggest the ambivalence, vacillation and equivocation that one can encounter in other works whose authors were human beings.

89- ...We have sent down to you a Book explaining all things, a guide, a mercy and glad tidings for those who submit.

16-The Honeybee, 89

CHAPTER 66

ELECTRIC LIGHT BULB, ELECTRICITY, RAPID TRANSMISSION OF MATERIAL AND NEW MEANS OF COMMUNICATION

35- God is the light of the heavens and the earth. The parable of His light is that of a niche in which is a lamp. The lamp is enclosed in glass. The glass is like a pear-like planet. Lit with the oil of a blessed tree, the olive, neither of the east, nor the west, whose oil appears to light up even though fire touches it not. Light upon light. God guides to His light whomever He wills. God sets forth parables for the people. God knows all things.

24-The Light, 35

We believe that there are implications in the Quran indicating certain important inventions that were to take place in the future for mankind. At the time of the Prophet, when these inventions were beyond human imagination, people could not have imagined them. How could it be possible to explain to these people what electricity and the electric light bulb were?

The verse above seems to hint at electricity and the light bulb. However, I am not claiming that this is its only significance. It is certain that the scope of it must be larger than that. While the verse points to a fundamental issue in referring to light, it also seems to have the connotation of an electric bulb and electricity.

Light ("*noor*" in Arabic) is described enclosed in a glass. The fuel of this light within the glass comes neither from the east nor from the west, as the fuel consumed at the time was olive oil, but the expression here seems to point to a source of energy other than olive oil. The expression east and west means the entire world. An energy whose origin is neither the east nor the west must be an unknown energy. When this fact is seen within the framework of the expression, **"to light up even though fire touches it not,"** one generated by an energy without fire suggests electricity.

This verse certainly has other connotations. But it is impossible not to think of electricity. At the end of the verse, mention is made of parables. Recourse to parables is a method used by the Quran to convey information to the public who may not be in a position to understand what is communicated.

The imaginative scene that this verse generates in our mind is the following: the electric bulb that is lit in a dark room without having recourse to a flame illuminates the entire medium. Likewise when we look at the universe around us without our being aware of God's existence, deprived of all faith, everything will look dark, void and suggestive of despair. Once we take cognizance of God's existence and are enlightened by religion, our world will be illuminated just as the dark room is lit up. An aimless life will become meaningful, despair will yield itself to hope, and the feeling of being in a void will be replaced by a sense of existence. That is, the dark will be turned into light.

RAPID TRANSFER OF THINGS

40- The one who had knowledge of the Book said, "I can bring it to you within the twinkling of an eye." When he saw it settled in front of him, he said, "This is a blessing from my Lord; He tests me whether I am grateful or ungrateful. Yet if one is grateful, he is grateful for himself, and if one is ungrateful, truly my Lord is Rich, Honorable."

27-The Ant, 40

The Prophet King Solomon wanted the throne of the Queen of Sheba brought to him as soon as possible. Someone came forth telling Solomon that he would bring it before the King could stand up. Upon this, the person "who was given knowledge of the Book" promised that he would bring it within the twinkling of an eye, and granted Solomon's wish.

Emphasis is made here to the knowledge of the person who performs this feat. It is not said that this so-called miracle was the doing of the Prophet or due to the jugglery of a jinn. What is of particular importance here is the fact that if one has the true knowledge of something, it is possible to convey it at a very high speed.

Thanks to the state-of-the-art science and technology in our age, the sound and image of a material in any part of the world can be transmitted at a speed almost equal to the one expressed in the verse. This is not the transportation of the matter itself, though. Could the transfer of matter itself be possible one day?

As a matter of fact, scientists have made some progress. For example, in 1993, researchers from Innsbruck University in Austria were able to transfer photons from one spot to another. They dreamed of conducting the transmission of atoms and molecules using the same method. In the future, even the teleportation of the human body is speculated.

The attitude of Solomon in the verse quoted must set an example for all scientists. What he saw led Solomon to realize that he was being tried as to whether he was ungrateful or grateful, and thus he decided to turn toward God, in thanks. A scientist should take cognizance of the fact that whatever he discovers or invents is due to the brain, eyes and hands given to him by God, within the laws He has laid down, and give thanks to Him.

NEW MEANS OF TRANSPORTATION

8- And the horses, the mules and the donkeys for you to ride and for splendor. Additionally, He creates what you do not know.

16-The Honeybee, 8

While enumerating the means of transportation of the past, God predicts that man will use other means in the future. We, who know how comfortable it is to travel by airplanes, trains, cars, etc., can easily understand the reason for the drawing of our attention to means of transportation unknown at the time.

When the universe was created, all scientific discoveries existed potentially. All the natural laws, materials used in the manufacture of a car, the possible shapes and designs and configurations of the materials in question, as well as the energy needed, like petroleum, to run the car were already there. The Creator of the world had arranged everything beforehand. Therefore it is incumbent upon us to give thanks to Him and not to be ungrateful.

6- Truly man is to his Lord ungrateful.

100-The Gallopers, 6

CHAPTER 67

THOSE WHO DISBELIEVE IN THE END OF THE UNIVERSE

3- Those who disbelieved said, "There is no coming of the Hour for us." Say, "No, by my Lord, the knower of the unseen, it will certainly come upon you."

34-Sheba, 3

50- If We give him a taste of mercy after suffering some adversity, he says, "This belongs to me. I do not think that the Hour will come. Even if I am returned to my Lord, I will find in Him better things." Certainly We will inform the disbelievers of all their works and We will afflict them with severe retribution.

41-Elucidated, 50

In the first part of our work we dwelt upon the creation of the universe. The time has come now to examine the end of the world and the universe as expressed in the Quran. We are fully convinced that there has been no other book in the entire history of mankind that has given such a detailed account of the beginning and end of the world. Delve into all the books in history preceding scientific data and you will see that there is none like the Quran. It was said that the Quran would provide the signs and evidence; here they are, then! Will these not suffice for someone who is unbiased?

It is man's habit, confined in his own time bracket, to consider everything around him as constant and static. At the time of the Prophet, speaking of the end of the world, and especially of the universe, would be beyond conception. People ignorant of the fact that the world was an object flying in space, considered it a safe and sound place under their feet. They could not have believed that the day would come when everything would vanish.

As the accumulation of knowledge increased, thanks to scientific discoveries, it became clear that the end of the universe and of our world was inevitable. No one of sound mind today would assert that the world will exist forever. Even if no other celestial phenomenon occurs, it is certain that once the energy of the sun is exhausted, the end of the world will become unavoidable. However, the way and the exact time of this occurrence cannot be predicted.

To give you an example, the laws of thermodynamics indicate that the end will come. A stove's heating of a room; our leaving a cup of tea to cool down are subject to this law. Especially Rudolf Clausius's studies have led to the adoption of a measure of the unavailable energy called entropy. The total entropy continuously increases in the universe. The sun's heat flows toward the cold of the universe and this process is irreversible...

LAWS OF THERMODYNAMICS SEEN UNDER THE LIGHT OF RELIGION AND PHILOSOPHY

Will this process go on forever? The answer will be "No." When heat reaches a constant temperature, there comes about a static state called "thermodynamic balance." The flow of heat from the sun and from the multitude of stars may last for billions of years, but it is not inexhaustible. At the end of a time bracket, the laws of thermodynamics will make the activities going on in the universe come to a standstill. Under the circumstances, we can make the following deductions:

1- That the universe had a beginning, and
2- That it will come to an end one day.

All religions that have expounded belief in one God throughout history have been defenders of these two arguments. The Quran had this to say about the beginning and end of the universe. (In the first three chapters we read the miraculous statements of the Quran about the beginning of the universe.) On the other hand, materialists claim that matter has existed since eternity and will continue to exist forever and ever. In other words, they deny the beginning that led to the idea of creation and the end of the world and the universe, the *sine qua non* of religion. (In the two verses quoted above we saw the objections raised at the time of the Prophet against him.) When, as a result of developments in astrophysics, it became clear that the universe did have in fact, a beginning and an end, some atheists tried to fit their theories to the new discoveries. However, it is evident that before this issue was scientifically established, the atheists were against this idea. Nevertheless, despite the data provided by scientific studies, there are still atheists who refuse to believe that the universe had a beginning and that it will have an end.

The laws of thermodynamics confirm the assertions of monotheistic religions. This is then the scientific evidence supporting the teachings of the three major monotheistic religions regarding the end of the world. Had the universe existed since eternity, according to the laws of thermodynamics, all actions in the entire universe would have come to a standstill by now (according to thermodynamic balance). The fact that there is still action in the universe shows that the universe had no eternal existence, but that it had a beginning. Given the fact that there is still action going on in the universe and that it had a beginning, the end of the universe must come- at least according to the laws of thermodynamics. However, it appears that we shall not have to wait for the consequence of the laws of thermodynamics (We shall come back to this point in Chapter 68 and 69).

CHAPTER 68

DEATH OF THE STARS AND THE SUN

8- When the stars are put out.

77-The Emissaries, 8

At the time of the descent of the Quran, people believed that the light of the stars would last forever. This at a time when the inner structure of the stars was a mystery and the fact that the energy of the stars would, one day, be exhausted was not known. The Quran's prediction about the end of the stars is a miraculous statement.

2- When the planets are scattered.

82-The Shattering, 2

While the verses speak of the putting out of stars, the planets, not light sources, will scatter. The Arabic word for a star is *"najm,"* while *"kavkab"* is a planet. Given the fact that the planets are dependent on a central star, when this star is no more, the planets will necessarily scatter. (There have been translators who translated both words as stars without heeding the difference between them.) Planets are not light sources, therefore their extinction is out of question. The Quran displays its miraculous attribute in all its statements.

1- When the sun is rolled.

81-The Rolling, 1

The Arabic word *"takwir"* refers to the wrapping of the turban around the head in a spiral form; it also means the rolling or winding of a thing into a ball or round mass, or around something. The scene describes how the end of the sun will come. Like all the other stars, our sun also consumes hydrogen atoms by transforming them into helium atoms and releasing energy in the form of radiation, heat and light. The transformation of hydrogen into helium stops with the exhaustion of the hydrogen. Even without the effect of other potential causes, the sun will have to come to an end for this reason. Before their extinction, the stars, according to their sizes, pass through such phases as red giant, white dwarf or black hole. In view of its magnitude, our sun must turn first into a red giant before dying.

The sun has been a subject of worship in the history of mankind. People who did not believe in the end of the universe considered the sun itself to be an immortal divinity and thought that the universe and the earth would last eternally; there have been those who believed in the transmigration of souls everlastingly. Having eventually been convinced by scientific discoveries that the world was doomed to die one day, the minds that idolized the sun and the belief in the eternal reincarnation cycle lost their support. The belief in the Hereafter described in the Quran and the end of the universe are interconnected as the stages of a system. Taking cognizance of the fact that the end of the universe will eventually come has reinforced the belief in the Hereafter.

7- And verily the Hour is coming, no doubt about it, and that God will resurrect those who are dead.

22-The Pilgrimage, 7

The description of the end of the universe in the Quran relating to the end of the sun and of the world is given in striking colors. What the people at the Prophet's time knew about astronomy could not possibly have permitted them to describe such occurrences. Muslims who lived at the time of the revelation of the Quran believed in all these, not because of scientific deductions but because they had faith in the fact that it was easy for God, the Creator of the heavens and the earth, to destroy them. All the statements of the Quran about the disappearance of the stars, the sun and the earth are corroborated today by scientific discoveries.

EARTHQUAKES WITH BOILING SEAS

4- When the earth will be shaken up.

56-The Inevitable, 4

When the Hour comes, the entire earth will be shaken by a terrible earthquake. The Quran says that the tremor will cause mountains to be pulverized, and men will run to and fro in panic. As for the sea, we have the following indications:

6- When the seas boil.

81-The Rolling, 6

3- When the seas are suffered to burst forth.

82-The Shattering, 3

An earthquake will pulverize mountains, hot lava will burst forth from many corners of the earth. Volcanoes will erupt and lava will rise from the sea. It is unlikely that the depiction of the end of the world was an exaggeration of natural disasters that Muhammad experienced in his lifetime. The area where Muhammad lived was not on a major earthquake fault-line, and those who spent most of their lives in the middle of desert, most likely, never witnessed the eruption of a volcano in mid-ocean!

5- When the wild beasts are summoned.

81-The Rolling, 5

The Quran draws our attention to the herding together of animals. We know today that animals react to a tremor even before we, as human beings, realize it. For instance, in the zoo in Seattle Woodland, the odd movements of elephants and the restlessness of gorillas in their cages were observed before the earthquake was felt by human beings. This is a domain in which further research studies are being conducted. In view of this statement of the Quran, we think that this research should be intensified.

3- And when the earth is flattened out.
4- And when it throws out whatever it contains and is empty.

84-The Splitting, 3-4

The contents of the earth, the magma, the molten rock, will rise to the surface as lava, as described in the verses quoted.

The Quran would like us to turn our attention to the most serious event of earth history to come. Advanced science has demonstrated that the end of the world and the universe is inevitable. No one can assert any longer that the stars and the sun will shine forever, and that the universe and the earth will abide to eternity.

18- Are they waiting until the Hour comes to them suddenly? Its signs have already appeared. How can they benefit then when it has come upon them?

47-Muhammad, 18

CHAPTER 69

FROM BIG BANG TO BIG CRUNCH

104- On that day We will fold the heaven, like the folding of a book. Just as We initiated the first creation, We will revert it. This is Our promise. We will certainly fulfill it.

21-The Prophets, 104

I would like to bring an interesting point to your attention. In the verse it is said that God will return it to its former state. Therefore, to be able to understand the end of the universe, we have to go back to the first three chapters of our book where the beginning of Creation is described. The fact that they appear in the same sura is meaningful (The beginning is explained in the sura The Prophets; verse 30, in the same sura, verse 104, the end is explained).

30- Do not these disbelievers see that the heavens and the earth were an integrated mass, which We then split, and from water We made all living things? Will they not believe even then?

21-The Prophets, 30

47- With power did We construct Heaven. Verily, We are expanding it.

51-The Dispersing, 47

We deduce from the above two verses;
1- that the universe was separated from a whole, and
2- that the universe formed following this separation is expanding.
The extraordinary miracle in these verses of the Quran was exam-

ined in the first three chapters. Now if we may be allowed to go back to the verse we quoted in this chapter, if the universe is going to regress to its original state, then:

1- the expanding universe will have to contract, and

2- the expanding universe will return to its primordial unity.

Experts versed in astrophysics will take cognizance of the magnificence of this verse. We know today that the universe is expanding. We also know that this expansion is the consequence of the acceleration generated by the Big Bang. We are faced with two alternatives here. According to one of them, the expanding universe will spread out to a vast expanse, all the stars will have exhausted their energies, the temperature will fall and thus the end will be reached. Following the exhaustion of the energy of the stars and the coming to a standstill of all actions, all celestial bodies will break apart and escape from gravitational force. This is called the "Open Universe Model." According to a second alternative, the expanding universe will stop because of the mutual attraction of all bodies, and the universe will contract to return to its primordial state.

ONE MIRACLE AFTER ANOTHER

It seems that the Quran's implication is inclined toward the second alternative. At a time when people believed that the earth stood on the horns of an ox or on a fish, the Quran's description of the event was incredible. There is no way this fact could have been rendered from the scientific knowledge base of the day, or have been a product of fancy or flight of thought. The source of this knowledge is not scientific observation but God's revelation. The verse under our scrutiny also gives an answer as to which of the two alternatives man should put faith in. The greatness of the Quran, which stated that the universe was created from the one primordial wholeness, that it expanded, and that it would shrink back -at a time when all scientific evidence was lacking- is understood better today with the advance of science and the discovery of the mystery of the universe.

The collapse of the universe is referred to as the "Closed Universe Model." The power to realize this folding up is gravity. As we know, all matter is in mutual attraction. When something is thrown into the air, the object thrown cannot help falling back after some time because of gravity; matter that has scattered in every possible direction in space following the Big Bang will retrace its steps in a given time to be folded up. We must remember that at the time of the descent of the Quran, the notion of gravity did not exist and that it was to be known some one thousand years later, thanks to Newton's discovery.

Once the expansion of the universe was established, scientists began to study whether the universe would continue to expand or come to a close by folding up. To this end, they tried to find out the critical density of matter in the universe and arrived at certain ratios that they called "Omega." If the density in the universe is at a certain level, the process of folding up will begin before the scattering of matter into infinity...

Humans are born, live and die and eventually return to the dust of which they were made. The same thing holds true for beasts and plants. It appears that the law that governs all living creatures is also applicable in the case of the universe. In the verse we examined, this event is stressed with the word "revert." Following are the verses in which this word is used.

27- And He is the One who first creates and then reverts it. This is very easy for Him. And to Him belongs the most sublime similitude, in the heavens and the earth. And He is the Almighty, Wise.

30-The Romans, 27

34- Say: "Can any of your idols initiate creation, then revert it?" say "It is God who initiates the creation, and then reverts it. Then, how could you deviate?"

10-Jonah, 34

HEAVEN RENT ASUNDER AND THE RED ROSE

37- When the heaven will split asunder, and become rosy red like the dregs of anointing oil.

55-Gracious, 37

The Quran speaks of the color of heaven on the day the solar system comes to an end. Heaven's "split asunder" is also mentioned in other verses of the Quran.

9- When the heaven split asunder.

77-The Emissaries, 9

16- When the heaven will crack and split asunder. That day it will be flimsy.

69-Incontestable, 16

I believe that these verses may be understood in two different ways. If we take heaven for the entire universe, one may think of the decay at the outer extremities of the universe in continuous expansion. (By this the decay in the vacuum structure of the universe may have been meant. However, I am not going to dwell on this long issue.) According to a second alternative, if we take heaven for the atmosphere of our earth, big earthquakes, activities on the surface of the earth will likely affect the atmosphere, which will be split asunder and the protective layer of the atmosphere will be peeled off. As a matter of fact, the atmosphere depends on the fine balance between the earth's gravitational force and the movement of molecules in the atmosphere. Any alteration in this balance will likely affect the atmosphere. Either of these two alternatives, or both, for that matter, may have been meant by the verses.

SUDDEN ARRIVAL

187- They ask you about the Hour and when it will come to pass. Say, "The knowledge thereof is with my Lord. Only He reveals its time. Heavy it is, in the heavens and the earth. It will come to you suddenly." They ask you as if you are well-informed of it. Say, "The knowledge thereof is with God. But most people do not know."

7-The Purgatory, 187

The Quran says that the process of the end of the world and the universe will begin all of a sudden, at a time which even the Prophet does not know. According to the theory of relativity, the fastest motion in the universe belongs to light, the speed of which is not surpassed by anything. The data we obtain from light-emitting objects and the reflection of light are the limits of our understanding of the phenomena taking place in the universe. If information about the time the Hour will take place is to be transmitted at the speed of light, we can never be informed of it before some time has elapsed. For instance, if the sun explodes this very moment and the beginning of the end has come, we will be aware of it only after the lapse of eight and a half minutes.

The same holds true for other phenomena that will likely occur, causing the destruction of the universe. If the process in question has started at some point in the universe, we cannot be aware of it for some time. A series of phenomena will occur before we are conscious of it, up until the time we are suddenly caught by it.

1- When the inevitable comes to pass.
2- There can be no denying of its befalling.
3- It will lower some, and raise others.
4- When the earth will be shaken up.

56-The Inevitable, 1-4

The end of the universe and of the world is the most serious event next to its formation. Riches, reputations, situations, families, beauty, ugliness, joy, distress will be no more; the entire universe will be transformed into a small unit. Superiority will no longer be measured by riches, possessions and high offices. Now, "superiority" will depend on the sort of life man has led. From the scenery of the end of the universe and the world described in the Quran, there are lessons to draw in this life of ours. All these are not for the mere sake of knowing. What is communicated has as its objective to move people and guide them to God. We must bear in mind the third verse of the 56th sura:

3- It will lower some, and raise others.

56-The Inevitable, 3

CHAPTER 70

LIKE LOCUSTS

7- They will come out of the graves with downcast eyes like an expanding swarm of locusts.

54-The Moon, 7

In the verse above, unbelievers are reminded that they will be resurrected and that it will be a difficult day for them. Imagine, billions of men rising from the dead, coming out of their graves! Confusion, perplexity, fear, remorse... Everybody on his own... The only help is from God. The day when high offices, families, riches and possessions have no value- the day of no return...

The resurrected are likened to locusts; why particularly locusts? Recent research benefiting from micro cameras conducted by a systematic observation of insects have given us an idea about the reason for the selection of locusts as an example. To begin with, swarms of locusts, billions of them together, give the impression of a vast rain cloud without end, a black mass stretching far and wide many kilometers! Locusts bury their eggs in the earth and their larvae spend some time under the ground before they eventually emerge to the surface.

Take for instance the locusts, part of the fauna of New England, USA; in the month of May of the year in which they attain their 17th year, these insects emerge from under the ground where they have been living for years and years. Suppose, you tell a man: "We'll shut you up in a dark cell without a wristwatch and you'll have no contact whatsoever with the outside world and you'll be released at the end of the 17th day." it is very doubtful that he will be able to know exactly the time when he will be let out. There is a similarity between the rebirth of locusts and man's resurrection.

-After a long time
-Under the ground
-Altogether
-Densely crowded
-They rise to the surface of the earth

The parables and metaphors in the Quran are many. These figures of speech are to help us to understand better the meanings of the verses.

43- And such are the parables We set forth for the people, but only those understand them who have knowledge.

29-The Spider, 43

27- We have put forth for the people every kind of parable in this Quran that they may take heed.

39-The Throngs, 27

THE MIRACLES CONTAINED IN THE QURAN ARE EVIDENCE PROVING THE COMING OF THE HEREAFTER

A great deal of space is reserved for the description of life Hereafter in the Quran. Next to the existence of God, the most important message is that there is an afterlife and that man will receive recompense or retribution there. 1400 years ago, the Quran elaborated on physics, embryology, geology and zoology. There was no inaccuracy or misreckoning in any of the information supplied in it. Everything is perfectly expressed in the most unambiguous way.

The greatest claim of the Quran is the declaration of God's existence and the fact that no partner should be attributed to Him. The Quran reflects the Omnipotence and Omniscience and Artistry of God: the One, the Eternal and the Absolute. The messages it contains enables masses of people to choose the right path, the path of the chosen. It has saved many people from perdition, idolatry and atheism while confirming the Scriptures and prophets that preceded it. In short, those who comprehend the importance of the question whether God exists or not, will also appreciate the importance of the Quran, since it provides a conclusive answer to that question:

1- The Quran's most important message is God's uniqueness and oneness. The Quran has guided millions of people in the right path.

2- The predictions it contains have no precedent. This very fact proves that its original source is God, and confirms that its messages are true.

All these miracles and the mission that the Quran has assumed prove that it is the word of God and that one should put his complete trust in it. The Quran's greatest message, next to that of the existence of God, is the existence of the Hereafter. Every miracle evidencing the reliability of the Quran is also a proof of the existence of the Hereafter and the Day of Judgment.

RE-CREATION

The evidence of a life after death or a Hereafter are many. One of the main signs is man's aspiration for immortality. God has provided water for the thirsty and food for the hungry. If He did not want to give, then He would not give the desire to want. It is again He who has created in man the aspiration for immortality. Since He has done so, His promise shall be fulfilled. God's promise is sure to be gratified.

The most important and self-contained evidence of the existence of the Hereafter is God's promise. Is it possible that God would disappoint the believers who trust God, dedicate themselves to God and seek the Hereafter in their actions, while justifying disbelievers who deny the Hereafter, who disregard His messages, who fabricate lies about Him and mock those who are in the right path? Lies are a proof of imperfection, while everything is perfect with God.

Both during the Prophet's time and thereafter there have been doubts about the possibility of the end of the universe and of the Hereafter. The Quran is categorical and explicit about this.

> **77- Does not the human being see that We created him from a tiny drop? Then he turns into a profound enemy.**
> **78 - And he makes comparisons for Us and forgets his own creation. He says, "Who can resurrect the bones after they are rotten?"**
> **79- Say, "He who created them the first time. He has knowledge of every creation."**
>
> *36-Ya-Seen, 77-79*

Creation of a life in the Hereafter is the easiest thing for God. To begin with, it is His promise. The very fact of creation should convince us that re-creation is not difficult for Him.

49- They said, "After we turn into bones and fragments, shall we be resurrected as a new creation?"
50- Say, "Even if you turn into rocks or iron."
51- "Or any kind of creation that you deem impossible to resurrect." They will then say, "Who will bring us back?" Say, "The one who created you in the first place."
17-The Children of Israel, 49-51

The Hereafter is not a problem for God. In the first place, it has been promised by God. Moreover, we all have need of it. The Hereafter is repeatedly emphasized in the Quran. And it is clear that creation is a very simple act for God.

3- "What! When we die and become dust? This returning is most far-fetched."
4- We know what the earth consumes of them; with Us is a protected record.
50-Qaf, 3-4

God has recorded even in a single DNA molecule all the information related to the human body. While the Quran gives us an impression of an afterlife through creation, it directs our attention to the process to which God had recourse in creating us. The cells in our body die and are immediately replaced by new ones. Today, the cells that constitute our body are not the same as those we were made of initially. The food we consume is continually transformed into a part of our system. The atoms of carbon, hydrogen, nitrogen, oxygen, and phosphorous flow in our body and are consumed, to finally return to dust. What remains unchanged is the essence we call "self" or "soul." Even when we are of this world God creates us every moment anew. Since He has promised to re-create us there is no doubt that He will.

33- Do they not realize that God, Who created the heavens and the earth and did not tire creating them, is able to revive the dead? Yes, verily He has power over all things.

46-The Dunes, 33

Creations in endless space, the greatness in the number of species and creatures make it evident that re-creation for God is as easy as the creation.

28- The creation and resurrection of all of you is the same as that of one person. God is Hearer, Seer.

31-Luqmaan, 28

LET'S GET READY TO DEPART

There are many subjects explicitly given in the Quran; however, the things that our five senses may fail to perceive are presented in metaphors (3- The Family of Imran, 7). In the description of paradise and hell, allegory is made to figures of speech (2- The Cow, 25). Blessings and rewards in the life Hereafter are described succinctly by metaphors. The exact rendering of the objects will take place when man is transferred there. Allegories made must not be taken fully literally. Bliss in heaven and remorse in hell are evident, although they will be understood in the Hereafter more clearly.

The scope of the account related to the Hereafter is far beyond what is said about paradise and hell. The description of a single province like the Bahamas would take a whole book thicker than the Quran itself. Had all the details of paradise and hell been given, they would have filled an encyclopedia of many volumes. Only the clues are given. The fact that only a few names of some fruits are mentioned does not mean that is all that paradise contains. The mere mention of the fact that everything that a human being may aspire to shall be there is enough. (21-The Prophets, 102; 42-Consultation, 22; 43-Vanity, 71; 50-Qaf, 35.)

In this brief earthly life of ours, the wisest act for us is to direct ourselves to God.

185- Every soul shall have to taste death, and you will get your recompense in full on the Day of The Resurrection. The one who is saved from the fire and admitted to paradise has attained a great triumph. The life of this world is no more than goods and chattels of deception.

3-The Family of Imran, 185

7- Those who disbelieved claim that they will not be resurrected! Yes indeed, by my Lord, you will be resurrected, and then informed of what you have done. And that is easy for God.

64-Mutual Blaming, 7

MATHEMATICAL MIRACLES

92- And to recite the Quran. Whoever comes to guidance does for himself; and if any stray, say, "I am only a warner."
93- Say, "All praise be to God. He will show you His signs, and you will recognize them. Your Lord is never unaware of anything you do."

27-The Ant, 92-93

Verse number 93 above predicts that God will reveal His signs sometime in the future. The miracles in the Quran could not have originated from the thoughts of the Prophet, for even if all the knowledge of the Prophet's entire era were collected together, this knowledge could not suffice to vie with these miracles. Had the author of these miracles been Muhammad of the deserts himself, he would have used these miracles in order to impress his own people, to demonstrate to them the perfection of the Quran and thus to put an end to their recalcitrance. The Muslim world itself was unaware of many of these miracles until quite recently, i.e. up until a hundred years ago. God reveals His miracles when the time is ripe. Persons of sound mind and clear conscience will appreciate these signs, praise God and thank Him.

20- They say, "How is it that no sign was sent to him by his Lord?" Whatever cannot be perceived belongs to God. So wait and I am waiting with you.

10-Jonah, 20

The fact that God will show His signs in the future is also confirmed in the above verse. Disbelievers insist on miracles, and yet when they see one performed they persist in their disbelief. It is clear that the insistence of disbelievers is far from an honest demand, and it is antagonism for antagonism's sake.

146- I will divert from My signs those who behave unjustly with arrogance on earth. Even though they see every kind of sign, they will not believe, and when they see the path of guidance, will not take it to be a way. But when they see the path of straying, they will adopt it as their path. This is so, for they have called Our signs lies, and have been heedless of them.

7-The Purgatory, 146

Persons unwilling to learn patent truths and those who deny God's religion say arrogantly, "We are self-sufficient and we have no need of a God." This behavior renders them blind to the miracles of the Quran. Even if they do see the miracles, they remain adamant because of their stubbornness.

The scientific and mathematical demonstrations of the Quran address man's reason. People who are suspicious of the potential of human intelligence, who think that religion is a way of belief utterly devoid of discursive reason, or those who consider religion as a source of profit cannot comprehend these miracles. Some false authorities, who see religion as a tool for their own benefit, manipulate the religion by denying direct access to it. Open access encourages questioning and intellectual reasoning; controversy undermines their authority and lessens their power and their ability to profit from the religion.

THE INCONTESTABLE CERTAINTIES OF MATHEMATICS

In this part of our book, I shall be dealing with the mathematical miracles in the Quran. Mathematics is a basic tool and a common language of all sciences. Mathematical certainty has always impressed philosophers throughout history. The importance of it was better appreciated after the 16th century. Great improvements were achieved in the sciences, thanks to the scientific approach that placed mathematics right in the center. Cars, trains, satellites, medications, means of communication and the technological wonders of the modern age owe their origins to mathematics. Without mathematics we could not understand the universe, nor could we come up with new inventions.

The value of mathematics was not entirely ignored in the past, but it was in the course of the last four centuries that it gained such ascendance. Today's scientific logic is a product of mathematics. Galileo, who played an important role in endowing mathematics with this central role, stated that mathematics is the language in which God wrote the universe. No other discipline has had a field of application of such scope. Philosophers, amongst others Pythagoras, sensed that the basic order of the universe was numerical, and they attached mystical meanings to mathematics. However, it was only in the recent past that scientific logic was constructed around mathematics. Descartes, one of the main advocates of translating science into the language of mathematics and one of those who combined arithmetic with geometry on Cartesian coordinates, said, *"Mathematics may and must be the common link among intellectual disciplines."*

Mathematics should be considered the biggest discovery of mankind. From Edison's electric bulb to race cars, from Einstein's theory of relativity to Newton's law of gravitation, all these owe their origin to the fundamental importance of mathematical language. The Quran mentioned the importance of mathematics 1400 years ago. It continuously draws our attention to the sensitive balance and the role of mathematics in the universe.

5- The sun and the moon are calculated.

55-Gracious, 5

In the process involving the movements of the sun, the world and the moon, mathematics has played a role of towering importance. It was discovered that God had expressed the universe in the language of mathematics. The Quran indicated this very important point 1400 years ago. The Quran sees no contradiction between the creation of the universe based on teleological causality and the definition of universal phenomena in terms of mathematical formulations.

If the universe is the product of God and expressed in the language of mathematics, we should not be surprised if God's book, the Quran, also used the same language. God displays His miracles with the incontestable certainty of mathematics. Moses had worked miracles in an age when magic was in fashion and converted the magicians, and the Quran displayed its mathematical miracles in an age when science and its language, mathematics, were at their peaks. Now that considerable advances have been made in mathematical logic, the importance of such miracles can be understood more clearly. People trying to antagonize religion by having recourse to science will be disarmed. God's plan is perfect. God's timing is perfect. God's miracles in His Book are perfect.

WHY MATHEMATICS?

In our age, every science is in pursuit of mathematical certainty and approval. Even if it fails to find that certainty, it envies those who have it. Some people searching for certainty in religion have also searched for a mathematical language. Carl Sagan is an author who writes about astronomy; his imaginative explanations in his book *Contact* are a good example of people's expectations of mathematical proofs from God.

"No, do not you see: This would be different. This is not just starting the universe out with some precise mathematical laws that determine physics and chemistry. This is a message. Whoever makes the universe hides messages in transcendental numbers so they'll be read fifteen billion years later when intelligent life finally evolves. I criticized you and Rankin the time we first met for not understanding this. If God wanted us to know that He existed, why didn't he send us an unambiguous message? I asked. Remember?"

"I remember very well. You think God is a mathematician."

"Something like that. If what we're told is true. If this is not a wild-goose chase. If there's a message hiding in pi and not one of the infinity of other transcendental numbers. That's a lot of ifs."

"You're looking for Revelation in arithmetic. I know a better way."

"Palmer, this is the only way. This is the only thing that would convince a skeptic. Imagine we find something. It doesn't have to be tremendously complicated. Just something more orderly than could accumulate by chance that many digits into pi. That's all we need. Then mathematicians all over the world can find exactly the same pattern or message or whatever it proves to be. Then there are no sectarian divisions. Everybody begins reading the same Scripture. No one could then argue that the key

miracle in religion was some conjurer's trick, or that later historians had falsified the record, or that it is just hysteria or delusion or a substitute parent for when we grow up. Everyone could be a believer." (Carl Sagan, *Contact*)

The conversation above is quoted from Carl Sagan, an astronomer not conversant with the Quran's mathematical miracles. In his work, he displays the imaginative approach of philosophers: God's mathematical evidence. As a universal language leaving no room for suspicion, mathematics has always attracted philosophers and scientists. The quotation above is a proof of this. God, well aware of the values and conditions of our time and of the desires of the human mind, answers this search for certainty with mathematics, at a time when this science is at its peak, and answers in a way that is not complicated and is impossible to imitate.

Some points must be added to Carl Sagan's quotation: Supposing that such a miracle did happen, it would be wrong to think that the public would lend credence to it. The psychology of the cynic who never gives in, who is always keen on finding loopholes and who avoids common sense, will be deaf and blind to clearest evidences.

NOT EVEN ONE SINGLE SURA CAN BE DUPLICATED

23- If you are in doubt of what We have revealed to Our Servant, then bring a sura like this, and call any witness you like, apart from God, if you are truthful.
24- But if you cannot, as indeed you cannot, then guard yourselves against the fire whose fuel is men and rocks, which has been prepared for the disbelievers.

2-The Cow, 23- 24

You will see very clearly that it is quite impossible to imitate even a single sura in the Quran when you start reading the sections of the present work on the Quran's mathematical miracles. Every sura happens to be encoded and the words used in them are interlocked in mathematical terms and every particular sura is locked in by a mathematical code. If you leave out a single sura from the Quran then the number of suras, 114 (the number 19x6) would suffer injury.

Assuming that the word "a day" (*yewm*) is used twice in this sura, with the dismissal of that sura, the frequency of the word "day" in the Quran, which is 365, would be reduced to 363, spoiling the mathematical code. Suppose that the word "world" is mentioned three times and the word "hereafter" is mentioned once. The frequency of those words in question totals 115 times for each. If that particular sura is left out, the frequency of the word "world" would be 112 and the word "hereafter" 114, and this would negate the whole system...

The removal of any one of the suras would spoil the whole mathematical miracle of the Quran. This means that each sura is an integral part of the whole truth. One sura means the entirety of the Quran. The entire mathematical miracle makes sure that every sura is indispensable. The remaining chapters, in which we are going to examine the mathematical miracles of this book, will show the reason why even a single sura cannot be eliminated. The perfection of the suras and the volume of mathematical miracles are of even greater scope. But even the ones mentioned in this book are enough to show why it is impossible to copy even a single sura. The reality is crystal clear for those who are willing to face it.

GO NOT AFTER THE THINGS OF WHICH YOU HAVE NO KNOWLEDGE

36- Do not follow that of which you have no knowledge. Because the ear, the eye and the heart, each will be questioned.

17-The Children of Israel, 36

The mathematical and scientific miracles God displays are for the people who use their minds and have the intention to see them. Stubborn deniers, people taking advantage of religion, and people who experience it by imitating the people around themselves cannot draw any benefit from these miracles unless they change their self-seeking attitudes. God despises people who imitate other people as ritual. The real value is in the people who do not expect any worldly benefits, who use their minds, explore, and search for evidence in the universe and in the holy books. May God protect us from people who sell their religion in consideration for dollars, euros and gold coins and seek reputation, and from those who represent religion as myths and dreams.

God sent us a book whose contents are endorsed by the miracles it reveals. It displays miracles and proofs coded mathematically within its text. The Quran is a guide for us.

50- For they say: "How is it no signs were sent down to him from his Lord?" Say: "The signs are with God. I am only a plain warner."
51- Is it not sufficient for them that We have revealed the Book to you which is read out to them? It is indeed a grace and reminder for people who believe.

29-The Spider, 50-51

NUMERICALLY STRUCTURED BOOK

The Quran's 83rd sura, "The Cheaters" speaks of "numerically structured books" in two instances. The Arabic of this word is *"kitabun marqum."* These verses are evidences of God's encoding the books, of His involving mathematics in the system:

7- Indeed, the book of the wicked is in Sijjeen.
8- Do you know what Sijjeen is?
9- A numerically structured book.

83-The Cheaters, 7- 9

17- They will be told, "This is what you used to deny."
18- Indeed, the book of the righteous will be in "Elleyyeen."
19- Do you know what "Elleyyeen" is?
20- A numerically structured book.
21- To be witnessed by those who are brought close.

83-The Cheaters, 17-21

The Quran speaks of numerically structured books with reference both to the good and to the evil. While those **"who are brought close"** can testify, the same is not made available for the evil characters. The evil characters call the proofs of God "legends" and deny their truth (*83-The Cheaters, 13*). The evidence in hand shows that the

Quran is a numerically structured scripture. There are those who confirm this while others assert that its contents are but legends and stories. It is a boon of God to be able to appreciate and to confirm these miracles.

EASY TO UNDERSTAND, IMPOSSIBLE TO IMITATE

We have divided the presentation of the mathematical miracles into two groups. The first group consists of the Mathematical Miracles in Lexical Concordance (*MMLC*). We shall tackle the subject from different angles: the concordance of words among themselves and the concordance of words with universal phenomena. These miracles are easy to understand but impossible to imitate. Even those who are not really interested in mathematics can easily understand the miracles in question. The second part takes up the "miracle of the number 19." We shall dwell particularly on number 19, a figure mentioned in the Quran. Anybody who can count from 1 to 19 can easily witness this miracle, easy to understand but impossible to imitate. We run across this mystery in many instances. But, to understand all the characteristics concerning this number one must have recourse to the theory of probability, and deeper research is needed.

While writing the mathematical sections of our book for the MMLC miracles, I had recourse to works like Abdülrezzak Nevfel's, and for the sections treating of the number 19, I used different studies, such as those of Cesar Majul, Rashad Khalifa, Edip Yuksel, Richard Voss and Milan Sulc. I did not include any of these people's ideas on religion in our book, as I do not want to get involved in any debates among believers, even though such a discussion could prove fruitful. But this is outside our main concern here.

Whatever the identities of the discoverers of these miracles were, the miracles the Quran contains will not be affected in any way because they are the Quran's miracles and they were there to be discovered. Their truth can be checked anytime. Even if the discoverer is an atheist, this would not hurt the truth. (For example, the word month is used 12 times in the Quran. It doesn't matter who discovers this fact because it has been there for 1400 years. It is very easy to check the truth of this.) Since the mathematical patterns are both physical facts understood by inductive and deductive reasoning and thus are verifiable and falsifiable, occasional errors made by a discoverer do not hurt the credibility of other findings. In short, this miracle is not dependent on the authority and credibility of the person but on the authority and credibility of the Quranic text, statistics, laws of probability, and reason.

Chronic skepticism is a widespread sickness in our age. The mathematical miracles of the Quran can be checked any time and this is the best answer for this skepticism. These miracles are not ephemeral phenomena. The Quran and its miracles are there and can be seen any time.

88- Say, "If all the humans and the jinns came together in order to produce a Quran like this, they would surely fail, no matter how much assistance they lent one another."

17-The Children of Israel, 88

MATHEMATICAL MIRACLES in LEXICAL CONCORDANCE (MMLC)

MMLC - 1

ONE DAY

The word "a day" (*yewm*) is used 365 times in the Quran. The figure 365 does not only represent the number of days in the calendar, but it is also the figure that shows the astronomical relationship between our world and the sun. When our world completes its turn around the sun, it has revolved 365 times around its own axis. In other words, when the world has completed its cycle around the sun, this means we have lived 365 days on earth. It is important that the word "a day" is used 365 times in the Quran, because the world's revolution around the sun takes 365 days.

The word	Number of occurrences
A day	365
The number of days in which the world completes its revolution around the sun?	365

MMLC - 2

DAYS

The different uses of the word "day" in the Quran is phenomenal. While the singular word "a day" is used 365 times, its plural (*eyyam, yewmeyn*) is used 30 times. This represents the number of the days in a month, which is 30. So it is meaningful that while the singular "day" (*yewm*) is mentioned 365 times, the plural of it (*eyyam, yewmeyn*) is mentioned 30 times.

In the solar calendar, the months have either 30 or 31 days and in the lunar calendar the months have either 29 or 30 days. So, the number 30 is the intersection group for both calendars. In the community to which the Quran was revealed, the lunar calendar was in use; the mention of "30" is therefore meaningful. It takes 29.53 days for the moon, the satellite in the sky, to make a month. The rounded figure is 30. With such mathematical miracles, we witness that the Quran calculates correctly this rounding up business. Likewise, the world completes its cycle around the sun in 365.25 days exactly. The rounded figure is 365.

The word	Number of occurrences
Days	30
Number of days in a month	30

MMLC - 3

THE DERIVATIVES OF THE WORD DAY

We saw that the singular "day" (*yewm*) is mentioned 365 times, and the plural of it, 30 times in the Quran. All of the derivatives of the word "day" are used 475 times. This means that the singular, plural and all the other derivatives add up to 475. 475 is equal to 19x25. (After we study this mathematical miracle in this section, we will also examine it in the "miracle of 19" section and show more clearly what the number 19 indicates.) Sometimes, the MMLC and the miracle of the number 19 may be interconnected, as in this example. Since the use of the word "day" shows the miraculous characteristic, apart from the miracle of the number 19, I have presented the discoveries on it in the MMLC section too. Like the multiplier 19, the number 25 also has a significant meaning. As I have already mentioned, days are formed as a result of the relationship between the earth and the sun. The earth revolves around its own axis 365 times while completing its cycle around the sun, and during this time the sun also revolves around itself. As the earth revolves around itself 365 times, how many times must the sun itself have revolved? 25 times exactly. This number, pointed out by the miracle that is easy to understand but impossible to imitate, was not known at the time of the descent of the Quran in the region in question. They had no idea about it. It is a miracle that the Quran, by references to repeated numbers, points out; and the fact that those numbers indicated things unknown at the time is another miracle.

On the other hand, the figure 19, multiplier of 25, has an important role within the context of the concept of the relationship between the sun / the earth and day. A Meton cycle—that is when the sun, the earth and the moon come to the same line,—occurs once in every 19

274

years. That is to say, the sun turns around itself the number 19x25=475 times in a Meton cycle (Read the next chapter, MMLC 4). Yes, exactly 475 times. This number is equal to the number of times the derivatives of the word "day" are used in the Quran.

The word	Number of occurrences
All the derivatives of the word "day"	475 (19x25)
How many times does the sun revolve around itself within a year?	25
How many times does the sun revolve around its own axis in a Meton cycle?	475 (19x25)

MMLC - 4

YEAR

The derivatives of the word "year" (*sinet, sinin*) are mentioned 19 times in the Quran. The solar and lunar calendars need correction because of the leap year. When the world revolves around the sun 365 times, the moon revolves around the earth and itself 12 times. This constitutes a year. But when the earth completes its revolution and arrives at the starting point, the moon is behind schedule. It takes the earth and the moon 19 years to meet at the same starting point. This cycle of 19 years is called the Meton cycle. The lunar calendar, re-arranged every 19 years, ends up with 7 leap years (355 days) and 12 full years (354 days) during this period. It is also another surprising characteristic of the miracles that the singular year (*sinet*) is used 7 times, whereas the plural year (*sinin*) is used 12 times in the Quran. And all the derivatives of the word "year" are used 19 times, an indication of the Meton cycle.

The word	Number of occurrences
Year	19
In how many years does a Meton cycle occur?	19

The earth lines up with the sun and the moon every 19 years. In the Quran, the words "sun" and "moon" are used in the same verses exactly 19 times; the same number that makes a "Meton cycle" corresponds to the number of times the word "year" is used in the Quran. It is interesting to note that on the 19th time, these two words are used together, we have the following verse:

9- And the <u>sun</u> and the <u>moon</u> are conjoined.

75-The Resurrection, 9

The overlapping of the meaning and of the mathematical concordance is a miracle. Now let us look at the table where the words "sun" and "moon" are used together (In the 41st sura, verse 37, these words are used twice).

Repetitions (times)	Suras	Verses
1	6	96
2	7	54
3	10	5
4	12	4
5	13	2
6	14	33
7	16	12
8	21	33
9	22	18
10	29	61
11	31	29
12	35	13
13	36	40
14	39	5
15	41	37
16	41	37
17	55	5
18	71	16
19	75	9

If you add up the numbers of the suras and the verses in which these words are used:

6+96+7+54+10+5+12+4+13+2+14+33+16+12+21+33+22+18+2
9+61+31+29+35+13+36+40+39+5+41+37+41+37+55+5+71+16+75
+9=1083 (19x57) and 57= the number 19x3.

Please keep in mind this concordance formed by the multiples of 19, and remember it, in the following chapters on the miraculous number of 19.

The MMLC in the Quran shows itself both in the sura and verse numbers. This proves that the Quran's miraculous order covers even the numbers of the suras and verses.

MMLC - 5

THAT DAY AND THE RESURRECTION DAY

We saw earlier that the word "day" in the Quran, with its singular, plural and derivative uses, constitutes a marvelous pattern. Apart from this, the phrases of the same word also produce mathematical miracles as well. For example, we see this miracle in phrases like "that day" used in connection with the end of the world (*yewme izin*) and "the day of resurrection" (*yewmul qiyameh*). Both phrases are used 70 times, out of the 475 occurrences of all the derivatives of the word "day." Here are two example verses for these words:

8- Many faces will be joyous on <u>that day</u>.

88-Overwhelming, 8

67- ...the whole earth is within His fist on <u>the day of res-urrection</u>.

39-The Throngs, 67

The word	Number of occurrences
That day	70
The day of resurrection	70

MMLC - 6

THE MOON

The word moon (*Qamar*), together with its derivatives, is used exactly 27 times in the Quran. This number is equal to the number that is the moon's ecliptic cycle around the world. The Quran indicates that both the sun and the moon follow courses exactly computed (*55-Gracious, 5*). The sun's and the moon's definition in terms of mathematics is interesting and the word "moon" is mathematically coded in the Quran.

The word	Number of occurrences
Moon	27
How long does the moon's ecliptic cycle take?	27

MMLC - 7

THE MONTH

The earth's revolution around the sun takes 365 days, while the moon's 12 revolutions around the earth takes 12 months in the lunar calendar. The Quran says that there are 12 months in a year. On the other hand, in the Quran, the word "a month" (*shehr*) is also mentioned 12 times to indicate that there are 12 months in a year. The following verse mentions this:

36- ...twelve is the number of months with God...

9-Repentance, 36

The word	Number of occurrences
A month	12
The number of the months or the number of the moon's revolutions around the world in a year	12

MMLC - 8

THE DATE OF THE LANDING ON THE MOON

In chapter 16, we studied the expressions in the Quran that alluded to man's landing on the moon. One of the most important among the signs is in the first verse of the sura the Moon (*Qamar*). The number of verses to be counted from this verse to the end of the Quran is 1389. The year 1389 in the Muslim calendar corresponds to the year 1969 in the Gregorian calendar. And the year 1969 was the year when man landed on the moon for the first time. (On the other hand, the number 1389 may also be pointing out that man will land on the moon 1389 years after this verse or after the Quran was revealed by God. This was because the Muslim calendar started at a time when the revelation was not completed.)

1- The Hour has come closer and the The Moon has split.

54-The Moon, 1

How many verses are there from the first verse of the sura The Moon until the end of the Quran?	1389
In which year of the Muslim calendar did the first man land on the moon?	1389

MMLC - 9

RATIO OF THE SEA AND LAND SURFACE

The word "the sea" (*al-bahr*) is used 32 times in the Quran. The word "*al-bahr*" is used both for sea and other waters like lakes and rivers. The word "*al-berr*" (the land) is used 12 times in the Quran.

The surface of the world is 510 million square kilometers. Approximately 360 million kilometers are made up of waters, like seas, lakes, etc. In addition, 15 million kilometers are ice-sheets; if we exclude these ice-sheets from the rest, approximately 135 million square kilometers are land.

The ratio of the words "*al-bahr*" (the land) and "*al-berr*" (the sea) in the Quran is 12/32 = 0.375. The ratio of the land and the sea in the world is 135 mill sq. km / 360 million sq. km=0.375. So, there is a very interesting harmony between the usages of these words in the Quran and the existing phenomena in the world.

22- He is the One who moves you across the <u>land</u> and the <u>sea</u>.

10-Jonah, 22

The word	Number of occurrences	The Ratio
Land	12	$\dfrac{12}{32} = 0.375$
Sea	32	

The Place	Surface of the Earth	The Ratio
Land (excluding ice sheets)	135 million square kilometers	$\dfrac{135}{360} = 0.375$
Sea	360 million square kilometers	

MMLC - 10

THE 309TH WORD

We have seen earlier that the mathematical miracle in lexical concordance can be presented in many different ways. The concordance in the Quran is sometimes referred to as lexical concordance with the universe, and sometimes merely as lexical concordance between words. We shall see a different type of evidence in this section. The 18th sura, The Cave, relates the story of seven sleepers who slept in a cave for 300 years and 9 years were added to this time period. (We shall see why this number was not given directly as 309, but mentioned as above, in the sections on the 19 miracle. If this number had been given as 309, then the total of the numbers given in the Quran would not be a multiple of 19.)

The youth who stay in a cave are mentioned in the 9th verse of the 18th sura. Up until the 25th verse, all the verses are about these young people and in the 25th verse, it is said that these youths stayed in the cave for 300+9 years. From the beginning of these young people's adventure until the end of the time they stayed in the cave, the story is told in 308 words and the 309th word is the word 300+9 years, which is the amount of time they stayed in the cave. The following verse is given below:

25- They stayed in the cave: <u>three hundred years and nine</u>.

18-The Cave, 25

How many years did the youngsters stay in the cave?	309
How many words are used from the beginning of the verses that describe the youngsters till the end of the time they stayed in the cave mentioned?	309

The verses describing the young people in the cave and expressing the number 309:

The Verses	Number of Words
9	10
10	16
11	7
12	9
13	11
14	19
15	19
16	19
17	34
18	22
19	37
20	13
21	32
22	33
23	7
24	17
25	3
TOTAL	**308+**

308+ (the 309th word gives the meaning of 309)

MMLC - 11

SEVEN HEAVENS

The Quran tells us that the heavens are created in seven layers. We studied this subject in our book's first section, chapter 17. The term "seven heavens" is used seven times in the Quran.

1- 2-The Cow, 29
2- 17-The Children of Israel, 44
3- 23-The Believers, 86
4- 41-Elucidated, 12
5- 65-Divorce, 12
6- 67-The Kingdom, 3
7- 71-Noah, 15

The word	Number of occurrences
Seven heavens	7
What is number the Quran gives for the number of heavens?	7

MMLC - 12

ATOMIC NUMBER OF IRON

Let us see first the verse that mentions the importance and character-istics of iron:

> 25- We have surely sent Our messengers with clear signs, and sent with them the book and the balance, so that man may stand by justice; and We sent down the iron, wherein there is strength, and many benefits for the people. So that God would know who will support Him and His messen-gers in secret. Verily God is Powerful, Almighty.
>
> *57-Iron, 25*

The verb *"inzal"* in the Quran is usually used to describe the action of coming from above the earth. The verb *"inzal"* refers to the fact that a creation in the world has taken place following an event exterior to the earth. The temperature of the earth was not sufficient, at the beginning, for the formation of iron. Not only the earth, but even a middle-sized star like our sun did not have the heat necessary for the formation of iron. That is why iron must have come to our planet, as well as to the entire solar system, from outer space. The iron we have in our planet today must have come to our solar system from other stars that had higher temperatures favorable for the formation of iron.

The Quran shows other mathematical miracles by pointing out iron's atomic number, 26, in different ways.

1. In the Quran, there is a mathematical value for every letter. (We will give all the letters and their numerical values in the part on 19.) The mathematical value for the word iron (*hadid*) is 26.

Ha	=	8
Dal	=	4
Ya	=	10
Dal	=	4
+		
Total	=	26

2. The verse that refers to iron is the 25th verse in the sura Hadid. If we count *Basmalah*, then that number is 26.

3. The name God mentioned in this sura for the 26th time is in the same verse. The atomic number of an element is the main character-istic of that element and is determined by the number of its protons, which are the building blocks of that element. Iron's atomic number is 26 because of its 26 protons. From the beginning of the sura Iron (*Hadid*) till the end of the verse of that sura that alludes to iron, the word God is used 26 times.

The word	Mathematical value of the word
Iron	26
Iron's atomic number	26
How many times is the word "God" used from the begin-ning of the sura until the end of the 25th verse, which is the only verse wherein the prop-erties of iron are mentioned?	26

MMLC - 13

IRON'S ISOTOPES

As iron's atomic number is encoded in the sura that mentions iron, there is also a sign in that sura about iron's isotopes.

The word "*al hadid*," which refers to a particular iron, has a mathematical value of 57. The article "*al*" corresponds to "the" in English. When the word *hadid* is used with the article "*al*," referring to a specific iron, the mathematical value turns out to be 57.

Alif	=	1
Lam	=	30
Ha	=	8
Dal	=	4
Ya	=	10
Dal	=	4
+		
Total	=	57

1. The sura Iron (*Hadid*) is the 57th sura of the Quran. And 57 is one of the isotopes of iron.

2. The sura Iron (*Hadid*) is the 58th sura from the end of the Quran. That is another isotope of iron.

3. This sura has 29 numbered verses. This number becomes 30 when the unnumbered *Basmalah* is counted. These two numbers (29 and 30) are equal to the neutron numbers of two isotopes of iron, from the total of four. The frequency of the word God in this sura gives the neutron number of the other isotope.

The word	Mathematical value of the word
The iron (al hadid)	57
One of iron's isotopes	57
What is the sura number of the sura the Iron?	57

MMLC - 14

THE HIGHEST DEGREE

One of the verses of the Quran points out that God is the possessor of the high degrees. The verse is:

15- <u>Possessor of the high degrees</u>, and Ruler of the whole dominion. He sends inspiration, bearing His commands, to whomever He chooses from among His servants to warn about the Day of Gathering.

40-The Believer, 15

"*Rafii al-Darajat*" is translated as "the possessor of the high degrees," but it can also be translated as "the one who increases the degrees." The word "*Rafii*" expresses highness and the word "*al-darajat*" expresses the degrees. The mathematical value of "*Rafii*," which states the highest degree, is 360. And this number is the equivalent of the conventionally accepted highest degree in the universe. The mathematical values are as follows:

Raf	=	200
Fa	=	80
Ya	=	10
Ayn	=	70
+		
Total	=	360

The word	Mathematical value of the word
Rafii	360
The conventionally accepted highest degree in the universe	360

MMLC - 15

THE SURA ON THE HONEYBEES

We observe that the honeybee is mentioned more specifically in the Quran than other animals (We presented this subject in the 41st and the 42nd chapters). There are many mentions of animals in the Quran but none of them play such a special part as the honeybee. The number of this sura is 16 and entitled The Honeybee (*Nahl*). The number of this sura equals the number of the chromosomes of the male honeybee. The number of chromosome of the female honeybee is (2n) which is equal to 32 (16x2). So the number of the sura indicates the number of chromosomes. The number of chromosomes is like the atomic number of that element, it cannot be changed. Everywhere in the world, the number of chromosomes of the male honeybee is 16 and every female honeybee has 32 chromosomes. On the other hand, the verse number of this sura is 128, this means; 8 times the number of chromosomes of the male honeybee (16) and also 4 times the number of chromosomes of the female honeybee (32). Just like the number of this sura, the verse number is proportional to the number of chromosomes of the honeybees.

In this sura, the verses 68 and 69 mention the honeybees. The first verse, 68, has 13 words. If we count the words from the beginning of this sura up to the word honeybee (*nahl*) in that verse, we come up with 884 letters. Let us see if this number has any meaning. This number is equal to the verse number multiplied by the number of words in that verse (68 x 13 = 884). Can this be coincidence? There are many different ways in which the Quran shows its mathematical miracles.

What is the number of the sura The Honeybee (Nahl)?	**16**
How many verses does the sura The Honeybee have?	128 (**16**x8)
The number of chromosomes of the male honeybee	**16**
The number of chromosomes of the female honeybee	32 (**16**x2)

MMLC - 16

THE WORLD AND THE HEREAFTER

The Quran speaks of two lives: the one in this "world" (*dunya*), which is finite, and the other in the "Hereafter" (*ahiret*), which is infinite. The relation between these words in the Quran is very clear. These two words, which are used sometimes together in a verse and sometimes separately, are mentioned 115 times each. There are two examples below:

185- ...The life of this <u>world</u> is no more than goods and chattels of deception.

3-The Family of Imran, 185

103- This should be a sign for those who fear the torment of the <u>Hereafter</u>...

11-Hud, 103

The word	Number of occurrences
World	115
Hereafter	115

MMLC - 17

ANGELS AND THE DEVIL

If you ask people what comes to their mind when they hear the word "angel," a majority of them will say "devil." All derivatives of these two interrelated words (angel/devil) are used in the Quran 88 times each. It is interesting to note that the most frequent form of these two words, *"al-shaytan"* and *"al-melaike,"* are used 68 times each in the Quran. Two examples for these words:

6- <u>The Devil</u> is certainly your enemy...

35-The Originator, 6

12- Thus, your Lord inspired <u>the angels</u>.

8-The Spoils of War, 12

The word	Number of occurrences
Angels	88
Devil	88

MMLC - 18

BENEFIT AND CORRUPTION

The word "benefit" (*naf*) with all its derivatives is used 50 times in the Quran. The same is true for the word "corrupt" (*fasad*), that is, it and its derivatives are used 50 times as well. Corruption (*fasad*) is a social evil and condemned by the Quran. A person cannot benefit (*naf*) from corruption (*fasad*). The result of corruption is the opposite of benefit.

55- And remind, for the reminder benefits the believers.
51-The Dispersing, 55

152- Who corrupt the land and do not reform it.
26-The Poets, 152

The word	Number of occurrences
Benefit	50
Corruption	50

MMLC - 19

SEXUAL CRIME, TRANSGRESSION AND WRATH

The word "sexual crime" (*fahsha*) and its derivatives are used 24 times in the Quran. The word "transgression" (*baghy*) and its derivatives are also used 24 times. Since these behaviors deserve wrath, the word "wrath" (*ghadab*) also is used 24 times in the Quran. The relationship between the words "sexual crime" (*fahsha*) and "transgression" is seen clearly in the verse below:

90- ...and forbidden <u>sexual crime</u>, impropriety and <u>transgression</u>...

16-The Honeybee, 90

An example for "wrath":

7- The path of those You have blessed, not of those who have deserved <u>wrath</u>, nor the strayers.

1-The Prologue, 7

The word	Number of occurrences
Sexual crime	24
Transgression	24
Wrath	24

MMLC - 20

DIRTINESS AND NASTINESS

In the Quran, the words "dirtiness" (*rijs*) and "nastiness" (*rijz*) have similar pronunciation and spelling: the word "*rijs*" refers to dirtiness brought by the human hand and the word "*rijz*" refers to nastiness caused by the dirtiness generated by the human hand. These two words are used 10 times. The two verses given below are examples of these words used in the Quran:

33- ...God desires to remove all <u>dirtiness</u> from you...
33-The Parties, 33

5- Forsake from <u>nastiness</u>.
74-The Hidden, 5

The word	Number of occurrences
Dirtiness	10
Nastiness	10

MMLC - 21

OPENLY AND PUBLICLY

The words "openly" and "publicly" have close meanings. The successive use of these words in the sura Noah, 8th and 9th verses, points to the relationship of these words. These two related words are used 16 times each in the Quran. The verses in which these words are used in succession are given below:

8- Then I called them <u>openly</u>.
9- Then I invited them <u>publicly</u> and in private.

71-Noah, 8- 9

The word	Number of occurrences
Openly	16
Publicy	16

MMLC - 22

SATAN AND SEEKING REFUGE

In the Quran, we are told that Satan (*Iblis*) is the enemy of mankind. Muslims should seek refuge (*euzu*) in God in order to be protected from the evil of Satan. The relationship between these two words is crystal clear for the people who know the Quran. These two words are used in equal numbers, i.e., 11 times each. Examples are given below:

50- ...they fell prostrate, except <u>Satan</u>. He was one of the jinns and rebelled against His Lord's command...

18-The Cave, 50

1- Say "I <u>seek refuge</u> in the Lord of the people."

114-People, 1

The word	Number of occurrences
Satan	11
Seek refuge	11

MMLC - 23

SORCERY AND DISCORD

From the Quran, we learn that "sorcery" is a "discord." It is in the same verse that these two words are used for the first time (2-The Cow, 102). In this verse, the relationship between these words is clear. These words and their derivatives are used 60 times each. The verse in which they are used for the first time is as follows:

102- ...Solomon, however, was not a disbeliever, while the devils were disbelievers. Thus, they taught the people <u>sorcery</u> that was sent down through the two angels of Babel, Harut and Marut, who, however, never taught it without saying: "We are only a <u>discord</u>. Be not then a disbeliever..."

2-The Cow, 102

The word	Number of occurrences
Sorcery	60
Discord	60

MMLC - 24

LANGUAGE AND ADVICE

In order to have someone do something, people use different methods like rewarding, punishing or advising. In rewarding, there is something pleasant, and in punishment there is something unpleasant. In the process of advising, language is used as a tool. The difference between advice and rewards and punishment is that advising is done by using the language as a tool, whereas many other tools can be used for the other two methods. These two connected words, "language" (*lisan*) and "advice" (*mawize*) are used in equal numbers, 25 times each. Two examples are given below from the Quran:

22- Among His signs are the creation of the heavens and earth, and the variations in your <u>languages</u> and your colors. Surely there are signs in these for those who understand.

30-The Romans, 22

63- God is fully aware of their innermost intentions. So do not mind them; <u>advise</u> them, and speak to them eloquent words that would touch their souls.

4-The Women, 63

The word	Number of occurrences
Language	25
Advice	25

MMLC - 25

SAY AND THEY SAID

Many sentences in the Quran are in the form of reported speech using the formula "they said" (*Qalu*) and yet many orders are expressed by another formula "say" (*Qul*). These two words, which have very clear relationships, are used many times in the Quran; 332 times each. The total number of uses of these two words is 664. This number is so big that it is even greater than the number of words used in the last 15 suras of the Quran. The mathematical miracle of the Quran has surrounded it in a unique way. The Quran itself is a total miracle, such a miracle that it is easy to understand and impossible to imitate.

The word	Number of occurrences
Say	332
They said	332

MMLC - 26

MERCY AND GUIDANCE

In the Quran, the words "mercy" (*rahmat*) and "guide" (*huda*) are used together in 13 verses. This, by itself, is enough to show the relation between these words. God's guidance of mankind is the biggest mercy for them. These two words are used in the Quran 79 times each in the same format. The words "*Rahman*" (Gracious), "*Raheem*" (Merciful) and other derivatives that come from the same stem of "RHM," are all used in such a way that they form a mathematical miracle. (We shall examine it in the next chapter and in the section on 19.) Below is an example of a verse where the words "mercy" and "guide" are used together:

77- It is a **guide** and **mercy** for the believers.

27-The Ant, 77

The word	Number of occurrences
Mercy	79
Guide	79

MMLC - 27

MERCY, MERCIFUL AND GRACIOUS

We saw in the previous chapter that the word in the form of "mercy" (*rahmat*), derived from the stem of "RHM," is used in 13 verses together with the word "guide" (*huda*), and that they are mentioned 79 times each. The derivatives of the word "mercy" (*rahmat*) are mentioned 114 times (*Rahmat* 79 times, *rahmatika* 3 times, *rahmatina* 5 times, *rahmatihi* 25 times, *rahmati* 2 times); God's attribute "Merciful" (*Raheem*) also comes from the same stem, RHM, and is used exactly 114 times, and God's attribute "Gracious" (*Rahman*) is used half the times these words are mentioned, viz. 57 times. The mathematically designed use of these words performs more detailed miracles regarding the code 19 in the Quran. (These are investigated in detail in the chapters on 19.)

1- In the name of God, <u>Gracious</u>, <u>Merciful</u>.

1-The Prologue, 1

The word	Number of occurrences
Mercy	114 (57x2)
Merciful	114 (57x2)
Gracious	57

MMLC - 28

RIGHTEOUSNESS AND REWARD

The word *"birr,"* which means righteousness, and all its derivatives are mentioned 20 times in the Quran. God informs us that we shall reap what we have sown in the next world. None of our good deeds will be left unrewarded. All the derivatives of the word "reward" (*tsawab*) are used in equal numbers, i.e., 20 times. Below are two verses in which these words are used:

2- ...but help one another in <u>righteousness</u> and piety...
5-The Feast, 2

195- ...and the best of <u>rewards</u> is with God.
3-The Family of Imran, 195

The word	Number of occurrences
Righteousness	20
Reward	20

MMLC - 29

HOPE AND FEAR

The Quran mentions that "hope" (*rayhaban*) and "fear" (*rahaban*) should co-exist in prayer ritual. Keeping these two conflicting feelings in balance will save us from despair on one hand and from being spoiled and arrogant on the other. These two words, used in conjunction and expressing two divergent feelings, are mentioned 8 times each in the Quran. Below is an example:

90- ...These were men who vied in good deeds with one another, and prayed to Us with <u>hope</u> and <u>fear</u>...

21-The Prophets, 90

The word	Number of occurrences
Hope	8
Fear	8

MMLC - 30

COLD AND HOT

If you ask someone to say the first thing that comes into his mind when he hears the word "cold," his answer will usually be "hot." One of these two opposites, "hot" (*hare*) is mentioned 4 times with all its derivatives, while the word "cold" (*berd*) is also mentioned 4 times with all its derivatives. Below, two verses are given as an example:

81- ...and clothes for protection against <u>the hot</u>.

16-The Honeybee, 81

69- We said "O fire, be <u>cold</u> and safe for Abraham."

21-The Prophets, 69

The word	Number of occurrences
Hot	4
Cold	4

MMLC - 31

SOW, GROW, AND FRUIT

The word "*harasa*" which refers to "sowing" is mentioned 14 times in the Quran. "*Zara'a*," which means growing of the crops from the earth, is also mentioned 14 times. The final result of all these steps, the "*fakeha*" (fruit), is again mentioned 14 times. The verses below contain examples for these words:

63- Have you noted the crops you <u>sow</u>?
64- Did you <u>grow</u> them, or did We?

56-The Inevitable, 63-64

73- You will have <u>fruits</u> in abundance there to eat.

43-Vanity, 73

The word	Number of occurrences
Sow	14
Grow	14
Fruit	14

MMLC - 32

TREE AND PLANT

The word *"shajar"* which means "tree" and all of its derivatives are mentioned 26 times in the Quran. The word *"nabaat"* which means "plant" and all of its derivatives are also used 26 times. Below are two verses as example for these words:

60- ...whereby We produce gardens full of beauty, you could not possibly manufacture their <u>trees</u>...

27-The Ant, 60

99- He sends down water from the sky, to produce with it all kinds of <u>plants</u>...

6-The Cattle, 99

The word	Number of occurrences
Tree	26
Plant	26

MMLC - 33

SIN AND SEXUAL CRIME, TRANSGRESSION, WRATH

We saw in MMLC 19 that the words "sexual crime" (*fahsha*), "transgression" (*baghy*) and "wrath" (*ghazub*) were mentioned 24 times each in the Quran. All these words are connected with the word "sin" (*al-itsm*). Especially since the words "sexual crime" (*fahsha*) and "transgression" (*baghy*) imply the word "sin" (*al-itsm*), their relationships are clear. And since behaviors that would entail wrath (*ghazab*) are also considered as sin, the word "wrath" (*ghazab*) is also related to the word "sin" (*al-itsm*). As the words related to sin are used 24 times each, the word "sin" (*al-itsm*) itself is used twice as many, viz. 48 times (24x2). As some words are used in equal numbers, forming a mathematical miracle, sometimes some others are mentioned twice as often to provide a different kind of evidence. We shall give some examples for this in the following chapters.

120- You should avoid both the visible and the invisible <u>sins</u>.

6-The Cattle, 120

The word	Number of occurrences
Sin	48 (24x2)
Sexual crime	24
Transgression	24
Wrath	24

MMLC - 34

THE RICH AND THE POOR

The word "rich" (*ghani*) in the Quran is mentioned 26 times. The opposite, "poor" (*faqr*) is mentioned 13 times, half as many. It is another sign from the Quran that these opposite words, which have a meaning relationship, also represent a numerical miracle. The verse below is an example:

> 38- You are invited to spend in the cause of God, but some of you turn stingy. The stingy are stingy towards their own souls. God is <u>rich</u> while you are <u>poor</u>.
>
> *47-Muhammad, 38*

The word	Number of occurrences
Rich	26 (**13x2**)
Poor	**13**

MMLC - 35

THAMUD AND THE NOISE

From the Quran, we learn that the people of Thamud were destroyed by a noise (*sayha*) sent upon them. By this definition, we learn that there is a relationship between the words "Thamud" and the "noise" (sayha). These words are presented as follows: Thamud is used 26 times, and the word "noise" (*sahya*) is used 13 times, half as many times. In the verses between 23 and 31 of the sura The Moon, the Quran speaks of Thamud, and the 31st verse says:

31- We sent a <u>noise</u> upon them, whereupon they became like harvested hay.

54-The Moon, 31

The word	Number of occurrences
Thamud	26 (**13x2**)
Noise	**13**

MMLC - 36

THE PEOPLE OF LOT AND
THE SHOWER OF ROCKS

In the previous chapter, I pointed out that between the 23rd and 31st verses of the sura The Moon, the Quran mentions Thamud. And in the 31st verse of the same sura, it is mentioned that Thamud was destroyed with a noise (*sayha*). We tried to show the numerical relationship between the words "Thamud" and the "noise." In the same sura, 3 verses later, in the 34th verse, it is mentioned that the people of Lot were destroyed by a shower of rocks (*hasiba*). In the Quran, while the phrases used for the people of Lot (*Qavmu Lot, Ihvanu Lot*) are mentioned 8 times, the term shower of rocks (*hasiba*) that destroyed that society is mentioned exactly half as many, viz, 4 times. It is important to notice that the destruction of Thamud and the people of Lot are mentioned in the same sura successively, and they both have the same lexical relationship between their names and the way they are destroyed. The verse of the sura The Moon that mentions the destruction of the people of Lot is given below:

34- We <u>showered them with rocks</u>. Only Lot's family was saved at dawn.

54-The Moon, 34

The word	Number of occurrences
The people of Lot	8 (4x2)
The shower of rocks	4

314

MMLC - 37

FORGIVE AND PAY

In the Quran, all the derivatives of the word *"ghafr"* (forgive) are mentioned 234 times. And all of the derivatives of the word *"ceza"* (pay), which is used both for retribution and reward, are mentioned 117 times, which is exactly half the number of times that "forgive" is used. Below are two verses in which these words are used:

28- My Lord, <u>forgive</u> me and my parents and anyone who enters my home as a believer, and all the believing men and women.

71-Noah, 28

123- Anyone who commits evil <u>pays</u> for it.

4-The Women, 123

The word	Number of occurrences
Forgive	234 (117x2)
Pay	117

MMLC - 38

DESTINATION AND FOREVER

The Quran states that God is our destination (*maseer*) and the place we will go is the Hereafter. It is one of the most important messages of the Quran that our final destiny (*maseer*) in the Hereafter will be forever (*abada*). These two words, destination (*maseer*) and forever (*abada*), which are interrelated, are used in the Quran in equal number, viz. 28 times each. Below are two examples:

43- We are the one who give life and death and to Us will be the <u>destination</u>.

50-Qaf, 43

9- ...Anyone who believed and did the right, He will remit his sins, and will admit him into gardens with flowing streams. They abide therein <u>forever</u>. This is the greatest triumph.

64-Mutual Blaming, 9

The word	Number of occurrences
Final destiny	28
Forever	28

MMLC - 39

ACT AND RESPONSE

The word "act" (*fi'l*) is mentioned 108 times in the Quran. The acts we perform will be responded (*ajr*) to, when the time comes. Whether we like or dislike the response (*ajr*), it will be the consequence of our acts (*fi'l*). And these two related words, "act" (*fi'l*) and "response" (*ajr*) are used in equal number in the Quran, 108 times each. It is the Quran's miracle to perform such a perfect mathematical pattern as a whole, even though it was completed piecemeal as circumstances necessitated.

There is no other book that contains a mathematical lexical concordance to this extent. The Quran not only presents accurate information from space high above to depths of the oceans, from mother's womb to animal kingdoms, it also shows mathematical miracles by using words and phrases in concordance. In addition, it accomplishes an important mission by introducing our Creator to us.

The word	Number of occurrences
Act	108
Response	108

MMLC - 40

SUN AND LIGHT

The sun is the most important source of light (*noor*) that comes to our world. Even the light (*noor*) from the moon is the sun's light because the moon only reflects the sun's light. Our sun is the source of light and heat. The relation between the words "sun" (*shams*) and "a light" (*noor*) is clear and these two words are used 33 times each. The singular form of light, "a light" is mentioned 33 times. Our sun is just one of the many light sources in the universe, but it is the most important one for us. Below are two examples:

37- Among His signs are the night and the day, and the sun and the moon.

41-Elucidated, 37

15- ... A light and a perspicacious Book has come to you.

5-The Feast, 15

The word	Number of occurrences
Sun	33
A light	33

MMLC - 41

ANNOYANCE AND REJOICE

The word "*dayq*," which means "annoyance and distress," and all of its derivatives are mentioned 13 times in the Quran. The opposite, "*tatmaa*" which means "rejoice" is also mentioned in equal number, viz. 13 times. These two verses below are examples:

127- **Do not grieve for them, and do not be <u>annoyed</u> by their schemes.**

16-The Honeybee, 127

28- **They are the ones whose hearts <u>rejoice</u> in remembering God...**

13-The Thunder, 28

The word	Number of occurrences
Annoyance	13
Rejoice	13

MMLC - 42

JUSTICE AND INJUSTICE

The word "*qist*," which means "justice," is mentioned 15 times in the Quran in its infinitive form. Its antonym, "*zulm*," which means "injustice," is also mentioned 15 times in the same form. The following verse is a good example of both words.

47- We will establish the scales of <u>justice</u> on the Day of the Resurrection. No soul will suffer any <u>injustice</u>. Even the equivalent of a mustard seed will be accounted for. We are the most efficient of reckoners.

21-The Prophets, 47

The word	Number of occurrences
Justice	15
Injustice	15

MMLC - 43

A FEW AND APPRECIATE

In the Quran, it is said that only a few of all men are appreciative. So, according to the Quranic text, there is a relation between the words "a few" and "appreciate."

The total number of the derivatives of "*qalil*" (a few) and "*shukr*" (appreciate) are just the same: 75 times each. The verse that connects these two words is like this:

13- Only <u>a few</u> of My servants are <u>appreciative</u>.

34-Sheba, 13

The word	Number of occurrences
A few	75
Appreciate	75

MMLC - 44

MESSENGER AND PEOPLE

Derivatives of the word "messenger" (*rasul*) are used 368 times. In the Quran, the words meaning "people" and all their derivatives are used 368 times. These words are derived from the roots "*nas*" and "*bashar*" (The derivatives of these words are as follows: *nas, insan, ins, unas, anasiyy, insiyy, bashar, basharan, basharayn*). A messenger is a person whose mission is to deliver God's message to men. The relationship between "people" and "messenger" is clear and this relation is reflected perfectly with the exact same use of these words in such a great number, 368 times each. Below are two examples where these two words are used:

168- O <u>people</u>, eat only the products of the earth that are lawful and good...

2-The Cow, 168

15- Whoever is guided is guided for his own good, and whoever goes astray does so to his own loss; and no sinner will bear the sins of anyone else. We never punish till We have sent a <u>messenger</u>.

17-The Children of Israel, 15

The word	Number of occurrences
Messenger	368
People	368

MMLC - 45

HARM AND BENEFIT

The word "*darr*" which means harm, and its opposite "*naf*" which means benefit, are used in these forms equally 9 times. The interesting point is that in 8 of these 9 repetitions, these two words are used emphasizing the opposite meanings involved and used in the same verse. If all these repetitions were in conjunction, there would be 9 repetition symmetrics in the use. So the 8 repetitions show the relation between these words and 1 separate use shows the mathematical relation. The verses where these two words are used in conjunction are as follows: 5-The Feast, 76; 7-The Purgatory, 188; 10-Jonah, 49; 13-The Thunder, 16; 20-Ta-He, 89; 25-The Distinguisher, 3; 34-Sheba, 42; and 48-Victory, 11. Apart from these 8 uses, the word "harm" (*darr*) is used in the sura The Jinn, 21st verse; and the word "benefit" (*naf*) is mentioned in the sura The Women, 11th verse, only once each. The following is an example of these words' being used together:

76- Say "Would you worship besides God powerless idols who can neither <u>harm</u> you, nor <u>benefit</u> you"

5-The Feast, 76

The word	Number of occurrences
Harm	9
Benefit	9

MMLC - 46

SABBATH

Although the Jewish people can work and lead a normal life 6 days of the week, rest and worship are foreseen for the seventh day, like abstaining from hunting. According to the Quran the said abstinences are only for the Jewish people. "Sabbath" is on the seventh day of the week and the word "*sebt*" is used exactly seven times. Following is an example:

124- The <u>Sabbath</u> was decreed only for those who had differed about it; and your Lord will judge them on the Day of the Resurrection regarding their disputes.

16-The Honeybee, 124

The word	Number of occurrences
Sabbath	7
How many days from one "Sabbath" to the next?	7

MMLC - 47

THE FIRST BLOW OF THE HORN AND THE SECOND BLOW OF THE HORN

We learn from the Quran that the horn will be blown twice (39-The Throngs, 68). The first blow will announce the beginning of the end of the universe, and the second blow will announce the rising of the dead. 5 of the 10 uses of this blow indicate the first blow while the other 5 indicate the second blow. In the sura the The Throngs, the 68th verse, where the two blows are mentioned, the word "*soor*" is used while describing the first blow, but it is not used to describe the second blow; in this manner the harmony of the words is maintained. The verse is:

68- **The horn is blown,** whereupon everyone in the heavens and the earth is struck dead, except those whom God wills. Then it is blown again, whereupon they rise up, looking.

39-The Throngs, 68

The word	Number of occurrences
The Horn (first blow)	5
The Horn (the second blow)	5

MMLC - 48

THE STAGES OF CREATION AND THE HUMAN BEING

Verse 67 of the sura The Believer and verse 14 of the sura The Believers refer to the stages of the creation of the human being. (We examined how miraculously the Quran speaks of the creation of man between chapters 46 and 52.) The words that describe the stages are mentioned as follows:

1- dust (*turab*) 17 times
2- drop (*nutfa*) 12 times
3- the hanging (*alaq*) 6 times
4- chewed lump of flesh (*mudga*) 3 times
5- bones (*ezam*) 15 times
6- flesh (*lahm*) 12 times.

These names of stages which man undergoes before his birth are used 65 times in total. And the word "human being" is also used 65 times in the Quran. Can all this be the consequence of coincidence? The two verses that reflect the stages of creation are as follows:

67- He is the One who created you from <u>dust</u>, and subsequently from a <u>drop</u>, then a <u>hanging</u>, then He brings you forth as a child...

40-The Believer, 67

14- Then We developed the <u>drop</u> into a <u>hanging</u>, then develop the <u>hanging</u> into a <u>chewed lump of flesh</u>, then created the <u>chewed lump of flesh</u> into <u>bones</u>, then covered the <u>bones</u> with <u>flesh</u>. Then formed him into a new creation. Most blessed is God, the best Creator.

23-The Believers, 14

The word	Number of occurrences
Dust	17
Drop	12
Hanging	6
Chewed lump of flesh	3
Bones	15
Flesh	12
Total =	65
Human being	65

MMLC - 49

INTOXICANTS, GAMBLING, IDOLS, FORTUNE ARROWS: DIRTINESS AND THE DEVIL'S LABOR

The 90th verse of the sura The Feast refers to: 1- intoxicants (*khamr*), 2- gambling (*maysir*), 3- idols (*ansab*), 4- fortune arrows (*azlam*); and then describes these with two adjectives: 1- the devil's work (*amelilsheytan*), 2- dirtiness (*rijs*).

The first four items mentioned above are used 12 times in total. The two qualities used for these four items are also used 12 times in the Quran. As can be seen here, the mathematical miracle of the Quran is not presented in one single form. God shows different creations in the universe, and different types of mathematical miracles in the Quran. The four items and the two adjectives are shown in the verse below:

90- O you who believe, <u>intoxicants</u>, <u>gambling</u>, <u>idols</u> and <u>fortune arrows</u> are <u>dirtiness</u> of the <u>devil's work</u>. So keep away from them, that you may prosper.

5-The Feast, 90

The word	Number of occurrences
Intoxicants	6
Gambling	3
Idols	1
Fortune arrows	2
Total =	12
Devil's labor	2
Dirtiness	10
Total =	12

MMLC - 50

ADAM AND JESUS

The 59th verse of the sura The Family of Imran points to a similarity between Adam and Jesus. There is no other comparison like that between any other two prophets in the Quran. How many times are these prophets' names used in the Quran? In equal number, exactly 25 times each. The verse that points to the similarity between Jesus and Adam is given below:

59- For God, the likeness of <u>Jesus</u> is as that of <u>Adam,</u> whom He created out of dust, then said to him, "Be," and he was.

3-The Family of Imran, 59

The word	Number of occurrences
Adam	25
Jesus	25

Some people declare Jesus the incarnation of God, as he was created without a father. This is in total disregard of the omnipotence of God. God gives Adam as an example, since he was created without either father or mother. By doing so, God shows how illogical it is to attribute divine qualities to Jesus. God, while referring to the similarity between Adam and Jesus, also supports this statement with a numerical symmetry, using both names 25 times each in the Quran. The mathematical pattern is not limited to this alone. Let's examine the table below:

ADAM			JESUS		
From the beginning	Sura number	Verse number	Sura number	Verse number	From the end
1	2	31	2	87	25
2	2	33	2	136	24
3	2	34	2	253	23
4	2	35	3	45	22
5	2	37	3	52	21
6	3	33	3	55	20
7	3	59	3	59	19
8	5	27	3	84	18
9	7	11	4	157	17
10	7	19	4	163	16
11	7	26	4	171	15
12	7	27	5	46	14
13	7	31	5	78	13
14	7	35	5	110	12
15	7	172	5	112	11
16	17	61	5	114	10
17	17	70	5	116	9
18	18	50	6	85	8
19	19	58	19	34	7
20	20	110	33	7	6
21	20	116	42	13	5
22	20	117	43	63	4
23	20	120	57	27	3
24	20	121	61	6	2
25	36	60	61	14	1

The 59th verse of The Family of Imran points out the relation between Adam and Jesus. It is the only verse in which these two names are mentioned together. In this verse, both of these two words are used for the seventh time from the beginning of the Quran. Also, if we count from the end of the Quran, it is in this verse that each of these words is used for the 19th time (This is another example how the miracle of 19 and the mathematical miracle in lexical concordance are used together).

And very surprisingly, the 19th occurrence of these words is in the sura Mary, which is the 19th sura of the Quran. These two names are used only once in the sura Mary, and it is the 19th repetition of these words in the Quran.

The number of the verses between these two words in the sura Mary is also interesting. The word Jesus is used in the 34th verse of the sura Mary, and the word Adam is used in the 58th verse. If we start to count from the 34th verse, the 58th verse is the 25th verse. And 25 is the frequency of these two words in the Quran.

We want to present another interesting point. Besides Jesus, this sura also refers to Mary in verse 34. Make a guess: How many times is the word Mary used in the Quran? Exactly 34 times. The verse is given below:

Verse number	Number
34	1
35	2
36	3
37	4
38	5
39	6
40	7
41	8
42	9
43	10
44	11
45	12
46	13
47	14
48	15
49	16
50	17
51	18
52	19
53	20
54	21
55	22
56	23
57	24
58	25

34- This was <u>Jesus</u>, son of <u>Mary</u>: A true account they squabble about.

19-Mary, 34

THE MIRACLE of 19

MATHEMATICS AND 19

In the previous part of this book, we examined the mathematical miracles of the Quran. We witnessed the mathematical miracles of the Quran, which are easy to understand but impossible to imitate. The mathematical miracles of the Quran can be comprehended easily by anyone who knows how to count and is conversant with figures. You do not need to be a mathematician in order to comprehend these miracles. However, we believe that people with a stronger mathematical background can best appreciate the glory of these miracles.

The miraculous structure formed by the "System 19" in the Quran is comprehensible but not amenable to emulation. In this part of the book, I will give more examples that will make the miracle easier to be witnessed. As this book will appeal to different reader groups, I shall also deal with subjects requiring greater initiation.

"*Mathematics is the language in which God wrote the universe*" is the famous saying of Galileo. The Quran's mathematical miracles confirm God's using the language, in which He also wrote the Universe, in His book. What these miracles teach us is not about the British Royal Family, the New York Stock Exchange or the matches of the champions' league! It is about the Creator of the universe, the reason for the creation and the life in the Hereafter, since all of these have been explained in the messages revealed in the Quran. And the miracle we are going to witness shows the impossibility of imitation of the Quran, of its composition beyond human capacity and its perfect preservation from human intervention.

As Hrovista of Gandersheim says, "*This discussion would be unprofitable if it did not lead us to appreciate the wisdom of our Creator, and the wondrous knowledge of the Author of the world, who in the begin-*

ning created the world out of nothing and set everything in number, measure and weight, and then in time and age of man formulated a science, which reveals fresh wonders the more we study it." Any subject that is not related to our Creator is meaningless since our main concern in this world should be the reason for our creation and our situation in the Hereafter. The miracles of the Quran will help us to accomplish our main goals regarding the fundamental issues of our lives.

EVIDENCE AND DISBELIEVERS

101- We narrate to you the history of those communities; their messengers went to them with clear signs but they were not to believe in what they had rejected before. God thus seals the hearts of the disbelievers.

7-The Purgatory, 101

God supported His messengers with corroborative signs. But the mentality that rejected these messages approached these signs with a ready-to-reject attitude and looked at them with prejudice. Instead of trying to understand them, those who received these signs tried their best to ignore and even oppose them. Every human being is in need of God's messages. A person who denies God, contradicts himself. The first thing that disbelievers should do is to avoid denial, and approach the proofs objectively. It is not logical to give up the eternal life God has promised because of arrogance and stubbornness.

118- Those who posses no knowledge have said, "Why does God not speak or show us a sign?" The same question has been asked by others before them, who were like them in their hearts. But to those who are firm in their faith, We have shown Our signs.

2-The Cow, 118

God shows His signs and miracles according to His unchanging system. It is in vain to expect God's miracles to be displayed to suit disbelievers' wishes, such as, "God should be visible and angels should come down from the heavens." God displays His evidence clearly to

335

the people who are ready to receive it. Mathematics, which is the origin of all sciences, has the most respectable place among all sciences, and especially the natural sciences depend on mathematical data. Even the most skeptical people yield to mathematical certainty. In the age we live in, God confirms that He wrote the Book He sent to humanity in the same language in which He wrote the universe. So the Book of God proves the correctness and reliability of its messages in a miraculous style.

38- Do they say that: "He has fabricated it?" Say to them, "Bring a sura (chapter) like this, and call anyone apart from God you can. If what you say is true."
39- Indeed, they have rejected what they have no knowledge about, whose explanation has not reached them yet. Thus, those before them disbelieved. Therefore, note the consequences for the unjust.

10-Jonah, 38-39

When disbelievers are insistent in their denial, instead of trying to comprehend what has been presented, they reject it immediately. Their denial is not justified. Arrogance, stubbornness and contradiction motivate them. The Quran informs us that such people will not demonstrate motivation objectively, and rationally evaluate the evidence; thus, they will continue to disbelieve.

109- They solemnly swear by God, that if a sign came to them, they would certainly believe in it. Say, "The signs are with God." For all you know, if a sign did come to them, they would continue to disbelieve.
110- We shall turn their hearts and their eyes, for they did not believe them at the very first; We leave them in their transgression, blundering.
111- Even if We sent down the angels to them, even if the dead spoke to them, even if We gathered all things before their eyes, they would not believe unless God willed it. For most of them are ignorant.

6-The Cattle, 109-111

IS IT JUSTIFIED TO SAY "WE ALREADY BELIEVE, NO NEED FOR PROOFS?"

Some people say, "We already believe in the Quran! Are proofs really necessary?" when they are informed about the mathematical and scientific miracles in the Quran. We have nothing to say to the people who state that they believe in the Quran without seeing any proofs, but if they say, "Are proofs really necessary?" then we should advise them, "Now, stop there!"

The Prophet Abraham is praised in the Quran for opposing the ignorance of idol worship promoted by his father and his community. But even Abraham, who was praised as a prophet in the Quran, once asked for signs or evidence from God. (See 2-The Cow, 260) We should ask the following question of the people who look down upon the divine evidence and who ask if proofs are really necessary, "Is your faith stronger than the faith of the Prophet Abraham?"

The believers should be grateful for God's signs and miracles. If God displays a sign, then He must have a reason. A person might pretend that he or she does not need miracles or divine signs, but then wouldn't it be better if he or she witnessed those miracles in order to share with others who are in desperate need of a divine sign or evidence? If believers do not appreciate the importance of God's miracles, who will?

The same is true for the miracle of the number 19, which we will examine in this chapter. The number 19 is a proof that the Quran has a miraculous structure. Besides, God draws attention to the number 19 in the Quran to strengthen the faith of the believers. (74-The Hidden, 31)

People who do not utilize their faculties of reasoning cannot witness the miracle of mathematics. The miracle in question challenges all imitation, while laying the cornerstone of truth. These miracles may not be accessible to those who attach excessive importance to the spiritual and economic support of their friends, of their respective communities and family members. These miracles may not be witnessed by those who are dependent on the approval of their communities; they disregard God's evidence and opt for conformity rather than discursive reason. Those who fear being rejected or rebuked by their communities and worry about how to answer people cannot witness God's miracles.

WHY 19?

When we talk about the miracle of 19 in the Quran and claim that the words, suras and verses in the Quran are related to the number 19 and its multiples, people ask us, "Why 19?" If this number were 11 or 23, then they would ask "why 11?" or "why 23?" The number in question however is 19. In the Quran, the 30th verse of the sura "The Hidden" says that **"Over it is 19."** The 31st verse of the same sura informs us about the functions of number 19. Nineteen is the only number in the Quran whose functions are commented upon. We will investigate the sura "The Hidden" in detail in the following chapters. The peculiar characteristics of 19 are sufficient as an answer to the question, "Why 19?" There is a reason why God chose 19 and emphasized it in His Book.

In addition to the fundamental reasons we will present in the following chapters, we can mention some other reasons for the question, "Why 19?" here.

Nineteen is a prime number, that is to say, 19 can be divided only by itself and by 1. (It is also the preference of banks and intelligence services to use prime numbers to form a security code.) If the code of the Quran had been formed by a composite number, then it would be debatable whether the code was formed by that composite or by its multiples. For example, the multipliers of 21 are 7 and 3. If the number 21 had formed the code of the Quran, then it would be questioned which number formed the code of the Quran, since every number that is the multiple of 21 is the multiple of 7 and 3.

The figures 1 and 9 form the number 19. 1 is the smallest and 9 is the biggest of single digit counting numbers. Moreover, the written forms of 1 and 9 are very similar in many languages. For instance, the numeral used for numbers in Arabic is very similar to the numerals widely used all over the world.

In addition to the properties mentioned, 19 has many other interesting characteristics. For example, there has been intriguing research on the number 19 in the table of elements of chemistry. But this is not the subject of our book, and we must conclude that further research has to be carried out.

We have witnessed the existence of a mathematical system in the Quran - without the knowledge of the code 19 - in the previous chapters of MMLC. Whoever examines whether or not the Quran draws attention to a specific number notices that the Quran indicates the number 19 in particular.

Here we are going to see that there are many patterns in the Quran formed by this number and its multiples. These patterns are the answer to the question, "Why 19?"

GOD IS ONE: 19

The basic message of the Quran is the unity of God. The unity of God is expressed by an Arabic word "*Wahid*" and the mathematical value of the word "*Wahid*" is 19. Let us explain what a mathematical value (GAMATRIA, ABJAD or ABCD) of a word means. Before adopting the Indian numeral system and improving it, at the time of Prophet Muhammad, Arabs used letters for both writing and mathematical operations. For example the letter "*Alif*" was equal to 1 in numerical value and the sound "*Waw*" was presented by the letter "w" and was equal to 6. You can see the mathematical equivalents of letters in Arabic below:

								Alif
								1

Ya	Ta	Ha	Ze	Waw	He	Dal	Jeem	Ba
10	9	8	7	6	5	4	3	2

Qaf	Sad	Fa	Ayn	Seen	Noon	Meem	Lam	Kaf
100	90	80	70	60	50	40	30	20

Ghayn	Za	Dad	Dhe	Kha	Tse	Te	Shin	Ra
1000	900	800	700	600	500	400	300	200

The word "*Wahid*" is written with the letters waw+alif+ha+dal, and the total numerical values of these letters are (6+1+8+4=19), as we have mentioned above.

Waw		Alif		Ha		Dal		Total
6	+	1	+	8	+	4	=	19

The word "*Wahid*" (One) whose mathematical value is 19, is used 19 times for God in the Quran. The list of these verses is given below in the table.

Serial Number	1	2	3	4	5	6	7	8	9	10
Sura and Verse number	2-163	4-171	5-73	6-19	12-39	13-16	14-48	14-52	16-22	16-51
Serial number	11	12	13	14	15	16	17	18	19	
Sura and Verse number	18-110	21-108	22-34	29-46	37-4	38-65	39-4	40-16	41-16	

Except for these verses, the word "*Wahid*" is used 7 times in the Quran, yet those uses do not refer to the names of God, but to objects, things like doors and eating materials.

The form "*Wahiden*," derived from the word "*wahid*," is used 5 times in the Quran, and it expresses God's unity. However, "*Wahiden*" is written with an additional "*alif*," and the mathematical value of this word is not 19. So only the word "*Wahid*" -the name of God whose mathematical value is 19- is used 19 times in the Quran. The total of all the forms of the word "*Wahid*" should not be multiples of 19 because only four names of God should be used as multiples. (We will examine the reason for this in the following pages dealing with the four names of God in a symmetric table.)

HOW 19 IS MENTIONED IN THE QURAN

Nineteen is a prime number that has interesting features, as I have mentioned above. The mathematical value of the word "*Wahid*," which expresses God's unity, is 19. How are the functions of 19 and the importance of 19 stressed in the Quran? The 74th sura "The Hidden" draws attention to the number 19:

24- And said, "This is nothing but the magic of old."
25- This is nothing but the word of a human.
26- Soon I will cast him into Saqar
27- Do you know what Saqar is?
28- It leaves nothing nor does it spare

29- It is tablets for people

30- Over it is 19

31- We appointed angels to be guardians of fire. And We assigned their number as a trial for disbelievers. So that those who were given the Book may arrive at certainty, and the believers may increase in faith, and to remove all traces of doubt from the hearts of the people of the Book and believers. And that those in whose hearts is a disease and the disbelievers may say, "What does God mean by this allegory?" God thus sends astray whomever He wills and guides whomever He wills. None knows the armies of your Lord, except He. This is a reminder for the people.

32- Absolutely, by the moon

33- And by the night as it passes

34- And the morning as it shines

35- This is one of the greatest

36- A warning to mankind

37- For those among you who wish to advance or regress.

74-The Hidden, 24-37

THE FUNCTIONS OF 19 ACCORDING TO THE QURAN

There are numbers other than 19 in the Quran, but most of them are used as adjectives (Four months, seven skies, a thousand months, etc.). However, in verse 30 of the sura "The Hidden," the number 19 is emphasized by the statement **"Over it is Nineteen"** and in the 31st verse, where the function and purpose of the number 19 is prophetically explained, the numerical aspect of the number 19 is again emphasized by the statement, **"We assigned their numbers..."**. For the number 19, the verse lists the following functions:

1. Believers may increase faith

2. Convincing the people of the Book (Jews, Christians)

3. Removal of all suspicions in the minds of believers and the people of the Book

4. It creates a situation in which disbelievers and people sick at heart ask, "What did God mean by this?" or "What is the use of it?"

These kinds of questions are not questions asked with honest intentions to learn the meaning of a Quranic assertion. It is just an approach taken by disbelievers in order to criticize religion and the believers. In other words, this is a rhetorical question that exposes their dogmatic prejudice and lack of understanding of the Quranic allegories. With this rhetorical question, they want to say that the Quranic assertion about the number 19 being an answer for skeptics regarding its authenticity does not make sense.

As you can see, 19 is an answer to the assertion that the Quran is the word of a man. A number as an answer... This dispels all suspicions! Just think how incredible it was for people to believe in the miracle of 19 prior to the discovery of this miracle. It took 1400 years to reveal this miracle, and when the time came, the miracle 19 in the sura "The Hidden" became manifest. Following this manifestation, the functions of 19 described as **"one of the greatest"** in the 35th verse of the sura "The Hidden," came into light. This miracle clears away the doubts of the believers and the people of the Book.

THE SURA "HIDDEN" AND THE DATE OF DISCOVERY OF NUMBER 19

The first time the code 19 in the Quran attracted attention was in 1974. After this discovery, scholars came up with many more observations of miraculous patterns. No wonder the name of the chapter prophesying it is "The Hidden" and it is the 74th sura of the Quran. When you place 74 beside 19, you have the number 1974, which is the date of the discovery of the miracle of 19, according to the Gregorian calendar. That is to say, the miracle had been hidden for 1974 years after the birth of Jesus Christ and was pointed out in the sura "The Hidden."

When this was discovered, the year according to the Muslim calendar was 1393. (The Muslim calendar starts with the hegira of the prophet Muhammad from Mecca to Medina). God started to reveal the Quran to the Prophet Muhammad 13 years before the hegira. In other words, this miracle was discovered 1406 years after God had started to reveal the Quran. What is 1406? 19 multiplied by 74 makes 1406!

The sura "The Hidden," which prophesies and explains the math-

The date of the discovery of the miracle 19	1974
When we put the number 19 together with 74, the number of the sura in which it is mentioned, what do we have?	19-74
How many years after the Quran's revelation was this miracle discovered?	19x74=1406

ematical miracle of the Quran, demonstrates many miraculous aspects. The first two verses of this sura are given below:

1- O! The Hidden
2- Arise and warn

74-The Hidden, 1-2

The first verse of the sura calls "the hidden," and the second verse pronounces that it is time to arise and start to warn. These two verses consist of 19 letters. Can you guess what the mathematical value of these two verses is? You may have difficulty being convinced when you hear it. Here, the mathematical value of these two verses is 1974.

Serial Number	1	2	3	4	5	6	7	8	9	10
Letter	Ya	Alif	Alif	Ya	He	Alif	Alif	Lam	Meem	Dal
Numerical Value	10	1	1	10	5	1	1	30	40	4

Serial Number	11	12	13	14	15	16	17	18	19	
Letter	Tse	Ra	Qaf	Meem	Fa	Alif	Noon	Dhe	Ra	
Numerical Value	500	200	100	40	80	1	50	700	200	Total 1974

During the gradual revelation of the Quran, the semantic unity was maintained in such a way that even the date of the discovery of miracle 19 was coded. The first two verses of this sura, informing of the unveiling of the secret, with their 19 letters indicate the code of the mathematical miracle, and with the numerical value of these letters indicate the year of its unveiling, 1974. Can you imagine a more elegant prophecy than this?

And again, 1974 is formed when 19 of the miracle 19 and 74 of the 74th sura are written together successively. And the first verse of the sura "The Hidden" is shown as (74;1). It is interesting to note that there are 741 verses counting from this verse till the end of the Quran, and when you multiply 19 and 39, you have 741 (741= 19x39)

ONE OF THE GREATEST

The magnificence of the miracle of 19, described as **"one of the greatest,"** is shown by the mathematical codes in the sura "The Hidden" in which this miracle is mentioned.

The sura addresses a prototype skeptic who says that the Quran is the word of a human, stating that he will be thrown into *"Saqar."* The 27th verse asks the question, **"Do you know what Saqar is?"** *"Saqar"* is said to be an exact and objective punishment that displays many scenes (tablets) for men. This punishment can be presumed to be hell itself or to be 19, which is an answer for disbelievers. With the meaning "hell," it includes everything and shows people what they have done in their past; or as "19," it protects all the Quran with a mathematical system and displays miracles, so it is a perfect reply to disbelievers claiming that **"This is nothing but the word of a human."** Since the 31st verse calls attention to the functions of 19, it does not matter which of these two meanings is given to *"Saqar."*

The word *"Saqar"* is important for the miracle of 19 in any given situation. *Saqar* is used four times in the whole Quran and three uses are in the sura "The Hidden." These three uses of the word *"Saqar"* are coded mathematically. In the said sura, *"Saqar"* is used in the 26th, 27th and 42nd verses. The total of the verse numbers of these three verses is 95 (19x5). And the total of the numerical values of these three verses is 1900. 1900 is equal to 19x100. If we add the numerical value of these 3 verses and the sura number of "The Hidden" (74), we have the date of the discovery of the miracle of number 19.

The numbers of the verses in which the word "saqar" is used in the sura The Hidden	Total
26 + 27 + 42	95 (19x5)

The mathematical values of the verses in which the word "saqar" is used in the sura The Hidden	
26 27 42 556 + 683 + 661	**Total** 1900 (19x100)

The mathematical values of the verses in which the word "saqar" is used in the sura The Hidden	The number of the sura The Hidden	Total
1900 +	74 The date of the discovery of the miracle of 19.	1974

OTHER MIRACLES IN THE SURA "THE HIDDEN"

While all the other verses of the sura "The Hidden" are very short, the 31st verse that mentions the functions of 19 is quite long. Although the 282nd verse of the sura The Cow is the longest verse of the Quran, this verse is six times longer when the verse average of the sura The Cow is considered. The 20th verse of the sura The Enwrapped is also long; it is eight times longer than the word average of the verses in that sura. The 31st verse of the sura "The Hidden," however, is more than twelve times longer than the word average of that sura. Thus, this verse has the largest number of words, when the word proportions of the verses are considered, in the entire Quran. The 31st verse of the sura "The Hidden," the only verse mentioning the function of number 19, is a special case. When we examine the number of letters and words in this verse, we witness that this verse is encoded with 19, as well as the fact that the verse mentions the functions of 19:

1) This verse consists of 57 words (19x3). Since this verse, which mentions the functions of 19, has 57 (19x3) words, and the preceding verse, **"Over it is Nineteen,"** consists of 3 words (in Arabic), 3 has a meaning here, because the number of words in this verse (57) is 3 times 19 words.

2) In the part of the verse that says, **"What does God mean by this allegory?"** the description of the functions of 19 ends. While this part of the verse consists of 38 (19x2) words, the remainder of it consists of 19 words.

3) It is very interesting that the number of words of the only verse mentioning the functions of 19 is equal to the number of the words of the first 19 verses in the sura "The Hidden," which consist of 57(19x3) words.

4) The first 30 verses of the sura "The Hidden," referring to the functions of 19, consist of 95 (19x5) words and this is another proof evidencing the fact God uses the code 19 many times in this sura.

5) The 30th verse of the sura "The Hidden" is the only verse referring to the number "19." From the beginning of the sura "The Hidden" till the beginning of the word "nineteen," there are 361 (19x19) letters. How great and detailed God's miracles are!

6) The sura "The Hidden" has 56 numbered verses and an unnumbered *Basmalah* at the beginning. Thus, the sura "The Hidden" has 56+1=57 (19x3) verses.

We would like to call your attention to two points that may not be as obvious as the particularities above. The 31st verse of the sura "The Hidden" is the last verse of the Quran whose words are a multiple of 19. In addition, the statement, **"None knows the armies of your Lord, except He,"** which is in the 31st verse of the sura "The Hidden," consists of 19 letters.

How many words are there in the 31st verse of the sura The Hidden, which mentions the functions of 19?	57 (19x3)
How many words are in the section that mentions the functions of 19 in the 31st verse of the sura The Hidden?	38 (19x2)
How many words are there in the first 19 verses of the sura The Hidden?	57 (19x3)
How many words are there from the beginning until the 31st verse of the sura The Hidden?	95 (19x5)
How many letters are there until the word "nineteen" in the sura The Hidden?	361 (19x19)
How many verses are there in the sura The Hidden? (Including Basmalah, which isn't numbered)	57 (19x3)

We have seen the sura "The Hidden" pointing to the number 19 as the basis of the mathematical miracles in the Quran, which includes many mathematical marvels. We would like to point out an interesting sign in this sura. When you think about the most important event in the world around 1974, the date of the discovery of the miracle of 19, you will see that man landed on the moon in 1969. This event is one of the most important events in the history of the world. Human beings went to the moon a short time after the discovery of the mathematical miracle that relates to the lexical concordance and a very short time before the discovery of 19. If we consider this, it is very significant that the Quran calls attention to the moon in the 32nd verse, just after the 31st verse of the sura "The Hidden" referring to the functions of 19. (We have examined the statements indicating that one day men would go to the moon in the Quran in the 16th chapter of this book.)

32- Absolutely, by the moon.

74-The Hidden, 32

EVERYTHING IS COUNTED

28- So that He may know that they have delivered their Lord's messages. He is fully aware of what they have. And the numbers of all things He has counted.

72-The Jinns, 28

The last word of this verse "*Adada*" (counted) is the last word of the sura Jinn. Because this verse is the last verse of the sura, this statement expressing that everything is counted and everything depends on numbers is very important with respect to the miracle of 19. Moreover, this statement displays some of the particulars related to 19:

1. All the forms of "*Adda*" (number) are used 57 (19x3) times in the Quran. One of these forms is in the statement "their number..." which is in the 31st verse of the sura "The Hidden." And this displays the relation between the miracle of 19 and the word "*adada.*"

2. The above mentioned verse is the 28th verse of the sura Jinn. The total of the figures forming 72 and 28 is 19 (7+2+2+8= 19)

3. The word "*adada*" is the 285th (19x5) word of the sura Jinn.

4. We have seen that the word "*adada*" is the last word of the last verse of the sura Jinn. The total number of letters of the last words belonging to each verse in the sura Jinn is 114 (19x6).

5. The 28 verses of the sura Jinn end with 28 words, yet some of these words are repeated. If we count these words excluding the repeated ones, the verses end with 19 words.

6. These words at the end of the sentences consist of 19 different letters (the Arabic alphabet has 28 letters).

7. The word "*adada*" is written with the letters "ayn+dal+dal+alif." If we add up the repetitions of these letters in the sura Jinn, we have 37+54+54+216 and the total of these numbers is 361 (19x19).

THE NUMBERS IN THE QURAN

We have seen that God made everything according to a numerically defined order and proportion. This fact led us to examine the numbers throughout the Quran, and we came up with some interesting results related to the code 19.

There are 30 whole numbers in the Quran. The total of these 30 whole numbers is a multiple of 19. (The numbers marked with an asterisk are used only once.)

$$
\begin{aligned}
&1\\
&2\\
&3\\
&4\\
&5\\
&6\\
&7\\
&8\\
&9\\
&10\\
&11*\\
&12\\
&19*\\
&20*\\
&30\\
&40\\
&50*\\
&60*\\
&70\\
&80*\\
&99*\\
&100\\
&200\\
&300*\\
&1000\\
&2000*\\
&3000*\\
&5000*\\
&50000*\\
+\ \ &100000*
\end{aligned}
$$

162.146= (19x8534)

349

It is mentioned in the sura "The Cave" that the youths stayed in a cave for 300 years, and 9 years were added to this number. In addition, the number 950, which is related to the Prophet Noah, is not given as 950, but in a form to be subtracted from, i.e. 1000 minus 50. Because the numbers are used in this way, the total of the numbers used in the Quran becomes a multiple of 19. This is a special feature of the Quran. The numbers 1000 and 9 are repeated many times in the Quran. If the numbers 309 and 950 had been mentioned directly, the total of the numbers in the Quran would not have been a multiple of 19.

Muslims have always been curious about why God did not say 950 and 309 directly, but said instead 1000 minus 50 and 300 plus 9. Thus, it is clear now why God said it this way. Apart from the special characteristic of 19 forming miracles, this is a proof that it is a special way of answering questions and solving problems.

Except for these 30 whole numbers, there are 8 fractional numbers in the Quran. The total of all the numbers is 30+8=38 (19x2). These fractions can be seen in the Quran as follow: 1/20, 1/8, 1/6, 1/5, 1/4, 1/3, 1/2, 2/3.

We would like to mention Milan Sulc's discovery here. Thirty is the 19th composite number. If we count the numbers which can be divided into their factors, again 30 is the 19th composite number (4,6,8,9,10,12,14,15,16,18,20,21,22,24,25,26,27,28, 30). Thus, the number 30, which is the number of whole numbers in the Quran, is again related to 19. The number 8, the number of fractional numbers in the Quran, is also the number that indicates the place of 19 among the prime numbers: (2,3,5,7,11,13,17,19). The total of all the numbers in the Quran is 38 (19x2). This is meaningful, because the numbers 30 and 8, which form 38, are also related to 19. We will witness the relation between 19 and the numbers 30 and 8 in the coming chapters. Some numbers that are not multiples of 19 in the Quran are especially related to 19. For example, the number 30 is the 19th composite number, and 8 is the index number of 19 in the list of prime numbers.

The total number of the numbers (whole and fractional) in the Quran	38 (19x2)

The Prophet Muhammad was one of the busiest personages in history. While it is very difficult to persuade a society to give up even smoking, a facile habit when compared to social changes, Prophet Muhammad changed all the religious and social systems of his society. Reforming his society was not his only duty. While doing so, he was solving personal conflicts, mediating between factions, signing agreements among tribes and religious groups, or defending his city against repeated war campaigns planned and executed by the Meccan oligarchy. During that time he was also explaining the verses of the Quran, being revealed in parts, to the people. It is really childish to suppose that a mathematician, having at his disposal a lot of spare time, formulated the system of 19 in the Quran, something beyond the ability and power of a human being. This miracle can neither be explained by coincidences nor by the work of a human being. Which book in the world has contained such a prophecy and miracle?

23- If you are in doubt of what We have revealed to Our Servant, then bring a sura like this, and call any witness, apart from God, you like, if you are truthful.
24- But if you cannot, as indeed you cannot, then guard yourselves against the fire whose fuel is men and rocks, which has been prepared for the disbelievers.

2-The Cow, 23- 24

BASMALAH AND THE SURAS

The Quran consists of 114 (19x6) suras. The number 114 is one of the most fundamental numbers in the Quran; the number of chapters that form the Quran is 6 times 19.

Another interesting point is that the sura "People," which is the 114th sura of the Quran, has only 6 verses. When we divide 114 by 19, it gives 6, and that is the number of verses that the last and 114th sura People has.

The number of suras in the Quran	114 (19x6)

The most frequently used and the most outstanding verse of the Quran is known by every Muslim by its abbreviated name *Basmalah*, which is read as **"Bismillahirrahmanirraheem."** We can easily say that the group of words whose repetition is most frequent in the world is *Basmalah*. It means **"In the name of God, Gracious, Merciful."** *Basmalah* is used 114(19x6) times in the Quran.

The number of Basmalahs in the Quran	114 (19x6)

One may say that this is not a proof related to the miracle of 19, since there are already 114 suras in the Quran and every sura has a *Basmalah* at the beginning, it is quite normal to have 114 *Basmalahs*. It can be said that there is a symmetrical relationship between the number of suras and the number of *Basmalahs*.

This is not true, however, as the sura "Repentance," the 9th sura of the Quran, is different and does not have a *Basmalah* at the beginning. Thus, the number of *Basmalahs* is 113 and 113 is not a multiple of 19. Please, see how this problem in the Quran was solved. God astonishes us by first formulating a problem and then solving it in a marvelous way.

The sura "The Ant" is the 27th sura of the Quran. In this sura *Basmalah* is used twice, once at the beginning and again in the 30th verse; in this way, the total number of *Basmalah* becomes 114 (19x6). Thirty, which is the number of the verse in which the missing *Basmalah* was found, is the 19th composite number as we have seen before. This means that 30 is the 19th number that has multipliers. For instance, 4(2x2), 12(4x3), 15(5x3), 27(9x3) are composite numbers. Please count again to see whether 30 is the 19th composite number or not: (4,6,8,9,10,12,14,15,16,18,20,21,22,24,25,26,27,28,30). When we count *Basmalahs* that are at the beginning of the suras, the number we arrive at is 113 and it is the 30th prime number. This number "113" sends us to the 30th verse for *Basmalah*. As I mentioned before, 30 is the 19th composite number.

The mathematical miracle God displays has a marvelous system: One *Basmalah* for every sura's introduction. The number of suras and *Basmalahs* are both 114. Although one sura spoils the symmetry of *Basmalah* as I have mentioned before, both the number of suras and the number of *Basmalahs* being multiples of 19 is the result of the miracles. We find the lost *Basmalah* in the 30th verse of the 27th sura, "The Ant."

30- It is from Solomon and it is <u>in the name of God, Gracious, Merciful</u>.

27-The Ant, 30

The missing *Basmalah* in the 19th sura is found in the 27th sura, which is 19 suras after the 9th sura.

1	2	3	4	5	6	7	8	9	10	11	12	13	14	15	16	17	18	19
9	10	11	12	13	14	15	16	17	18	19	20	21	22	23	24	25	26	27

And if we add the verse number, which is 30, and the 27 of the 27th sura, we have 30+27=57(19x3)

The sura number where we find the missing Basmalah	The verse number of the missing Basmalah	Total
27 +	30	57 (19x3)

If we add all the sura numbers from the 9th sura to the 27th sura (9+10+11+12+...+24+25+26+27), we have 342 (19x8). It would be a mistake to consider this an additional miracle; since every consecutive 19 numbers' total is a multiple of 19 as every consecutive 17 numbers' total is a multiple of 17. Yet the number 342 has an additional feature. There are 342 (19x8) words from the beginning of the 27th sura to the *Basmalah* in the 30th verse. This is another element of the miracle, of course.

There are 342 words from the beginning of the sura "The Ant" to the lost *Basmalah*, and this number is a multiple of 19. This number (342) is equal to the total of the sura numbers from the sura "Repentance," which has no *Basmalah*, to the sura "The Ant" in which the lost *Basmalah* is found. These two features are independent of one another.

The total of the suras from the sura where there is no *Basmalah* to the sura where the lost *Basmalah* is found (9+10+11......+25+26+27)	342
The word number from the beginning of the sura "The Ant" till the verse where the lost *Basmalah* is found	342 (19x18)

WHAT DID THE DISCOVERY OF THE MISSING BASMALAH TEACH US?

The discovery of the missing *Basmalah* enabled us to understand the functions of the code 19 in the Quran. Let us summarize what we have covered:

1. People have been inquiring for 1400 years about the missing *Basmalah* at the beginning of the sura Repentance. Some thought it was a mistake; or they even thought that they should add a *Basmalah* to the beginning of the sura "Repentance." However, if there was a *Basmalah* at the beginning of the sura "Repentance," there would be 115 *Basmalahs* in the Quran: 115 is not a multiple of 19 and the system would be broken. The role of 19 is to protect the Quran from changes. This feature is a miracle that has functions for solving problems and for answering questions.

2. Whether the order of the suras in the Quran was arranged divinely or not is a subject of historical discussion. The miracle of 19 solves this problem also. The configurations that have emerged during the discovery of the missing *Basmalah* prove that the order of the suras was determined by God. (In the coming pages of this book we will see that many aspects of the miracle of 19 certify this.)

3. The importance of the *Basmalah* for the code 19 is understood with the help of these data. As we shall soon see, many data like this discovery of the missing *Basmalah* depend on the *Basmalah*, the keyword of the Quran.

4. In light of these data, it is understood that *Basmalahs* are not placed at the beginning of the suras arbitrarily.

5. We should not be apprehensive about dealing with problems related to the mathematical system of the Quran. The more we try to solve the problems in the Quran that have the appearance of mysteries, the more we come to understand the miracles of the Quran.

6. The examples we have examined have shown that anybody who knows how to count to 19 and knows the four arithmetical operations can be a witness to many points related to the code 19 in the Quran and appreciate many aspects of this miracle, as they are comprehensible and cannot be imitated. (There are also subjects that can be better understood with the help of a specific mathematical background, such as prime numbers and composite numbers.)

THE NUMBER OF LETTERS IN THE BASMALAH

As I have said before, the *Basmalah* is the group of words most frequently repeated by Muslims. All around the world Muslims recite it when they pray, when they read the Quran or before they intend to do something in their daily lives. We do not know of any other phrase that is repeated as often as *Basmalah* in any other language or religion in the world. One who recites the Quran notices the importance of this word (or group of words), so often repeated in the Quran. The *Basmalah* is like a password or a seal.

The number of letters in *Basmalah* is related to the miracle of 19, like the frequency of occurrences of *Basmalah*. The *Basmalah* consists of 19 letters:

If you do not know the Arabic alphabet, you can learn the Arabic letters in a few days. A child of six or seven can learn the letters and

1	2	3	4	5	6	7	8	9	10
Ba	Seen	Meem	Alif	Lam	Lam	He	Alif	Lam	Ra
11	12	13	14	15	16	17	18	19	
Ha	Meem	Noon	Alif	Lam	Ra	Ha	Ya	Meem	

THE QURAN: UNCHALLENGEABLE MIRACLE

their pronunciation in a few days. It takes only a few hours to learn the letters in the Quran and their corresponding mathematical values (*abjad*).

DIAMONDS AND GLASS

Much of the data about the miracle of 19 in the Quran is like diamonds. However, you can encounter people who try to augment the number of miracles by presenting some mathematical facts as miracles. Two kinds of people confuse diamonds and glass. The one who seeks an opportunity to deny the miracle of 19 in the Quran picks up only the splinters of glass from the mixture and says, "They are but splinters of glass, they are worthless." However, a diamond has its own value even though it may be mixed with splinters of glass. One who denies the value of a diamond neither does harm to the diamonds nor makes these diamonds worthless. The value of all the examples about the miracle of 19 I give in this book are not equal to one another. We tried to exclude worthless splinters, yet some of our examples may be like crystals beside these valuable diamonds. Please do not forget that not every diamond has the same value but that, rather, each diamond has a different value. For instance, the symmetric table with four parts about the names of God is worth a fortune.

As I will mention soon, the word "God" (Allah) is used 2698 (19x142) times in the Quran. This is a very important point in the scheme of the 19-based system. Furthermore, if we examine the first verses of all the suras in the Quran we see "God" mentioned 42 times. If we write 1 and 42 together, we have the number 142 and this number is the coefficient of the occurrence of the word "God" in the Quran. The second proof is not such a fundamental one as the occurrence of the word "God," that is, 2698 (19x142). Yet we should not ignore these kinds of signs because they support the main idea. This fact does not make the main point insignificant, but on the contrary supports it. However, trying to present the perfection of the Quran with the second kind of sign would be a product of ill-intention. These secondary signs are not like splinters of glass, nor are they of the same value as the ideas they support.

We should be careful not to give an opportunity to people who are ill-intentioned when we speak about the miracle of 19. (We excluded many examples that are like crystals.) We should state that no two samples are equal and some samples of inferior value do not damage the main value of the miracle of 19.

People unaware of probability calculations can present the ordinary signs as miracles. On the other hand, to present the extraordinary signs and the coding system of the Quran as an ordinary event cannot be considered a good intention. It is wrong to mix glass with diamonds and it is even worse to pretend that diamonds are glass.

THE WORDS IN THE BASMALAH

The *Basmalah* is the word group that is repeated most frequently in the world and it has a special place in the Quran. The number of letters and the number of repetitions of the *Basmalah* are again related to the code 19. *Basmalah* consists of 4 words. These words are 1) Name 2) God 3) Gracious 4) Merciful respectively. Please, be ready to witness now an important miracle. How many times are these 4 words repeated in the Quran?

Did God not say that He would dispel all suspicions and strengthen the faith of believers? Do we not see that 19 is a reply to disbe-

The word	Number of occurrences
Name	19 (19x1)
God	2698 (19x142)
Gracious	57 (19x3)
Merciful	114 (19x6)
The total of the coefficients of these words 1 + 142 + 3 + 6 = 152 (19x8)	

lievers in the sura "The Hidden?" We hope that you have started to comprehend the greatness of the number 19 that God calls attention to in the 35th verse of the sura "The Hidden:" **"This is one of the greatest."**

In addition to this, you will witness many significant mathematical phenomena in the coming chapters. Let us point out some aspects of the use of these four words in the Quran.

THE WORD "NAME" AND 19

The simple form of the word "name" is used 19 times in the Quran. This simple form consists of the letters *Alif*, *Seen*, and *Meem*. This characteristic of the word "name" shows that for mathematical use, the written forms should be taken into consideration.

When the word "name" is combined with the letter *Ba*, as in *Basmalah*, the letter "*Alif*" disappears and it is written as *Ba-Seen-Meem*. In the numbered verses, this use can be seen 3 times. (These numbered verses are 1:1; 11:41; 27:30.) After investigating the verses with these 3 "*Bsm*"s, we understand that "*Bsm*" has another characteristic.

God has given both the form (*Alif-Seen-Meem*) and (*Ba-Seen-Meem*) special missions for the code 19.

The number of verses between the first Bsm (1-The Prologue, 1) and the second Bsm (11-Hud, 41)	1520 (19x80)
The number of verses between the 2nd Bsm (11-Hud, 41) and the 3rd Bsm (27-The Ant, 30)	1691 (19x89)
The number of verses from the 3rd Bsm (27-The Ant, 30) to the end of the Quran	3135 (19x165)

The sura "The Hanging," which is the 96th sura, has an exceptional place. The word "*Bism*" in its first numbered verse, with its form "*Ba-Alif-Seen-Meem*," is used differently from the rest of the spellings of "*Ba-Seen-Meem*" throughout the Quran. Here, the word "in the name" is written "*Ba-Alif-Seen-Meem*," and this word is counted together with the frequency of other "name"s. This proves that the word "*Bsm*" written with three letters, "*Ba-Seen-Meem*," without the letter "*Alif*," throughout the Quran is intentionally written differently as "*Ba-Alif-Seen-Meem*" with the letter "*Alif*" in the first verse of the sura the "The Hanging," and this shows the wisdom of God. Thus, the code 19 teaches us the wisdom of this exceptional position in the sura the "The Hanging" that was not deciphered for 1400 years.

Since there are only two occurrences of "*Basmalah*" in the numbered verses in the Quran, two of the three occurrences of the form of "*Bsm*" without *Alif* are in these numbered *Basmalahs* that are *Bismillahirrahmanirraheem* (1:1; 27:30). The other "*Bsm*" without *Alif* is found in the phrase "*BISMILLAH*" (11: 41).

If we divide the Quran into two parts according to these two numbered *Basmalahs* (1:1; 27:30), the total number of the words "Name+God+Gracious+Merciful" in each of these parts is the multiple of 19.

The number of words from the first Bismillahirrahmanirraheem to the 2nd one				
Name	God	Gracious	Merciful	Total
9 +	1814 +	35 +	80	= 1938 (19x102)

The total of the words from the 2nd Bismillahirrahmanirraheem till the end of the Quran				
Name	God	Gracious	Merciful	Total
10 +	884 +	22 +	34	= 950 (19x50)

THE WORD "GOD" AND 19

"God" is the most frequently used word in the Quran. The word "God" and all its derivatives are used a total of 2698 (19x142) times in the Quran. Today, it is possible to check this number with the help of a computer and with careful calculations. Some people claim that the miracle of 19 related to *Basmalah* came into existence by chance, but the probability calculations debunk the assertions of these people.

If we look into the first verses of the suras and examine how many of them include the word "God," we come up with 42 suras. The numbers of this study are 1 (for verses) and 42 (for the number of the suras). If we write these numbers consecutively we get 142, and this number is the coefficient of the word "God" in the Quran. It is clear that even the coefficient of the word "God" is guaranteed and coded separately in the Quran.

Furthermore, the sum of the verse numbers where the word "God" occurs is 118123 (19x6217).

The sum of the numbers of the verses which contain "God"	118123 (19x6217)

We will witness the importance of the suras starting with initial letters for the code 19 in the next chapters. As you know, some of the suras in the Quran begin with "*Alif-Lam-Meem*" or "*Qaf*" or with some other initial letters. The first of these initial letters is in the 1st verse of the second sura "The Cow" and it is "*Alif-Lam-Meem*." The last of these initial letters is "*Noon*" in the first verse of the 68th sura "The Pen." Between this first and the last initial letter, the word "God" is used 2641 (19x139) times. And in the rest of the Quran the word "God" is used 57 (19x3) times.

From the first initial lettered verse (2-The Cow, 1) till the last one (68-The Pen, 1), the number of times the word "God" is used	2641 (19x139)

GRACIOUS, MERCIFUL: THE TOTAL OF THE COEFFICIENTS AND 19

The words "Gracious" (*Rahman*) and "Merciful" (*Raheem*), which are parts of the *Basmalah,* are used in multiples of 19. "Gracious" is used 57 (19x3) times and "Merciful" is used 114 (19x6) times. The 114 occurrences of "Merciful" are twice that of "Gracious." (I explained this in MMLC 27.) Like the afore-mentioned names of God, the word that shows the mercy of God and its derivatives appear 114 times (19x6) in the entire Quran.

The number of occurrences of the word "mercy" and all of its derivatives	114 (19x6)

Aside from that, the frequencies of each of these four words in *Basmalah* are multiples of 19. It is also noteworthy that the total of the coefficients of these words is 152 (19x8) [Name (1) + God (142) + Gracious (3)+ Merciful (6)] = 152; God displays the miracle and intactness of the Quran with these words. The total of the coefficients of these words, being a multiple of 19, confirms once again the correctness of the operation. The number "8" has a special meaning: when we multiply 19 with 8, it makes 152, and this number exists in all the coefficients in the *Basmalah.* We have seen that one of the most important characteristics of 19 is that it is a prime number. If you want to know where 19 stands in the order of prime numbers let us write all the prime numbers till 19.

The order of numbers	1	2	3	4	5	6	7	8
The order of prime numbers	2	3	5	7	11	13	17	19

A prime number is an integer that is not divisible without remainder by any other integer except 1 and that integer itself. If you are not interested in mathematics, you may consult someone who knows prime numbers.

THE NUMBER OF VERSES WITH THE WORD BASMALAH

We have seen that the words "Name+God+Gracious+Merciful" forming "Bismillahirrahmanirraheem" are coded with 19. These words are used throughout the Quran. In some verses, the word "God" is used more than once and in some verses both "God" and "Merciful" or "Gracious" are used together. Katerina Kullman, a Swedish muslim, was curious about how many verses have at least one of these four words and she was the first person who witnessed this interesting characteristic. If you write two 19s consecutively, you get the number 1919 and this number is the number of verses which have at least one of the four words that form *Basmalah*.

The number of verses where at least one of the four words of Basmalah is used	1919 (19x101)

We counted the words in the numbered verses and found out that the words forming the *Basmalah* were the multiples of 19. It is clear that the *Basmalah* is the first numbered verse of sura "The Prologue," which is the first sura. Many people probably have not understood why the *Basmalah* is numbered only in the sura "The Prologue" all through the Quran. And some people have thought that the *Basmalah* that is at the beginning of the sura "The Prologue" was numbered by mistake, or that other *Basmalahs* were placed at the beginning of other suras to imitate the sura "The Prologue." The code 19 provides a conclusive explanation for this peculiarity and puts an end to all the debates and suspicion on this subject. Does God not say in the 31st verse of the sura "The Hidden" that 19 will dispel the suspicions?

While the words forming the *Basmalah* are counted within the numbered verses in the Quran, the enumeration of the letters in the suras starting with initial letters includes only that sura and its *Basmalah*. If we add the words "Name+God+Gracious+Merciful" in these suras (suras starting with initial letters) according to the method of the suras which have initial letters, we come up with the multiple of 19.

The total of the words that form Basmalah in the suras that start with the initial letters (numbered verses + unnumbered Basmalahs)				
Name	God	Gracious	Merciful	Total
31 +	1121 +	66 +	74	= 1292 (19x68)

The result is 1292 (19x68). Besides the code 19, the number 68 is also important for this product since this case includes 29 suras that start with initial letters. The last of these 29 suras is the sura "The Pen," which is the 68th sura. The total number of occurrences of those four words in the suras with initial letters, from the first sura with initial letters (the 2nd sura) to the last one (the 68th sura), is 1292 (19x68).

THE NAMES OF GOD

The Quran with its mathematical code is an extraordinary book. It is miraculous in such a way that it points to scientific issues and explains scientific subjects that could not have been known about in the 7th century. This Book answers such questions as where we came from, why we exist and what we should do. This Book describes the existence, the unity, the power and the mercy of God. The Quran speaks of God, and introduces God as the Merciful, the Creator and the Forgiver. The description of God is the most important message of the Quran. Since God is the most important issue of the Quran, now let us examine the repetitions of some of God's names (attributes) in the Quran and their numerical values.

Let us remember what the numerical value of a word is. The 28 letters of the Arabic Alphabet have numerical values from 1 to 9, from 10 to 20 and from 100 to 1000. When the Quran was revealed, the same letters were also used for mathematical purposes. In this way, every letter, every word and every sentence has a numerical value. (People used such methods as writing in red ink or drawing a line on those letters in order to avoid confusion between the letters for mathematics and for writing.)

Although people believe that God has 99 names, there are in fact more names of God in the Quran.

THE MAGNIFICENT TABLE

When we examine the number of repetitions and the numerical values of the names of God according to the code 19, we are presented with a magnificent table. Dr. Cesar Adib Majul, former rector and professor of philosophy and logic at the Philippine Islands Islamic Research University and visiting professor at Cornell University, is the first person to have discovered this table. Later, Edip Yuksel, a Turkish author, completed the table with further research and observation. We can describe this extraordinary mathematical relation briefly as follows:

1. The repetitions of only 4 names of God are a multiple of 19 in the Quran.

2. The mathematical values of only 4 names of God are a multiple of 19.

3. The numbers which are the multiple of 19 in each group consisting of 4 words are equal to each other.

4. The multiples of 19 in the repetition of words point to *Basmalah*. (This shows why "Gracious" (*Rahman*) and "Merciful" (*Raheem*), the names of God, were chosen in *Basmalah*.)

5. All the coefficients on both sides of the table are equal to the coefficients of the *Basmalah*.

	The names of God repeated are the multiples of 19	Number of repetitions and mathematical values	The names of God of which mathematical values are multiples of 19
Name	Shahid	19 (19x1)	Waheed
	Allah	2698 (19x142)	Zul Fadl Al-Azim
	Rahman	57 (19x3)	Majid
	Raheem	114 (19x6)	Jaami
The total of coefficients 152 (19x8)		The total of the all numbers on the table $4^2 \times 19^2 = 5776$	

If we pay attention to these names in the table, we see that the number of repetitions of the word "Witness" (*Shahid*) is equal to the number of the repetitions of the word "Name" (*Ism*) that is in *Basmalah*, yet the word "Name" is not one of the names of God. Although the word "name" is part of *Basmalah*, we cannot include it in this list because it is not one of God's names.

Thus, while examining *Basmalah*, we have witnessed the code 19 in the Quran, and while examining the names of God, we have come across *Basmalah* again. This is a table of great beauty.

29- It is tablets for people
30- Over it is 19

74-The Hidden, 29-30

I think the symmetry of this table may provide new lessons regarding the meaning of *Basmalah* and divine attributes. The word "Witness" (*Shahid*) and the word "One" (*Wahid*) show that this miracle testifies to the unity of God, since this miracle proves the veracity of the messages of the Quran and the veracity of the messages proves the unity of God. The unity of God is the most important message of the Quran. "Possessor of Infinite Grace" (*Zul Fadl Al-Azim*), the numerical value of which equals the frequency of the name "God" (Allah) of the *Basmalah*, certifies that this miracle points to benevolence. The name "Glorious" (*Majid*), similar to "Gracious" (*Rahman*), is an adjective God uses, and this adjective defines the Quran in the first verse of the sura Qaf, which is very significant for the mathematical miracles. (We will refer to the letter "*Qaf*" in the chapter on the initial letters.) The number corresponding to the frequency of occurrence of the divine attribute "Merciful" (*Raheem*) and the numerical value of its symmetrical counterpart "Gatherer" (*Jaami*) is 114, and this number is equal to the number of the suras in the Quran. The Quran is the miracle and statement of God and consists of 114 suras. God, who gathered the Quran, will also gather people on the resurrection day and will evaluate their deeds on the Day of Judgment.

WHY IS THE BASMALAH LIKE THIS?

Some people may have wondered why the *Basmalah* consists of the words "*Bismi-llah-irrahman-irraheem*" and they may have wondered why *Basmalah* is not like "*Bismi-llah-alaziz-alhakim*" or "*Bismi-rab-gafurin-karim*" or "*Bismi-ssami.*" God has more than 100 names in the Quran. Why then are only the "God-Gracious-Merciful" names used in *Basmalah*? Why did the *Basmalah* not consist of another two names or five names of God? Why did *Basmalah* consist merely of these three names? What is the wisdom of God?

The findings about 19 help us witness the wisdom of God. The three names of God that form the *Basmalah* are repeated as multiples of 19. The other name "Witness" (*Shahid*) is not used in the *Basmalah* and is repeated exactly as many as times as the word "Name" (*Ism*). This enhances the miracle because it replaces the name "Ism" in the table which gives the names of God. As we have seen before, the total number of repetitions of the names, "God" (Allah), "Gracious" (*Rahman*) and "Merciful" (*Raheem*) are used as multiples of 19. As the coefficient of "*Ism*" in the *Basmalah*, whose coefficient is 1, is replaced with the word "Witness" (*Shahid*), with a coefficient of 1 again, as in the table of the names of God, the total of the coefficients of that table remains the same, 152 (19x8), since these two words have the same coefficients. By this means, both the coefficient of the *Basmalah* and the coefficient of the total of the table of God's names, each of which is formed of 4 words, are the same; that is, they are multiples of 19.

We have seen that all the suras except the sura "Repentance" have a *Basmalah* at the beginning, and that the missing *Basmalah* is found 19 suras later. This special condition adds many new characteristics to the miracle of the Quran. If all the suras had *Basmalah* at the beginning, then having 114 *Basmalahs* would be quite normal because of the symmetric structure, and consequently we would not pay any attention to the number of *Basmalahs*. The same is true for the table of God's names. To have 3 common and 1 different value upsets the symmetry, but on the other hand, the miracle of the concordance between two different subjects like the names of God and the *Basmalah* enhances the value of the miracle.

In this way the code of 19 explains the wisdom behind why the *Basmalah*, the most oft-repeated phrase in the world, is formed as it is.

We believe that there is much to be said about this subject. But it is important that the first rational explanation of why the *Basmalah* is formed like this is made with the help of code 19.

The most repeated group of words in the world is God's revelation and it is coded with 19. Some people may think that God chose *Basmalah* just because it is coded with 19. Others may think that just because God chose those words, *Basmalah* is coded with 19. We believe that both these explanations should be considered as arrangements of the Eternal Might.

THE ASPECTS WHICH THE PROBABILITY CALCULATIONS SHOW

Let us examine the magnificent table that presents the names of God with the probability calculations, in order to show the greatness of the miracle 19 and how it is that such a miracle could be the result of coincidence.

— Since the probabity is $1/19$ for any word in *Basmalah* to be repeated as a multiple of 19, for four words it is $1/19^4$

— If we take into account this probability, along with the probability of the repetition of the word witness (*Shahid*), which replaces the word "name," to be 19 too, then our probability is $1/19^5$

— Both in the *Basmalah* and in the table of God's attributes, the coefficients of the 4 words are $1+142+3+6= 152$ (19x8). The probability of the coefficient number being a multiple of 19 is $1/19$. If we add this to the previous number, then we have $1/19^6$

— We have to calculate the numerical value of God's attributes separately on the right side, because these numbers are not only multiples of 19, but they also exactly correspond to the same numbers on the left side. The biggest mathematical value of any of God's names is 2698. There are 2698 whole numbers up to 2698. We can show our set like this:$(1,2,3,4,......,2696,2697,2698)$. The probability of finding exactly the number that we want from this set of numbers is $1/2698$. If we repeat this operation four times then the probability of finding the numbers we want is $1/2698^4$. The probability we have found up to now is $1/19^6 \times 1/2698^4$.

Here is the result... Read it if you can!

1/2,492,811,198,929,644,375,696

This unreadable number is sufficient in itself to show how impossible it is to form even a single 19 table by chance. Since this number represents the probability of forming a single table like that, who can come up with the assertion that there is not a 19 code in the Quran, which Quran itself says that it will dispel suspicion? Even the probability of a single table shows the Quran's miracle and how unchangeable it is.

And there is one point that we did not take into consideration. Four out of all names of God are on the left hand side of the table and four are on the right hand side. Even if one of the other names were equal to a multiple of 19, according to the frequency or the numerical value of the words, the symmetry and the coefficient of 1+142+3+6=152 (19x8) would be spoiled. So, it is necessary for approximately 200 (100x2) names not to be multiples of 19 for the table to be acceptable. Thus we should take this point into consideration as well. It is a high probability for a name not to be a multiple of 19. But if we make a calculation for 200 words:

$$18^{200} / 19^{200} = 1/49,684.$$

There are other aspects that would lessen the probability. For example, the total of the four values on both sides is 5776 (5776 = 4^2 x 19^2). In this table, a system with 19, with symmetry of four numbers on each side, can be seen. If we take the numbers 4 and 19 shown by this table, and if we multiplied by the number 2 to the second power, which shows the two sides, it would be equal to the total of all the numbers. It is seen that by doing so we could add a few digits to the denominator. But, because it would be difficult to show why we added this result to the probability, and because of the complexity of the calculation, we did not add this to the final result. Apart from this, we mentioned that 19 was the 8th prime number. On the two sides of the table we examined eight names of God, and the total of the coefficients on both sides was 152 (19x8). But we did not take these aspects, which could lessen the probability, into consideration.

WHAT KIND OF LOGIC DO YOU HAVE?

Do not forget that this probability is the result of a single table. If we calculated the probability of all the phenomena related to 19 in the Quran, the number would be astronomical. This probability is much smaller than finding one single grain of sand after hiding it somewhere in the world. And it is even smaller than finding a piece of an atom randomly, after hiding it in a galaxy somewhere in the universe. The number of particles of the atoms in the universe is thought to be 10^{80}. If we brought all the tables related to 19 together, the probability of forming a mathematical pattern coincidentally like the one we have would be even smaller than $1/10^{80}$. We wonder what kind of logic you might have. Do you think that the Prophet was the first inventor of the computer, or that he was hiding a computer in the sand dunes of the desert in order to perform a miracle like this? Or do you think that we should accept a probability smaller than one over the total of all sub-atomic particles in the universe in order to ignore the Quran's miracle? Or will you accept this great miracle of the Quran and appreciate that all humans and jinns could not compose anything like it, even if they worked together? What kind of logic do you possess? What kind of logic would you prefer to possess?

88- Say, "If all the humans and the jinns came together in order to produce a Quran like this, they would surely fail, no matter how much assistance they lent one another."

17-The Children of Israel, 88

ENDLESS MIRACLES IN THE BASMALAH

Many more aspects of the miracle appear when the *Basmalah* is investigated. One of the points of the 30th verse of the sura "The Hidden" (**Over it is 19**) that attracts our attention is the *Basmalah*. It consists of 19 letters. *Basmalah* is written at the top of the suras, and it shows that the Quran has not changed and that it has a mathematical code and mathematical miracles.

Now, let us examine the internal mathematical patterns of the *Basmalah*, based on the code 19. *Basmalah*, a phrase that is repeated daily by hundreds of millions of people around the world, is a treasure trove of splendid diamonds. Let us examine the words forming *Basmalah* and their mathematical values:

Number	Letters of the words	Number of Letters	Number of Letters Mathematical Value	Total
1	Ba, Seen, Meem	3	2, 60, 40	102
2	Alif, Lam, Lam, He	4	1, 30, 30, 5	66
3	Alif, Lam, Ra, Ha, Meem, Noon	6	1, 30, 200, 8, 40, 50	329
4	Alif, Lam, Ra, Ha, Ya, Meem	6	1, 30, 200, 8, 10, 40	289
	Total	19		786

The mathematical value of the words "God," "Gracious," and "Merciful," which form the names of God in *Basmalah*, is a multiple of 19:

The mathematical value of God's names which form Basmalah			
God	Gracious	Merciful	Total
66 +	329 +	289 =	684 (19x36)

There are numerous 19-based numerical phenomena in *Basmalah*. Some of these are as follows:

1. If we write the number of the letters of the words in *Basmalah* after their serial numbers, we get an eight-digit number and this number is a multiple of 19:

$$1\ 3\ 2\ 4\ 3\ 6\ 4\ 6 = 19 \times 19x36686$$

2. Now, let us replace the number of the letters of these words with their total mathematical values. The number we get is a fifteen-digit number and this number is a multiple of 19: 1 102 2 66 3 329 4 289 = 19 x 5801401752331

3. Now, let us replace the total mathematical value of the words with the mathematical value of each letter. For example, in place of 102, which is the total mathematical value of the first word, let's write

2, 60, 40 which are the mathematical values of each letter in that word. We get a thirty-seven-digit number and this number is a multiple of 19 (You can check these divisions in a computer. We wonder whether some disbelievers will claim that the Prophet Muhammad discovered the computer 1400 years ago!)

1 2 60 40 2 1 30 30 5 3 1 30 200 8 40 50 4 1 30 200 8 10 40 = 19 x 6633695422...

4. Let us write the total number of letters in that word instead of the number of letters of each word we used in the first example. For instance, let us write 7(4+3), which is the total number of letters of the first and second words in the place of 4, which is the number of letters of the second word. This ten-digit number is also a multiple of 19: 1 3 2 7 3 13 4 19 = 19 x 69858601

5. Now, let us replace the mathematical value of each word used in the second example with the total mathematical value of these words. We get a sixteen-digit number, and this number is a multiple of 19. Then, we use the total mathematical value, as we used the total number of letters in the fourth example:

1 102 2 168 3 497 4 786= 19 x 58011412367094.

6. In the third example, we wrote the mathematical value of each word after the serial number of each word. Now, let's write in front of these mathematical values, the letter number of that mathematical value. The number we have is an exact multiple of 19: 112260340 21123033045 311230320048540650 411230320048510640= 19x 590843895848581....

7. Now, add the number of letters and the mathematical value of the letters in the first two examples. And then write this total number after the serial number of the words. For example, take 3, which is the total of the letters of the first word, and 102, which is the mathematical value of these three letters. Add 3 and 102. You get 105. Write this number (105) after the first word. This number is also an exact multiple of 19:

1105 270 3335 4295= 19 x 5817212281805

8. If you write the serial numbers of each letter in *Basmalah* from 1 to 19 after the mathematical value of each letter of the *Basmalah*, you get a 62 digit number and this number is also a multiple of 19:

2 1 60 2 40 3 1 4 30 5 30 6 5 7 1 8 30 9 200 10 8 11 40 12 50 13 1 14 30 15 200 16 8 17 10 18 40 19= 19x 113696858647648......

9. If you write the serial numbers of the words (1, 2, 3, 4) after the

parts pointing out each word in the number above, you get a sixty-six digit number and this number is an exact multiple of 19:

21 602 403 1 14 305 306 57 2 18 309 20010 811 4012 5013 3 114 3015 20016 817 1018 1019 4=19x113696858496344.....

10. In the ninth example, we wrote the serial numbers of the words (1, 2, 3, 4) after the mathematical values and the number of letters. Now, let us replace the serial numbers of the words with the mathematical value of each word (102, 66, 329, 289). The number we get is again an exact multiple of 19: 21 602 403 102 14 305 306 5766 18 309 20010 811 4012 5013 329 114 3015 20016 8 17 1018 4019 289=19x113696858432332....

Abdullah Arık deals with the mathematical structure of *Basmalah* in detail in his book, *"Beyond Probability."* We are going to limit our discussion here, however, since too much detail may bore and confuse some people.

The 19-based peculiarities of this verse consisting of 19 letters and 4 words are amazing. As we always remember the mercy of God when we say **"Bismillahirrahmanirraheem" (in the name of God, Gracious, Merciful)**, we can remember that God shows His incredible miracles and He displays His mercy. The *Basmalah*, which shines brightly with its 19 letters on every sura, is a significant part of the code 19 protecting the Quran.

30- Over it is 19.

74-The Hidden, 30

SURA THE PROLOGUE AND 19

The first sura of the Quran is the sura The Prologue. All the suras are introduced by *Basmalah*, but the only numbered *Basmalah* is in the sura The Prologue. (The *Basmalah* which is in the 30th verse of the 27th sura is also numbered, but it is not at the beginning of the sura). What we have learned before about the code 19 proves that this exceptional situation of the sura The Prologue is intentional. Thus, the code 19 helps us to understand an exceptional situation that has puzzled some Muslims for 1400 years. The mathematical characteristics of the sura The Prologue:

1. Prove that the *Basmalah* is the first verse of the sura The Prologue. (Contrary to some scholars who considered it just an unnumbered repeating verse; the followers of some sects, thus, do not recite *Basmalah* loudly when they recite The Prologue sura.)

2. Point out the miraculous structure of the sura The Prologue.

3. Prove that the sequence of the suras is arranged by God.

We can confidently say that The Prologue sura is the text that is repeated the most frequently in the world. We do not know any other texts that are repeated as frequently as this in any religion or community. People have repeated this text for more than 1400 years. The Prologue sura is read every day many times in almost every prayer. It is the sura that is recited the most frequently, and it is the text repeated the most frequently in the world. We give the translation of the sura The Prologue before we deal with its mathematical structure.

1- In the name of God, Gracious, Merciful.
2- Praise be to God, Lord of the worlds.
3- He is Gracious, Merciful.
4- Master of the Day of Religion.
5- Only You we worship, only You we ask for help.
6- Guide us to the right path,
7- The path of those You have blessed, not of those who have deserved wrath, nor the strayers.

1-The Prologue, 1-7

Let's give some examples of the mathematical system of this meaningful text:

1. If we write the verse numbers successively after the number "1," which is the sura number, the number we arrive at is an exact multiple of 19:

$$1\ 1\ 2\ 3\ 4\ 5\ 6\ 7 = 19 \times 591293$$

2. If we write the number of the letters of each verse side by side after number "1," which is the sura number, the fifteen digit number we get is also a multiple of 19 :

$$1\ 19\ 17\ 12\ 11\ 19\ 18\ 43 = 19 \times 6272169010097$$

3. If we write the mathematical value of each verse after the num-

ber of the letters of each verse, the number we get is a multiple of 19:

119 786 17 581 12 618 11 241 19 836 18 1072 43 6009=
19x630453556901378...

4. If we write the verse numbers before the number of the letters in the previous example, the number we get is an exact multiple of 19:

1 1 19 786 2 17 581 3 12 618 4 11 241 5 19 836 6 18 1072 7 43 6009= 19x589361167148059...

5. If we write the total number of verses and the letters and the total mathematical value side by side after the sura number (1) of the sura The Prologue, the number we arrive at is an exact multiple of 19:

1 7 139 10143 = 19x90205797

6. If we write the number of verses (7) and the number of words (29) respectively after the sura number (1) of the sura The Prologue, the number we get will be an exact multiple of 19:

1 7 29 = 19x91

7. If we write the number of verses (7) and the number of words in each of the seven verses (4 4 2 3 4 3 9) respectively after the sura number (1), the number we get is an exact multiple of 19:

1 7 4 4 2 3 4 3 9 = 19x9180181

This miraculous structure brings to mind the following:

23- If you are in doubt of what We have revealed to Our Servant, then bring a sura like this, and call any witness, apart from God, you like, if you are truthful.

2-The Cow, 23

THE PROBLEMS ABOUT 19 THAT REQUIRE SOLUTION

The findings related to 19 are sufficient in themselves to show the greatness of the miracle of 19. But more studies should be conducted. If we study further the aspects that suggest a problem, the greatness of the miracle of 19 will become even clearer. We have seen how the code 19 solved certain problems and we will continue seeing more in the coming chapters. In this part of our book, I am going to discuss three subjects that seem to be problematic. New discoveries of 19 have already solved many problematic issues related to 19 before, and we believe that further research will help resolve the following three points.

1) The first problem is about the counting of "*Alif*"s. Some words in Arabic can be written with or without "*Alif*," yet they are pronounced in the same way. In addition, the letter "*Hamza*," which is pronounced like the letter "*Alif*," was added to the Quran in order to allow people to read the Quran more easily. However, these additions do not change the number of words, the meanings, or the pronunciations of words in the Quran. Since the number of "*Alif*"s in some words is controversial, this causes some problems in the number of occurrences of this letter in some suras that have *Alif* as the initial letter. The number of initial letters in the suras is one of the most fundamental characteristics of the code 19. The suras having the initial letter "*Alif*" call for a closer examination. Although Rashad Khalifa stated that the number of suras with the beginning letter "*Alif*" was a multiple of 19, I believe that the counting was done hurriedly.

2) Whether the 128th and 129th verses of the sura Repentance belong to the Quran or not is the most important problem related to the code 19. Only two of the more than 6000 verses of the Quran are in doubt, and this shows that people who look into the code 19 do not abstain from discussing the matter; this also shows the greatness of the miracle (2 in 6000 is 1 in 3000). The wisdom of this discussion might be as follows: This discussion caused the code 19 to be open to debate among Muslims, and by being open to discussion, possible manipulations are prevented. Doubts cause incorrect calculations and weak mathematical results to be eliminated easily, since everything is inspected more carefully. So the data we have are the most reliable ones. Moreover, people's doubts stimulated researchers and new students to discover new connections related to the code 19. People who have doubts about the code 19 should be careful. People who are impatient could be victims of haste; they could think that the first splinter they find is a diamond. And if these people act impatiently and are stubborn, they may swerve from the right path. Obduracy is the most important enemy of rational judgment. The code 19 in the Quran is appreciated from a rational and mathematically trained perspective. There is no place for stubbornness in a mathematical and rational enterprise. In addition, during the discussions about the code 19, displaying aggressive moods and accusing people of infidelity is wrong. I hope that we will eliminate many mistakes if Muslims end up

understanding the code 19 and researchers do more studies on it in the Quran, yet all the corrections and critiques should be done within the limits of rationality, excluding obduracy and insult.

3) The other problem is about the counting of the letter "*Noon*" in the sura The Pen, the 68th sura, which is the last sura with initial letters. It begins with the initial letter "*Noon.*" The number of the letter "*Noon*" in this sura is 113 (19x7), but it is claimed that the letter "*Noon*" which is at the beginning was written originally with two "*Noon*"s. Present copies of the Quran have this initial letter with one "*Noon.*" It is claimed that the mathematical code corrects this error. Many more numerical values related to this subject should be studied, and whether the initial letter "*Noon*" at the beginning of the sura The Pen was written with one or two "*Noons*" in the ancient copies of the Quran should be investigated. We are waiting for conclusive evidence on this; consequently I will not deal with the counting of the letter "*Noon*" in the suras beginning with the letter "*Noon.*"

SURAS THAT HAVE INITIAL LETTERS AND 19

The Quran's initial letters have been one of its more curious aspects. Some suras are introduced with initial letters like "*Qaf*" and "*Alif-Lam-Meem:*" What the initial letters represent was a mystery until the manifestation of code 19. When code 19 became manifest, it was understood that the initial letters had a significant role with reference to the miracle of 19. You can see the suras and verses with initial letters in the Quran in the table below:

Sura Number	Sura Name	Beginning Letters	Total
2	The Cow	Alif-Lam-Meem	286
3	The Family of Imran	Alif-Lam-Meem	200
7	The Purgatory	Alif-Lam-Meem-Sad	206
10	Jonah	Alif-Lam-Ra	109
11	Hud	Alif-Lam-Ra	123
12	Joseph	Alif-Lam-Ra	111
13	The Thunder	Alif-Lam-Meem-Ra	43
14	Abraham	Alif-Lam-Ra	52
15	Hijr	Alif-Lam-Ra	99
19	Mary	Kaf He-Ya-Ayn-Sad	98
20	Ta-He	Ta-He	135
26	The Poets	Ta-Seen-Meem	227
27	The Ant	Ta-Seen	93
28	The History	Ta-Seen-Meem	88
29	The Spider	Alif-Lam-Meem	69
30	The Romans	Alif-Lam-Meem	60
31	Luqman	Alif-Lam-Meem	34
32	The Prostration	Alif-Lam-Meem	30
36	Ya-Seen	Ya-Seen	83
38	Sad	Sad	88
40	The Believer	Ha-Meem	85
41	Elucidated	Ha-Meem	54
42	Consultation	Ha-Meem/Ayn-Seen-Qaf	53
43	Vanity	Ha-Meem	89
44	Smoke	Ha-Meem	59
45	Kneeling	Ha-Meem	37
46	The Dunes	Ha-Meem	35
50	Qaf	Qaf	45
68	The Pen	Noon	52

There are 29 suras with initial letters and the total number of verses having initial letters is 30. We mentioned before that 30 was the 19th composite number. The initial letters themselves form independent verses without any other words in 19 of those 29 suras (for example, **"Alif, Lam, Meem"** is a verse in itself in the sura The Cow). In the other 10 suras, there are some words after the initial letters (for example, the first verse of the sura Qaf states, **"Qaf, the Glorious Quran"**).

The number of suras with initial letters as verse	19

The verses draw attention to the Quran (by using the words "Quran" or "Book") in 9 out of 10 suras that have initial letters together with words. The total of the sura numbers of these 9 suras is the number 190 (10+11+12+13+14+15+27+38+50= 190), and 190 is 10 x 19.

The total number of initial lettered suras that refer to the Quran together with initial letters	190 (19x10)

The initial letters can be grouped according to their repetitions. One group consists of initial letters repeated only once, and the other group consists of initial letters repeated more than once. The initial letters repeated more than once consist of four groups: *"Alif, Lam, Meem,"* *"Ta, Seen, Meem,"* *"Ha, Meem,"* *"Alif, Lam, Ra."* The number of verses belonging to the suras having these 4 groups of initial letters is 1900 (19 x 100).

The total of the verses in suras which have the repeated initial letter groups	1900 (19x100)

There are 67 suras between the second sura of the Quran, which has the first initial letters (2nd sura), and the 68th sura, which has the last initial letters. The number 67 is the 19th prime number. Because 29 of these 67 suras begin with initial letters, there are only (67-29=38), 38(19x2) suras that are not introduced with initial letters between the suras with initial letters.

The suras that do not have initial letters, between the suras with initial letters	38 (19x2)

I mentioned that I was not going to deal with the counting of the letter "*Alif*" in the Quran since there is difficulty in its counting. The difficulty is due to the additional "*Alif*"s inserted in later versions of the Quran to accommodate non-Arabs, and the need for a comprehensive, comparative and critical study of the oldest available versions. However, I can show that the suras introduced with the initial letter "*Alif*" are related to the code 19. For instance, the total of the sura numbers of the suras starting with the initial letter "*Alif*" is an exact multiple of the number 19. [2+3+7+10+11+12+13+14+15+29+30+31+32 =209(19x11)]

The total of the verse numbers where the letter "*Alif*" is used as initial letter	209 (19x11)

If we examine the number of verses in the suras that begin with initial letters, we see that the 28th and 38th suras consist of 88 verses each, and the 14th and 68th suras consist of 52 verses each. Thus, we see that there are 27 different numbers in the number of the verses of the suras starting with initial letters. The total number of the verses, excluding repetitions, is 2603(19x137).

The total of the verses in the initial lettered suras, excluding repetitions	2603 (19x137)

There are many characteristics that are related to the code 19 in the suras introduced with initial letters. All these examples show that the row of the suras and the number of verses in the Quran are arranged in a given order. There are 14 combinations of initial letters in the Quran and the total number of initial letters in these combinations is 38(19x2). And if we multiply the serial numbers of these combinations and the number of the initial letters in each combination and then add all these results, it makes up 247(19x13). Look at the following table:

THE QURAN: UNCHALLENGEABLE MIRACLE

Row Number	Initial letters	Number of letters in the group	The multiplication of the row number and the number of letters
1	Alif-Lam-Meem	3	1 x 3 = 3
2	Alif-Lam-Meem-Sad	4	2 x 4 = 8
3	Alif-Lam-Ra	3	3 x 3 = 9
4	Alif-Lam-Meem-Ra	4	4 x 4 = 16
5	Kaf-He-Ya-Ayn-Sad	5	5 x 5 = 25
6	Ta-He	2	6 x 2 = 12
7	Ta-Seen-Meem	3	7 x 3 = 21
8	Ta-Seen	2	8 x 2 = 16
9	Ya-Seen	2	9 x 2 = 18
10	Sad	1	10 x 1 = 10
11	Ha-Meem	2	11 x 2 = 22
12	Ha-Meem/Ayn-Seen-Qaf	5	12 x 5 = 60
13	Qaf	1	13 x 1 = 13
14	Noon	1	14 x 1 = 14
	Total	38 (19x2)	247 (19x13)

THE SURA YA-SEEN AND 19

The sura Ya-Seen is one of the most frequently recited suras. It is introduced with the initial letters "*Ya-Seen.*" The letter "*Ya*" is used 237 times and the letter "*Seen*" is used 48 times. If we add 237 and 48, it makes 285(19x15), which is an exact multiple of 19.

The sura Ya-Seen contains many scientific signs. I advise you to read this sura and try to understand it. Unfortunately, people always

The total of the occurrence of "Ya" and "Seen" initial letters all through the sura Ya-Seen		
Ya	Seen	Total
237 +	48	285 (19x15)

recite this sura after a person dies and they do not even try to understand the meaning of it. However, it is very interesting that God says that the Quran was revealed for the living.

69- We did not teach him myths, nor is it worthy of him. This is nothing but a reminder and a Quran making things clear.
70- To warn the <u>living</u> and justify the word against those who do not believe.

36-Ya-Seen, 69-70

THE SURA MARY AND NUMBER 19

The sura "Mary" is the 19th sura and is introduced with the initial letters "*Kaf, He, Ya, Ayn, Sad.*" This sura, whose sura number is important, has the longest combination of initial letters in one verse. (The combination, "*Ha, Meem, -Ayn, Seen, Qaf*" in the 42nd sura is used in two verses.) These 5 letters are used 798 (19x42) times throughout the sura Mary.

The total of the initial letters throughout the sura Mary					
Kaf	He	Ya	Ayn	Sad	Total
137 +	175 +	343 +	117 +	26	798 (19x42)

Additionally, in the 19th sura, if we put the mathematical values of "*Kaf, He, Ya, Ayn, Sad*" next to each other we get 20 5 10 70 90= 19x10795110.

There are minor attributes in which the miracle of 19 is made manifest along with the basic characteristics of these suras. But in order not to exceed the limits of our book or to distract our readers' minds from the fundamental subjects, I shall leave many of those attributes out.

THE BEGINNING LETTERS AYN-SEEN-QAF

The initial letters *"Ayn-Seen-Qaf"* are used in the 42nd sura (Consultation). The combination *"Ayn-Seen-Qaf"* has a characteristic that other combinations of initial letters do not have. While all the other combinations of initial letters are used only in the first verse of the suras, the combination *"Ayn-Seen-Qaf"* is used as the second verse of the 42nd sura. And these initial letters are used 209 (19x11) times in that sura. 209 is an exact multiple of 19.

The total of the initial letters, Ayn-Seen-Qaf, which form the second verse of the sura Consultation			
Ayn	Seen	Qaf	Total
98 +	54 +	57	209 (19x11)

THE INITIAL LETTER "SAD" AND THE MISTAKE THAT IS CORRECTED

Among the initial lettered suras, only three have one letter as their first verses. These three letters are *"Sad,"* *"Qaf"* and *"Noon."* These letters are used in the 38th, 50th and 68th suras. I shall now examine the letter *"Sad."* The sura that begins with the letter *"Sad"* is called also *"Sad."*

The letter *"Sad"* is used in the 38th sura by itself and it is also used in the combination *"Alif-Lam-Meem-Sad"* in the sura The Purgatory, which is the 7th sura, and in the combination *"Kaf-He-Ya-Ayn-Sad"* in the sura Mary, which is the 19th sura. The total number of occurrences of the letter *"Sad"* used in these 3 suras is 152 (19x8). This number is a multiple of 19.

The total "Sad" letters in the suras which have "Sad" initials			
7th sura The Purgatory	19th sura Mary	38th sura Sad	Total
97 +	26 +	29 =	152 (19x8)

If you count the letter "*Sad*" in some copies of the Quran, you will see that there are not 97 but, 98 "*Sad*"s in the sura The Purgatory. The reason for this is that the word "*Bastatan*" was written with the letter "*Sad*" instead of "*Seen*" by mistake in the 69th verse. In many copies, the letter "*Seen*" was added over that word and an explanation was written next to this word. This explanation says "*Yuqrau bi-s seeni*," that is to say, you should read this word with the letter "*Seen*" even though it is written with "*Sad*." So there are people who claim that the word "*Bastatan*" in the 69th verse of the sura The Purgatory is written with the letter "*Sad*" and pronounced with the letter "*Seen*" and some others say the word "*Bastatan*" is written with both letters "*Sad*" and "*Seen*."

The Quran is not the work of man. It is the revelation of God and the code 19 solves the problem in this verse. This word is written with "*Seen*" in Arabic dictionaries. After the code 19 was discovered concerning the initial letters, an old copy of the Quran was examined to solve this problem. It was discovered that the word "*Bastatan*" was written with the letter "*Seen*" in the Tashkent copy of the Quran, one of the oldest copies in the world. It is understood that, while copying

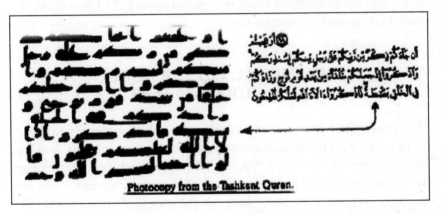

Photocopy from the Tashkent Quran.

In one of the oldest copies of Quran, the Tashkent copy, the word "*Bastatan*" is written with "*Seen*."

the Quran, certain copyists confused the letter "*Sad*" with the letter "*Seen*." We assume that the person who noticed this mistake wrote the letter "*Seen*" over the letter "*Sad*" to correct this mistake, yet people copying the Quran wrote it with the letter "*Sad*," as they did not understand that a correction had been made in the spelling of this word. However, this word was written with the letter "*Seen*" in some copies of the Quran. It is clear that there were discussions on this topic because a *hadith* was fabricated that says that it is correct to write the word "*Bastatan*" with the letter "*Sad.*" The code 19 solves this problem and proves that all these *hadiths* were fabricated.

There are some lessons to be taken from this correction:

1. The code 19 finds and corrects even the smallest mistakes performed by man in the Quran.
2. The code 19 is not a mere embellishment. It is a miraculous code having active, protective and corrective duties.
3. It is clear that God protects the Quran as He says: **"Surely, We have sent down Reminder, We. And We will assuredly guard it"** in the 9th verse of the sura Al-Hijr, which is the 15th sura of the Quran. The Quran is protected with the code 19 and other mathematical miracles. Man can make mistakes. The code that God draws attention to and placed into the Quran corrects these mistakes. (The mistake in the word "*Bastatan*" is good proof of the fact that human beings had made mistakes while they were copying the Quran, but the mathematical code corrected them.)

THE INITIAL LETTER "QAF," THE QURAN AND 19

The letter "*Qaf*" is one of the initial or introductory letters that performs easy to understand, but impossible to imitate miracles, and it is the first letter of the word "Quran." It is believed that it represents the Quran itself, as it is the first letter of the word "Quran." The letter "*Qaf*" is used as an initial letter in the sura *Qaf*, which is the 50th sura. Below is the first verse of this sura:

1- Qaf, the Glorious Quran

50-Qaf, 1

If you count the letter "*Qaf*"s in this sura, you will get 57(19x3). You do not need to know Arabic in order to count the "*Qaf*"s in this sura. Take the Quran and look for two dots over the round letters in the 50th sura. Only the letter "*Qaf*" has two dots over the round letters, so you can count easily.

The number of letter "Qaf" used in the sura Qaf
57 (19x3)

It is very significant that the Quran is described as "Glorious" (*Majid*) in the first verse of the sura Qaf, which has the initial letter "*Qaf*," because the numerical value of the adjective "Glorious" (*Majid*) is 57 (19x3).

The numerical value of the word "Majid"				
Meem	Jeem	Ya	Dal	Total
40 +	3 +	10 +	4	57 (19x3)

This form of the word "Quran," as used in this first verse, is mentioned 57(19x3) times in the Quran (I do not include the one in sura Jonah, since that refers to "another Quran").

The number of times the form "Quran" is used throughout the Quran
57 (19x3)

These numbers bring to mind two very short and interesting verses:

1- Gracious
2- Taught the Quran

55-Gracious, 1-2

If you remember the preceding chapters of this book, you recall the word "Gracious" (*Rahman*) is used 57(19x3) times also. Both the words "Gracious" (*Rahman*) and the simple form of the word "Quran" are used 57 times each (I should remind the reader that I excluded the word "Quran" written with an extra "Alif" as

"*Quranen*" and the other form, "*Quranehu*," attached to the pronoun "He").

And, if we examine the word "taught" (*Alleme*), which is also in the verse, to see how many times it is used to refer "God's teaching," we reach the number 19 (see 2-31, 2-32, 2-239, 2-251, 2-282, 4-113, 5-4, 5-110, 12-37, 12-68, 12-101, 18-65, 21-80, 36-69, 53-5, 55-2, 55-4, 96-4, 96-5).

These two verses mentioning the teaching of the Quran are also related to the multiples of 19.

Word	Gracious ⟶	Taught ⟶	Quran
Number of repetitions	57(19x3)	19(19x1)	57(19x3)

ENDLESS MIRACLES IN ONE LETTER

We have seen that there are 57 "*Qaf*" letters in the sura Qaf, and this is a multiple of 19, and the initial letter "*Qaf*" is the first letter of the word "Quran." The letter *Qaf* is also used in the form "*Ayn-Seen-Qaf*" in the 2nd verse of the sura Consultation. Make a guess how many times the letter "*Qaf*" is used in the sura Consultation. It is used 57 (19x3) times.

The number of "Qaf"s used in the sura Consultation
57 (19x3)

It is seen that the letter "*Qaf*," which is the first letter of the word "Quran," and which itself represents the Quran, is used in two suras as an initial letter. If we add the numbers of the "*Qaf*" letters in these suras together, we get 114 (19x6). As you know, 114 is the number of suras in the Quran. This means that the letter "*Qaf*" is used once for each sura.

The sura Qaf with the initial letter "*Qaf*" is the 50th sura and has 45 verses. 50+45=95 (19x5). The other sura with the initial letter "*Qaf*" is the sura Consultation, the 42nd sura, and this sura has 53 verses. 42+53 = 95 (19x5)

The total number of the verses and sura numbers which have "Qaf" as initial letter		
Number of the sura	Number of the verses	Total
50 +	45	= 95 (19x15)
42 +	53	= 95 (19x15)

As it can be seen, the letter "*Qaf*" is coded with the number 19 and "*Qaf*" initialed suras have numerical symmetries. All these data demonstrate to people whose eyes are not blinded by prejudice that in the Quran the sequence of the suras, the number of words, verses and the letters are all arranged in perfect order. This perfect system is the proof that that system could not have been arranged by a person who lived in the middle of the desert 1400 years ago, even if he had had a computer at his disposal.

Prophet Lot's community is called "*Qavmi-Lut*" throughout the Quran. But the term "*Ihvanu-Lut*" is used instead of "*Qavmi-Lut*" in the sura Qaf (50-Qaf, 13). *Ihvanu-Lut* has the same meaning as "*Qavmi-Lut.*" "*Qavmi-Lut*" is written with the letter "*Qaf,*" but there is no "*Qaf*" letter, in the term "*Ihvanu-Lut.*" If God had used the term "*Qavmi-Lut*" in the 13th verse of this sura, there would have been 58 "*Qaf*" letters instead of 57 and it would have spoiled the code 19. God shows that He formed the code 19 in the Quran in order to present a miracle. However, some of the so called devoted people want to surrender to their sheiks, dervishes and mullahs instead of the Quran, and they want the Quran to be read like a storybook that teaches nothing. Since they try to include their traditions in their religion, as if their traditions were sacred, they do not want a rational structure to rule over religion. For that reason, they see the code 19 as their biggest enemy, since it leads people to think. While God draws attention to the code 19 and its functions in the Quran and presents all these data for us, some people still act as they did in the past. They do not want to think about the code 19 and they do not even want to evaluate it simply because it may cause them to change their points of view and lead them to a rational way. I would like to remind these people of the following verse:

18- They are the ones who listen to the word and then follow the best. These are the ones who have been guided by God. These are the ones who possess intelligence.

39-The Throngs, 18

THE 19TH LETTER

Just the examination of the initial letter "*Qaf*" is enough to show that a mathematical system protects the Quran. The examination of this sole letter shows that the Quran rejects all foreign intervention related to the number of letters, the order of suras, the verse number of the suras and the repetition of the words.

If we continue to look into the letter "*Qaf*," we shall see more interesting things. We saw that the numerical value of the letters was important for the mathematical system of the Quran. The letter "*Qaf*" is the 19th letter in the table showing the numerical value of letters, and its numerical value is 100.

Serial Number	1	2	3	4	5	6	7	8	9	10
Letter	Alif	Ba	Jeem	Dal	He	Waw	Ze	Ha	Ta	Ya
Numerical Value	1	2	3	4	5	6	7	8	9	10

Serial Number	11	12	13	14	15	16	17	18	19
Letter	Kaf	Lam	Meem	Noon	Seen	Ayn	Fa	Sad	Qaf
Numerical Value	20	30	40	50	60	70	80	90	100

Thus, the letter "*Qaf*," symbolizing the Quran, has a special place since this letter is the 19th letter in the table showing the numerical value of letters. If we count the letter "*Qaf*" in the 19th verses throughout the Quran, we have 76(19x4), and this number is an exact multiple of 19.

The number of occurrences of the letter "Qaf" used in the 19th verses throughout the Quran
76 (19x4)

On the other hand, the total number of the letter "*Qaf*"s in the suras whose index numbers are multiples of 19 is 228 (19x12), and this number is an exact multiple of 19.

The total number of occurrences of the letter "Qaf" in the suras whose index numbers are multiples of the number 19						
19	38	57	76	95	114	Total
86 +	74 +	49 +	15 +	3 +	1	= 228 (19x12)

We see some people saying, "Is 19 so important? Does the code 19 cover all the Quran? Even if this miracle exists, it is not very important." These people who claim that the code 19 is not very important should read the information about the miracle of 19 in this book carefully. We expect that when God displays a miracle, it should be overwhelming. The data available shows that God displays an important and remarkable miracle. Believers do not look down upon the proofs God presents, and they thank God as God presents these proofs.

THE WORD "QURAN" AND NUMBER 19

The word "*Quran*" has two other derivations besides the form "*Quran,.*" These are "*Quranehu*" and "*Quranen.*" "*Quranen*" is used 8 times and "*Quranehu*" is used twice in the Quran. (The 15th verse of the sura Jonah is not included, as it mentions "another *Quran*." In addition, the 31st verse of the 13th sura is not included, as it describes a nonexistent type of "*Quran*" that destroys mountains and brings dead people back to life. The 44th verse of the 41st sura is also excluded, as it describes a nonexistent "*Quran*" as well, which is a "*Quran*" in another language. These descriptions do not describe the "*Quran*" revealed to Prophet Muhammad, therefore they are not included.)

We saw that 19 is a prime number and the factors of 19 cannot be separated. (A prime number is a number which is divisible only by itself and "1." A prime number produces numbers; it does not derivate from other numbers.) The number "67," which is the number of all the derivations of the word "Quran," is a prime number and has an interesting characteristic. The number "67" is the 19th prime number.

Prime number row	1	2	3	4	5	6	7	8	9
Prime number	2	3	5	7	11	13	17	19	23

Prime number row	10	11	12	13	14	15	16	17	18	19
Prime number	29	31	37	41	43	47	53	59	61	67

The word "*Quran*"'s simple form, which is also used in the first verse of the sura Qaf together with the initial letter *Qaf*, is used 57 (19x3) times throughout the Quran. Other forms or derivatives of "*Quran*" are used 67 times, and as I mentioned before, the number 67 happens to be the 19th prime number. Thus, this data draws attention to prime numbers and certifies the importance we give to them.

We saw before that the word "glorious" (*majid*), whose numerical value is 57, completes the word "*Quran*" in the sura Qaf. The word "glorious" (*majid*) completes once more the word "*Quran*" in the 21st verse of the 85th sura. The interesting point is that the completed word "Quran" in the 21st verse is the last use of that word and it is the 57th use in the Quran. As a result, the word "glorious" (*majid*) with a numerical value of 57 completes the word "*Quran*" twice (57x2) in the Quran; the number we get is 114 (19x6) and this is the number of suras in the Quran.

The Quran has many names or attributes such as "Reminder" (*Zikir*) and "Light" (*Nur*). The studies so far have shown that the number of these names was about 57. In light of the given data, I hope that this number will be 57. God knows the truth. I think that, if meticulous research is carried out on this subject, the names of the Quran will present a table which depends on the code 19, as the names of God present one.

I would like to give some interesting hints to researchers who wish to examine the names of the Quran. My wish is that there will be meticulous researchers who find other miraculous data related to the code 19 in the Quran. I shall examine the 19th, 38th, 57th (these numbers are multiples of 19) and 50th uses of the derivations of the word "*Quran*." The 50th use of the derivations of the word "*Quran*" is important because it combines the word "Glorious" (*Majid*) and the letter "*Qaf*" that we examined in the first verse of the sura Qaf. (All the derivations of the Quran consist of the form "*Quran*" and the form "*Quranen*" written with an extra letter "*Alif*" and the form "*Quranehu*" written with an extra letter "He")

The 19th derivation of "*Quran*" (17th sura, 60th verse)
The 38th derivation of "*Quran*" (36th sura, 2nd verse) 36+2=38(19x2)
The 50th derivation of "*Quran*" (50th sura, 1st verse) Qaf, Al-Quran, Majid
The 57th derivation of "*Quran*" (56th sura, 77th verse) 56+77=133(19x7)

And then, the 19th, 38th, 50th and 57th uses of the "*Quran*" form are examined.

The 19th "*Quran*" form (17th sura, 78th verse) 17+78=95(19x5)
The 38th "*Quran*" form (38th sura, 1st verse)
The 50th "*Quran*" form (55th sura, 2nd verse) 55+2=57(19x3)
The 57th "*Quran*" form (85th sura, 21st verse) Majid

The total of the sura and verse numbers is a multiple of 19 in four of these eight uses.

It is interesting that the 50th use in the first table is seen in the first verse of the 50th sura, and the 38th use in the second table is seen in the first verse of the 38th sura.

As I have mentioned, the form *"Quran,"* the letter *"Qaf"* and the word "Glorious" (*Majid*), whose numerical value is 57, are used in the first verse of the 50th sura. When the word "Glorious" (*Majid*) completes the word *"Quran,"* which is the 57th derivation of the form *"Quran,"* the number "57" here is equal to the numerical value of the word "Glorious" (*Majid=57*).

More studies should be conducted on the word *"Quran"* and the adjectives used to define the Quran. God displayed the code 19 in detail while researchers were examining the names of God, so we hope that God will display the code 19 in further detail as the names of the Quran are examined. God knows the truth.

THE INITIAL LETTERS "HA-MEEM" AND 19

Seven successive suras begin with the initial letters *"Ha-Meem."* These suras are the 40th, 41st, 42nd, 43rd, 44th, 45th and 46th suras. The verses of all these suras are introduced by two letters: *"Ha-Meem"*

Here, the total number of letters *"Ha"* and *"Meem"* used in these 7 suras is 2147 (113x19), and this number is an exact multiple of 19.

The code 19 demonstrates an interlocking mathematical system in the seven suras starting with the initial letters *"Ha-Meem."* The system involves both the divisibility of the frequencies of letters by 19, and a unique mathematical formula.

When Milan Sulc added together the values of the digits of all the letters *"Ha"* and *"Meem,"* he got the number "113," which is a multiple of 19. Please see the table below:

Sura number	Ha	Meem	The total of digits	Total
40	64	380	6+4+3+8+0	21
41	48	276	4+8+2+7+6	27
42	53	300	5+3+3+0+0	11
43	44	324	4+4+3+2+4	17
44	16	150	1+6+1+5+0	13
45	31	200	3+1+2+0+0	6
46	36	225	3+6+2+2+5	18
Total	292	1855		113
General Total	2147 (19x113)			

If we examine the 42nd sura, we see this sura has a difference. The first verse of this sura is introduced with the initial letters "*Ha-Meem*," and the second verse has the initial letters "*Ayn-Seen-Qaf*" (This sura is the only sura that has initial letters in the second verse). Thus, initial letters "*Ha-Meem*" are used in the 40th, 41st and 42nd suras in succession, and we can think that the initial letters in the second verse of the 42nd sura (*Ayn-Seen-Qaf*) divide "*Ha-Meem*" initialed suras into two groups: three suras (40, 41, 42) and four suras (43, 44, 45, 46) which follow each other. It is very interesting to note that if we divide the suras in this manner, there are 1121(19x59) letters "*Ha Meem*" in the suras forming the first group and this number (1121) is an exact multiple of 19, and there are 1026(19x54) letters "*Ha Meem*" in the suras forming the second group and this number (1026) is also an exact multiple of 19. Moreover, the total of the digits in the first table below is 59 (When we multiply 59 with the number 19, we get the total of the initials in the first group), and the total of the digits in the second table below is 54 (When we multiply 54 by 19, we get the total of the initials in the second group).

29- It is tablets for people
30- Over it is 19

74-The Hidden, 29-30

The following tables will better demonstrate:

Sura number	Ha	Meem	The total of digits	Total
40	64	380	6+4+3+8+0	21
41	48	276	4+8+2+7+6	27
42	53	300	5+3+3+0+0	11
Total	165	956		59
General Total	1121 (19x 59)			

Sura number	Ha	Meem	The total of digits	Total
43	44	324	4+4+3+2+4	17
44	16	150	1+6+1+5+0	13
45	31	200	3+1+2+0+0	6
46	36	225	3+6+2+2+5	18
Total	127	899		54
General Total	1026 (19x 54)			

The Probability Calculation of the Initials "Ha" and "Meem"

1- The probability of the totals of the "*Ha*"-"*Meem*" letters in the 7 suras in succession being a multiple of 19 is 1/ 19. In these suras the said letters are used 2147 (113x19) times.

2- There is no apparent reason for the total of digits in the frequencies of combination letters (*Ha, Meem*) of the seven chapters to be 113 as well. We have to calculate the probability of getting the number 113 for the total of digits. We have to find in which interval that number has the probability of occurrence, in order to be able to calculate the probability in question.

We know that the total number of repetitions of letters "*Ha*" and "*Meem*" is 2147. No matter how those letters are distributed throughout the suras, 2147 will not be spoiled, and the probability of that number's being a multiple of 19 will still be 1/19. But the total of digits of letter numbers in each sura may total up to 113; that number could be inferior or superior to 113. I prepared two imaginary tables in order to show how inferior or superior the total of the digits could be when the total of "*Ha*" and "*Meem*" initials is 2147. By doing so, we will learn the extent of the interval and we will be able to make the probability calculation of digits.

The example for the inferior number

Sura number	Ha	Meem	The total of digits	Total
40	101	400	1+0+1+4+0+0	6
41	100	301	1+0+0+3+0+1	5
42	100	100	1+0+0+1+0+0	2
43	102	110	1+0+2+1+1+0	5
44	101	320	1+0+1+3+2+0	7
45	100	112	1+0+0+1+1+2	5
46	100	100	1+0+0+1+0+0	2
Total	704	1443		**32**
General Total	2147 (19x **113**)			

The example for the superior number

Sura number	Ha	Meem	The total of digits	Total
40	99	198	9+9+1+9+8	36
41	99	298	9+9+2+9+8	37
42	99	298	9+9+2+9+8	37
43	99	198	9+9+1+9+8	36
44	99	198	9+9+1+9+8	36
45	99	198	9+9+1+9+8	36
46	99	66	9+9+6+6	30
Total	693	1454		**248**
General Total	2147 (19x **113**)			

In order to have 113, our interval is approximately between 32 and 248. This interval consists of more than 200 numbers. I will round it to 200 in order to make our calculation easier. So the probability of getting a whole number like 113 from this interval is 1/200.

Up till now, our probability calculation has been equal to 1/19 x 1/200.

3- When we remember that the 2nd verse of the 42nd sura divides the "*Ha-Meem*" initialed suras into two equal parts, and when we examine the first part of the 40th, 41st and 42nd suras, we see that the total of the initials used here is 1121 (59x19), and that is a multiple of 19. When we add this to our probability calculation, the result is 1/19 x 1/200 x 1/19.

You should be careful in one respect; we are calculating only for the first group, which consists of three suras whose initials are a multiple of 19. But we should not calculate the second group's initials' being a multiple of 19. Because if a whole is a multiple of 19 and if one part of this whole is a multiple of 19 as well, then the other part is automatically a multiple of 19, too. This is a mathematical property. We calculated the probability of the whole as the multiple of 19 (our calculation for the seven suras), then we calculated the probability for the first part (first three suras) so we should not add the second part (the last four suras) to our reckoning.

We saw that in the first "*Ha-Meem*" group, the total of digits of the numbers indicating the frequency of initial letters is 59, which is the same as the total of the repetition numbers for that particular group. Thus, we should add this point to our probability calculation. If we make imaginary tables as before, we shall see that there is an interval that consists of more than 50 whole numbers. So the probability of having a number like 59 from this interval can be represented by 1/50. While we add this result to our probability, we should not add the same probability to the second table.

Let us calculate now the probability of "*Ha-Meem*" initials that occur in the Quran according to our previous explanations:

$$1/19 \times 1/200 \times 1/19 \times 1/50 = 1/3,610,000$$

This shows that the code 19 presents a probability of 1/3,610,000 with its relation to "*Ha-Meem*" initials. Even this small part of code

19 is miraculous. If we calculated all the probabilities of the data related to code 19, imagine what the result would be!

If we group *"Ha-Meem"* initialed suras as 41-42-43 and 40 44-45-46, we are faced with the same characteristics. Let's look at the tables:

Sura number	Ha	Meem	The total of digits	Total
41	48	276	4+8+2+7+6	27
42	53	300	5+3+3+0+0	11
43	44	324	4+4+3+2+4	17
Total	145	900		55
Grand Total	1045 (19x 55)			

Sura number	Ha	Meem	The total of digits	Total
40	64	380	6+4+3+8+0	21
44	16	150	1+6+1+5+0	13
45	31	200	3+1+2+0+0	6
46	36	225	3+6+2+2+5	18
Total	147	955		58
Grand Total	1102 (19x 58)			

Some of you may wonder why I did not include these tables in our probability calculation. If we add these tables to our calculation we have to multiply 1/19 x 1/50 = 1/950 with our result. When we divided the suras as 40-41-42 and 43-44-45-46 we had a logical reason. But dividing in this manner we cannot come up with any logical reason. Maybe someone can find a reason for this, as this division may be related to the meanings of the suras or something similar. But as I could not find a reason, I did not take the previous tables into account.

For 1400 years, people wondered why there were initial letters at the beginnings of 29 suras. The reason for this is now clarified by the code 19. For those who want to go further and be free from their suspicions and closer to God, 19 is a mediator.

35- This is one of the greatest
36- A warning to mankind
37- For those among you who wish to advance or regress.
74-The Hidden, 35-37

We obtain mathematical data on the number 19 mostly from *Basmalah* and initial letters. The *Basmalah* with its 19 letters, and the initial letters which are at the beginning of the suras guard the Quran against any harm.

30- Over it is 19.
74-The Hidden, 30

There are other miraculous formations related to 19 besides the *Bamalah* and the initial letters. The information I gave about the numbers in the Quran and the remarkable points in the sura The Hidden are perfect examples. Since the scope of our book is not large enough to give all the data on 19, I have to limit its content about this miracle.

THE 19TH SURA FROM THE END: THE HANGING

When we count back from the end of the Quran 19 suras, we come across the sura Alaq (The Hanging). The number of verses in the sura The Hanging is 19.

How many verses are there in the 19th sura from the end?	19

The first 5 verses of the sura The Hanging are said to be the first verses to be revealed; that may well be so, since these first 5 verses consist of 19 words and 76 (19x4) letters. Since I obtained this information from a *hadith*, I can not attest to its validity, as some people may object. But it is interesting that the 19th sura from the end consists of 19 verses.

In addition, the only sura whose last word is "God" is the 82nd sura (The Shattering), and this sura consists of 19 verses. This sura is the first sura of the Quran that has 19 verses. And the word "God," used as the last word of this sura, is the 19th occurence of the word "God" in the Quran when counted from the end.

How many verses are there in the sura the Shattering?	19
When we count back from the end of the Quran, how many times does the word "God" appear until the last word "God" in the sura The Shattering?	19

Additionally, if we look at every sura from the beginning of the Quran with a prime number as its number of verses, the 19th such sura is 82 (The Shattering), and this sura is the first one having the prime number 19 as its number of verses.

The mathematical miracle of the Quran proves that the number of verses and the order of suras are arranged by God. All the data we have seen throughout this book prove this.

Some researchers wrote all the verse numbers consecutively according to various rules and formed new numbers, which were multiples of 19. In order to use these numbers, this operation needs to be valid in the light of probability calculations. As I have no such probability calculation, I abstain from commenting on these numbers. Let us give an example of this hypothesis: If we write the verse numbers of a sura one by one after the total number of verses of each sura (such as 7123456728861234...), we arrive at a number consisting of 12692 (19x668) figures and this number is said to be an exact multiple of 19. This hypothesis seems interesting, but I make no claims since I have not taken into account the numbers consisting of many figures within the limits of the probability calculation, and I have not checked the numbers for their correctness.

As I mentioned before, I have not discussed in this book all the claims and data that are related to the code 19. The code 19 in the

Quran has more aspects than are covered by this book. I plan to write a detailed book about this subject in the future.

SIGN, EVIDENCE, WORD AND 19

As I have mentioned, most of the words rendered as "sign" or "miracle" in the translations of the Quran stem from only one word in Arabic: "*ayat.*" I stated that 19 was a miracle of God. Here, the word "miracle or sign" (*ayat*) related to 19 is used 380 (19x20) times to mean the signs of God. (This word means the sign of kingdom in verse 2:248 and it also implies the signs that human beings display in verse 26:128. Since these usages do not mean the signs of God, the count does not include them).

The number of uses of the word "ayat," which implies the signs (miracles) of God	380 (19x20)

The miracle of 19 is a clear evidence of God. The word "*bayyina*" (evidence) is used 19 times in the Quran.

The number of uses of the word "bayyina"(evidence)	19

The Quran is the word of God and 19 is the miracle manifesting itself in the words of God. As you can see, there is a connection between the word "word" (*kalam*) and 19. The words "*kalam, kalimah*" are used 38 (19x2) times to mean the words of God. (These words are used 12 times to mean the words of human beings.)

The number of uses of "word" (kalam, kalimah) which imply the words of God	38 (19x2)

RELATIONSHIP BETWEEN GOD AND MAN AND 19

We can witness code 19 in the verbs that show the relation between God and man in the Quran. As we have seen in the last example and in others prior to that, the code 19 is not only related to the counting of words, but the meanings and the contexts of the words are important as well. For instance, as we have seen, the two "*ayat*" words (sign) are used to indicate the "signs" human beings show. When we exclude these two words, the number is 380 (19x20). It had to be like this since 19 is a sign of God. Consequently, the word "*ayat*" related to 19 is the word "*ayat*" meaning the sign of God. Of course, when the word "ayat" is counted, it is the word "*ayat*" meaning the proof of God that is counted.

Now, we should examine whether the verbs indicating the relationship between God and man are related to the code 19 or not; for this, the verbs emphasizing the relationship between God and man should be counted. Let us examine six examples, which were studied extensively by Prof. Adib Majul:

The verb **"amara:"** This verb is used for the orders that God gives. It is used with this meaning 38 (19x2) times. In its other meaning, denoting orders given by others, it is used 35 times.

How many times is the verb "amara" used to indicate God's orders?	38 (19x2)

The sura and the verse numbers of the suras having the verb "*amara*," that signifies God's orders to man:

Serial number	1	2	3	4	5	6	7	8	9	10
Sura and verse numbers	2-27	2-67	2-68	2-222	3-80	3-80	4-58	4-60	5-117	6-14
Serial number	11	12	13	14	15	16	17	18	19	20
Sura and verse numbers	6-71	6-163	7-12	7-28	7-29	9-31	10-72	10-104	11-112	12-40
Serial number	21	22	23	24	25	26	27	28	29	30
Sura and verse numbers	13-21	13-25	13-36	15-94	16-50	16-90	17-16	27-91	27-91	39-11
Serial number	31	32	33	34	35	36	37	**38** (19x2)		
Sura and verse numbers	39-12	40-66	42-15	42-15	66-6	66-6	80-23	98-5		

The verb **"hakama:"** This verb is used 19 times to mean divine commands and judgment. The commands and judgment of the Book (the Quran) are God's commands; in other words, God instructs us by means of the Book. Thus, instructing and judging by means of the Book are added to this enumeration. Apart from these uses, this verb is used 19 times.

How many times is the verb "Hakama" used to indicate the relationship between God and humans?	19

The sura and the verse numbers where the verb *"hakama"* shows the relationship between God and man:

Serial number	1	2	3	4	5	6	7	8	9	10
Sura and verse numbers	2-113	2-213	3-23	3-55	4-141	5-1	7-87	10-109	12-80	13-41

Serial number	11	12	13	14	15	16	17	18	19
Sura and verse numbers	16-124	22-56	22-69	24-48	24-51	39-3	39-46	40-48	60-10

The verb **"khalaqa:"** This verb related to God's creation is used 171 (19x9) times. Apart from these uses, this verb is used 13 times in reference to creations by those other than God, to express and comment upon the fact that idols cannot create, or as an expression to describe disbelievers' beliefs about idols' creation.

How many times is the word "khalaqa" used for God's creation?	171 (19x9)

The verb **"qada:"** This verb explains God's determination. This verb is used 38 (19x2) times in relation to God.

How many times is the word "qada" used for God's determination?	38 (19x2)

The sura and verse numbers where the word "*qada*" is used:

Serial number	1	2	3	4	5	6	7	8	9	10
Sura and verse numbers	2-117	2-210	3-47	6-2	6-8	6-60	8-42	8-44	10-11	10-19
Serial number	11	12	13	14	15	16	17	18	19	20
Sura and verse numbers	10-47	10-54	10-93	11-44	11-110	14-22	15-66	17-4	17-23	19-35
Serial number	21	22	23	24	25	26	27	28	29	30
Sura and verse numbers	19-39	20-114	27-78	28-44	33-36	34-14	35-36	39-42	39-69	39-75
Serial number	31	32	33	34	35	36	37	38	(19x2)	
Sura and verse numbers	40-20	40-68	40-78	41-12	41-45	42-21	42-14	45-17		

The verb **"allame:"** This verb means to teach. This verb is used 19 times to express that God teaches directly or by means of His angels. And this verb is used three times to indicate the teachings of human beings (5-4, 20-71 and 26-49).

How many times is the word "allame" used for God's teaching?	19

The sura and the verse numbers where the verb "*allame*" is used:

Serial number	1	2	3	4	5	6	7	8	9	10
Sura and verse numbers	2-31	2-32	2-239	2-251	2-282	4-113	5-4	5-110	12-37	12-68
Serial number	11	12	13	14	15	16	17	18	19	
Sura and verse numbers	12-101	18-65	21-80	36-69	53-5	55-2	55-4	96-4	96-5	

The verb **"ehteda:"** This verb is used 38 (19x2) times to mean God's guiding the righteous. It is used once to mean Jews' and Christians' presentation of a wrong way as a righteous one (2-135).

How many times is the word "ehteda" used for God's guidance?	38 (19x2)

The sura and the verse numbers where the verb "*ehteda*" is used to mean God's guidance:

Serial number	1	2	3	4	5	6	7	8	9	10
Sura and verse numbers	2-53	2-137	2-150	2-170	3-20	3-103	4-98	5-104	5-105	6-97
Serial number	11	12	13	14	15	16	17	18	19	20
Sura and verse numbers	7-43	7-158	10-108	10-108	16-15	16-16	17-15	17-15	18-57	19-76
Serial number	21	22	23	24	25	26	27	28	29	30
Sura and verse numbers	20-82	20-135	21-31	23-49	24-54	27-24	27-41	27-41	27-92	27-92
Serial number	31	32	33	34	35	36	37	38 (19x2)		
Sura and verse numbers	28-64	32-3	34-50	39-41	43-10	46-11	47-17	53-30		

These represent a partial summary of Cesar Adib Majul's work on the relation between 19 and the verbs that indicate God's signs, orders, teachings, creation, determination, judgment, and guidance. Obviously, all evidence related to the code 19 has not been discovered yet and further research is necessary. The data I have presented are sufficient to show that this evidence is magnificent and cannot be imitated. I hope that these examples will encourage researchers to study the mathematical structure and the related semantic fields of the Quran further.

35- This is one of the greatest
36- A warning to mankind
37- For those among you who wish to advance or regress.
74-The Hidden, 35-37

EVEN AND ODD NUMBERS

3- By the even and the odd

89-The Dawn, 3

As you see, the 3rd verse of the 89th sura in the Quran draws attention to the "even" and "odd" numbers. The word *"wa"* in Arabic is used to emphasize the words that succeed it when it is used at the beginning of a sentence (I translated the word *"wa"* as *"by"*). Korosh Cemnishon and Abdullah Jalghoom were inspired by the verse I mentioned above and examined the suras and verses of the Quran according to even and odd numbers. This examination proves that both the sura numbers and the verse numbers were arranged in perfect order.

When we want to show the sura numbers and the number of verses, we indicate them in figures, for example; the sura The Prologue 1:7 (the 1st sura and 7 verses) and the sura The Cow 2:286 (the 2nd sura and the 286 verses). In the table below, we add 1 and 7 (the sura number and the number of the verses of the sura The Prologue) and we get the number "8." Since the number "8" is an even number, we write it on the place reserved for even numbers. And we add 3 and 200 (the sura number and the number of the verses of the sura The Family of Imran), then we get the number "203." As this number is an odd number, we will write it in the place where odd numbers are. We have done the same operation for all other suras and verses of the Quran, as you can see in the table below. I think that this table alone is enough to show that the order of suras and verse numbers are protected and the Quran has a miraculous mathematical structure.

Sura number	Total of verses	Total	Even	Odd
1	7	8	8	-
2	286	288	288	-
3	200	203	-	203
4	176	180	180	-
5	120	125	-	125
6	165	171	-	171
. . . .				
57	29	86	86	-
. . . .				
109	6	115	-	115
110	3	113	-	113
111	5	116	116	-
112	4	116	116	-
113	5	118	118	-
114	6	120	120	-
Total 6555	6234	-	6234	6555

The total of sura numbers in the Quran is 6555; the total of the odd numbers in the table is also 6555. These two numbers are equal, although independent from each other. Moreover, the total of the number of verses in the Quran is 6234 and the total of the even numbers in the table is 6234. They did not have to be equal but they are. The equality of these numbers is one of the countless proofs that all the sura numbers and the number of the verses of the Quran are arranged by divine wisdom.

We know that the number of the suras in the Quran is 114 (19x6). If we write 19 in the form of 10+9, we have 6x(10+9). From this equation we obtain 60, and this number represents the number of suras whose total verses are even numbers. From this equation we also obtain 54, which is the number of the suras whose total verses consist of odd numbers. The sura numbers of 30 of these 60 suras are odd numbers and the sura numbers of the other 30 of these 60 suras are even numbers. The sura numbers of 27 of the 54 suras are odd numbers and the sura numbers of 27 of these 54 suras are even numbers. And their frequency may be given as follows: 3x(10+9). Thus, we get 30 and 27.

$$114=6x19=6x(10+9)=(6x10)+(6x9)=60+54$$
$$57=3x19=3x(10+9)=(3x10)+(3x9)=30+27$$

We have four groups. Let us give an example for each group:

1. Suras with odd numbers- the number of verses with odd numbers. Example: The sura The Prologue (1st sura, 7 verses)
2. Suras with odd numbers- the number of verses with even numbers. Example: The Family of Imran (3rd sura, 200 verses)
3. Suras with even numbers- the number of verses with odd numbers. Example: The Cattle (6th sura, 165 verses)
4. Suras with even numbers- the number of verses with even numbers. Example: The Women (4th sura, 176 verses)

We can show the table that contains the four groups:

114 SURAS			
60 (THE SURAS WITH AN EVEN NUMBER OF VERSES)		54 (THE SURAS WITH AN ODD NUMBER OF VERSES)	
30 EVEN NUMBERED SURAS	30 ODD NUMBERED SURAS	27 EVEN NUMBERED SURAS	27 ODD NUMBERED SURAS

If you change the place of a single verse in a sura, the system is upset. For instance, if the sura The Prologue consisted of 8 verses, the system would change, and if the sura The Family of Imran were the

2nd sura (it is the 3rd sura of the Quran), this mathematical system would change again. Only if we added 2 or 4 verses (even numbers) to an even total or subtracted 2 or 4 verses from an even total, the numbers in the table above would not change. However, if we added any number to the odd totals, all the data in the table would change. If we changed the places of a sura whose sura number is an even number and a sura whose sura number is an odd number, all the data would change and the system would be upset once again. To insist that the origin of such a table is by coincidence may be due to ignorance of the probability assumptions or a result of pure stubbornness. God draws our attention to the fact that He has numerically structured the Book (83rd sura, 9th and 20th verses). He also refers to the "even" and "odd" numbers. These tables we examine will help us to perceive the wisdom of God.

We can examine the suras in two groups:

1. Homogeneous Suras.
2. Heterogeneous Suras.

The homogeneous suras consist of the suras whose sura number and total verse number are both odd or are both even. The heterogeneous suras consist of the suras whose sura number is even when the total verse number is odd, or vice versa. There are 57 homogeneous and 57 heterogeneous suras. You can understand this better by following the table:

114 SURAS			
HOMOGENOUS SURAS		**HETEROGENEOUS SURAS**	
57 SURAS		57 SURAS	
30 SURAS even sura number even total verses	27 SURAS odd sura number odd total verses	30 SURAS even sura number odd total verses	27 SURAS odd sura number even total verses

As the total of the sura numbers and verse numbers are meaningful in relation to their being even and odd, so the number of even and odd suras and the number of even and odd verses are meaningful, as can be seen in the symmetrical tables. We should add that there is more, and this proves the divine design regarding even and odd.

We have seen that the total of the sura numbers in the Quran is 6555. This number is also equal to the total of the odd numbers on the table. The total of the numbers in succession is counted with the help of the following formula: $nx(n+1)/2$. Thus, we can count the total of the sura numbers in the Quran like this:

$$114x(114+1)/2=6555$$

Jordanian researcher Jalghoom thought that there were 60 suras that had verses whose total number was an even number and 54 suras that had verses whose total number was an odd number. And then he divided this formula into two parts and wrote them as follows:

$$60x(114+1)/2=3450$$
$$54x(114+1)/2=3105$$
$$Total=6555$$

Here, we come across an interesting conclusion: the total of the sura numbers of the suras with verses whose total number is an even number is 3450, and the total of the sura numbers of the suras with verses whose total number is an odd number is 3105.

Let us explain the example I have given above in terms of its conclusion: let us take the 3rd and 17th suras. The 3rd sura consists of 200 verses; that means that the 3rd sura is a sura with verses whose total number is an even number. The 17th sura consists of 111 verses; that means that the 17th sura is a sura with verses whose total number is an odd number. Let us suppose that the sura numbers of these suras were exchanged. In that case, if you added the sura numbers of the suras with verses whose total number is an even number, the result would be 3464. If you added the sura numbers of suras with verses whose total number is an odd number, it would make 3091. Thus, the data we have in that equation would change.

It means that even if you changed the order of two suras in the Quran, this mathematical table would have to change. And this shows that the sura numbers of the Quran were arranged by heavenly means and that this arrangement will not accept even a single change.

If we divide the Quran into two parts, the first part ends at the 57th sura, the sura Iron (*Hadid*). If we add the sura numbers of the first 57 suras, it makes 1653. If we multiply the sura number of the sura Iron (57) with the number of verses in the Iron sura (29), we have: 57x29=1653 (19x87). Thus, when we examine the Quran by dividing it into two parts, the sura Iron implies that we are going to have interesting mathematical data.

The total of the numbers of suras in the first half of the Quran (1+2+3+.................+55+56+57)	1653 (19x87)
Multiplication result of the last sura's number(57) in the first half of the Quran by the number(29) of verses in that sura	1653 (19x87)

There are 29 odd-numbered and 28 even-numbered suras in the first part of the Quran. There are 28 odd-numbered and 29 even-numbered suras in the second part of the Quran. This is because of a mathematical property, because all numbers following one another show this characteristic. However, it is interesting that while there are 28 "heterogeneous" and 29 "homogeneous" suras in the first part of the Quran, there are 29 "heterogeneous" and 28 "homogeneous" suras in the second part. This conclusion is not the result of a mathematical property. This is one of the endless miracles of the Quran. (Please remember the table about homogeneous and heterogeneous suras.)

Please examine the table:

114 SURAS			
First half of the Quran		**Second half of the Quran**	
29 odd numbered suras	28 even numbered suras	29 even numbered suras	28 odd numbered suras
29 homogenous suras	28 heteregenous suras	29 heteregenous suras	28 homogenous suras

The examination of the sura numbers and the number of verses in the Quran as "odd" and "even" is enough to prove that the order of suras and the number of verses in the Quran were arranged by heavenly means and the mathematical system protects this structure. This book presents endless examples showing that it is beyond human ability and was revealed by The Creator.

FRIGHTENED ONES

In this book, I have tried to give the basic data for the mathematical code in the Quran, to make the book readable. I also wanted to address a different reader group who are interested in mathematics; I examined subjects relating to prime numbers and probability calculations which require some knowledge of mathematics. I tried to present the subject as simply as I could. If you have any difficulty in understanding certain parts of the book, I advise you to look through the parts that seem clear to you and read the parts that seem difficult with someone who has knowledge about these subjects.

This mathematical miracle of the Quran is common to all Muslims (submitters to God alone) regardless of which religious sect they adhere to, since this miracle belongs to the Quran and the Quran has drawn attention to it. Nonetheless, besides disbelievers, I see a great number of people who believe in Islam but do not appreciate this miracle as they should. Many people are blindfolded to this miracle: they are like people who think that the sun will vanish if they close their eyes. Thus, the sura expressing the code 19 in the Quran draws attention to the people who turn a deaf ear to the messages of God:

49- Why then do they turn away from the Reminder?
50- As though they are frightened asses
51- Fleeing from a lion

74-The Hidden, 49-51

The miracles cannot be understood by people who approach them like football fanatics. The miracles performed by the prophets prior to Muhammad caused an increase in the fanaticism of many disbelievers. To understand these miracles, one must have a careful mind and a conscience free from prejudice, stubbornness and arrogance. The people who approach them saying, "How can I deny?" instead of saying, "How can I understand? What is the truth?" can never profit from miracles. These people, instead of asking, "How can I become a person of whom God may approve?" ask, "How can I ingratiate myself with relatives and friends?" The people afraid of being in conflict with their surroundings rather than with God cannot understand God's signs.

WHAT HAVE WE GAINED SO FAR?

We have seen that the mathematical code in the Quran is not a mere embellishment. The Quran draws our attention to 19, saying that, **"This is one of the greatest."** (74:35). And we have seen again that the mathematical code in the Quran is a system that actually protects the Quran and corrects man's mistakes. This system presents the wisdom that has been a subject of wonder for 1400 years. We have examined the data about the miracle of 19 and other mathematical data in the Quran throughout the book. I shall give ten examples of what we have gained from the mathematical miracle of the Quran:

1. The claim of the 23rd and 24th verses of the sura The Cow that people will not be able to imitate even one sura of the Quran is confirmed rationally and objectively by the mathematical miracle of the

412

Quran. It is now understood that all the suras, and even the verses of the Quran, are like the pieces of a big puzzle. If you destroy even one piece, you destroy the entire mathematical system in the Quran. The existence of this mathematical system in the Quran depends on every one of these parts, so one sura of the Quran represents the whole system. The Creator of the whole system is the Creator of each sura. Even one sura has all the power of the system. What a fascinating system it is!

2. Once the code 19 was understood, the reason why the 30th and 31st verses of the sura The Hidden drew attention to 19 became clearer: it is a figure that has been changing wrong beliefs and has been instrumental in dispelling traces of doubt in the hearts of monotheists.

3. The meaning of the verse; **"Surely, We have sent down a Reminder, We, and We are protecting it"** (15:9) is understood better when it was proven. that God protects the Quran with a mathematical code. For example, the code 19 proved that the word *"bastatan"* in the Quran was not written with the letter *"Sad,"* but with the letter *"Seen."* This shows that the code 19 is an active protector. God states in the verses that He protects the Quran Personally. It is clear that the code that the Quran calls attention to and that God placed in the Quran, protects the Quran. The mathematical miracle has helped us to understand this fact.

4. The code 19 has shown why the Quran consisted of 114 suras and it has also proved that the number of verses and the order of the suras in the Quran were arranged by heavenly means.

5. It is now understood why the *Basmalah* is in the form of **"Bismillahirrahmanirraheem"** and why it is not in the form of *"Bismihuazizulkarim"* or *"Bismihusubhanehu."* It shows why the *Basmalah* does not consist of other names of God. The group of words most frequently repeated in the world is coded by 19 and is miraculous.

6. The miracle of 19 explains why the *Basmalah* was not at the beginning of the sura Repentance, which is the 9th sura of the Quran, although it is at the beginning of all the other suras. (Please remember the missing *Basmalah* is in the sura the The Ant, which is the 19th sura from the 9th sura).

7. The code 19 has given the reason why some numbers in the Quran were mentioned in a different way. For instance, the number 309 in the 18th sura is described as 300 and 9. The wisdom of these

unique expressions of numbers has been understood thanks to the code 19 (If the number 309 had been stated directly, then the total of the numbers in the Quran would not be a multiple of 19).

8. The reason why some suras in the Quran started with initial letters was a cause for wonder for 1400 years. Before the code 19 in the Quran was discovered, there was groundless speculation. This secret, which had remained hidden for 1400 years, was revealed thanks to 19, which is described as **"one of the greatest"** in the Quran.

9. The probability calculations emphasize that it is impossible for man to have created this miracle, that is not a matter of coincidence. This shows why the person who said, **"This is nothing but the word of a human,"** (74-The Hidden, 25) was answered by the code 19. Moreover, code 19 gives visual presentations, we can see these presentations in the tables, all data indicated and verified, so that the following verse is understood better: **"It is tablets for people."** (74-The Hidden, 29).

10. Besides the Quran's literary appeal, which can only be understood with a good knowledge of Arabic, the mathematical miracle uses the universal language of mathematics. For the universal Book a universal miracle! God, who wrote the universe in the language of mathematics, also wrote the Book He sent down for guidance in the language of mathematics, and the data we produced about the mathematical code in the Quran proves this miracle.

THE LAST WORDS

FROM THE BIG BANG TO MOTHER'S WOMB, FROM UNDER THE SEAS TO MATHEMATICS

Throughout this book, I have examined subjects like the creation of the universe with the Big Bang, the account of our development in our mother's wombs, the description of the inner waves in the seas, the mathematical miracle in lexical concordance and finally, the miracle 19. We have witnessed the extraordinary evidence of the Quran on different subjects. The Quran is sufficient for people who look for signs and miracles to believe in religion.

> **51- Is it not sufficient for them that We have revealed the Book to you which is read out to them? It is indeed a grace and reminder for people who believe.**
>
> *29-The Spider, 51*

The book that presents all these miracles is coded miraculously in a mathematical system. The Quran, which describes the disbelievers' psychology, tells us that all these people who do not have any intention of believing in spite of all these miracles will continue not to believe. There is an example in the Quran that describes the disbelievers' minds in their own words:

> **132- They said: "No matter what kind of sign you show us, to bewitch us, we will not believe in you."**
>
> *7-The Purgatory, 132*

THE PATHS IN FRONT OF US

You have read about the miracles of the Quran in this book. Now there are several options before us. I can sum up our ideas about these options as follows:

1- **You can deny that the Quran is God's miraculous book**: If you choose this option, your life Hereafter will be in peril. The Quran, that shows all these signs, is at the same time a hope for mankind. The Quran tells us over and over again that we will not vanish after we die, and that the Creator who created us will recreate us. Disbelieving and rejecting the message of the Quran, its prophecies and miracles is the result of a stubbornness that will only injure the disbeliever.

2- **You can witness God's miracle and you can accept that the Quran is God's word. But you will continue not to spare enough time for God and religion and you do not apply the Quran's message to your life even though you believe in it**: This means you have not profited enough from the Quran and from its miracles. Do not forget that these signs approve the Quran's message. The Quran tells us that the existence of God is more important than anything else, and that even though this world will end one day, life in the other world will last forever. You should consider the importance of God's existence, the other world, the shortness of this world's life, death, and the fact that all our organs and our body are given to us by God. You should also consider that the miracles of the Quran are the signs that prove the Quran's message.

3- **You can see God's miracle and you can accept that the Quran is God's word. You will try to remember God and live as He has ordered. But as time passes, you can get used to the Quran's miracles and the impact of those miracles may sink into oblivion. Then God may not be in your mind as often as He had been and you may start adopting an attitude and lifestyle in contradiction to God's law**: Therefore our advice to you is to read the Quran frequently. You should go over the Quran's miracles and remember that even though time passes, the Quran and its miracles will not lose any of their value.

4- **You can accept that the Quran is God's word and His miracle and you can intend to live as the Quran orders, either before reading this book or after reading it**: This is what the Quran wants.

Our intention in writing this book was to make a contribution, although on a humble scale. To turn to the Creator every second for a lifetime... We must not forget the blessing and generosity of our Creator. We must always appreciate having faith based on knowledge and being blessed by eternal hope. We must always feel the gratitude of being created out of nothing.

THE BIGGEST CLAIM:
AN UNCHALLENGEABLE MIRACLE

To say that the Quran is God's word is a big assertion. We can even show two alternatives for those who deny that the Quran is the word God:

1. Either the Quran is the greatest truth (What can be more important than the words of the Creator of all things?)

2. Or the Quran is the greatest lie. (What can be a bigger lie than saying that it is from God?) There is no bigger deception than attributing it to Him, since there cannot be a greater entity than He.

No one can say that the Quran is an ordinary book. Even disbelievers do not accept this. And all the signs we have seen throughout this book take place in the Book (the Quran), which has the greatest claim and is the most extraordinary book. All the signs throughout the book demonstrate that the Quran's claim is true; this book with its ultimate claim is an unchallengeable miracle. A "lie" does not and cannot suit a book that is 100% correct on subjects so different from each other. After all the things we have learned in this book, let us answer the questions we ask. (Some of the answers we gave for the Quran are also acceptable for the other books God sent through the other prophets.)

Is there another book that places God in the center of life and gives Him the value He deserves?

- No.

- Is there another book on earth with a greater claim than this?

- No.

- Is there another book on earth that explains events that could not be known 1400 years ago, all of its information true, from the depths of space to beneath the seas, from development in our mother's wombs to the end of the universe?

- No

- Is there any other serious book that gives meaning to life, says there is an afterlife and gives mankind the hope it needs?
- No
- Is there another book that, while achieving all these, also has a mathematical code system and maintains the wholeness in its meaning and code?
- No
- Is there another book that confirms all the prophets throughout history, Noah, Moses and Jesus... the prophets who brought a common message? A book that approves of all the prophets and their books, since it is the last book?
- No
- Is there really another reliable book that we can choose as a guide for ourselves?
- No
- Does the Quran have an alternative?
- No
- Do the disbelievers have any excuse?
- No

All the data show that the book that has the ultimate claim is also the ultimate and unchallengeable miracle. The miracles of the Quran never end; a new miracle is revealed every day:

88- Say, "If all the humans and the jinns came together in order to produce a Quran like this, they would surely fail, no matter how much assistance they lent one another."
17-The Children of Israel, 88

GUIDE TO PRONUNCIATION

For proper names and some other words in this book, original Turkish spelling has been used. The following is a short guide to pronouncing these words.

Vowels in Turkish are pronounced as in French or German:
a - as in father
e - as in met
i - as in big
o - between the o in role or the au in author
u - as in rule

In addition, there are three other vowels that do not occur in English:
ı - undotted i, pronounced as the vowel sound in the second syllables of words such as herbal or function
ö - as in German
ü - as in German

Consonants are pronounced as in English, except for the following:
c - as j in jam, e.g. cami (mosque) = jahmy
ç - as ch in chat, e.g. çorba (soup) = chorba
g - as in get, never as in gem
ğ - is almost silent and tends to lengthen the preceding vowel
ş - as in sugar, e.g. çeşme (fountain) = cheshme

BIBLIOGRAPHY

Adair, K. Robert. *The Great Design*. New York: Oxford University Press, 1982.

Adler, Irwing. *The Sun and its Family*. New York: Signet Books, 1962.

Ahmed, Ali. *Al Quran: A Contemporary Translation*. New Jersey: Princeton University Press, 1994.

Alberts, Bruce. *Molecular Biology of the Cell*. New York: Gorland Publisher, 1994.

Ali, Yusuf A. *The Holy Quran: Translation and Commentary*. Durban: Islamic Propagation Centre International.

Alpher, Ralph A., Robert Herman. *Genesis of the Big Bang*. New York: Oxford University Press, 2001.

Al-Rehaili, Abdullah M. *This is the Truth*. 3rd ed. Alharamain Islamic Foundation, 1999.

Aquinas. *Selected Philosophical Writings*. Ed: Timothy McDermeott. Oxford: 1998.

Arık, Abdullah. *Beyond Probability*. Tucson: 2000.

Aristotle. *Metafizik*. Trans. Ahmet Arslan. Istanbul: Sosyal Yayınları, 1996.

— *Physics*. Trans. Robin Waterfield. New York: Oxford University Press, 1996.

Armstrong, Karen. *A History of God*. New York: Knopf Press, 1994.

Aron, Raymond. *Main Currents in Sociological Thought*. translated by Richard Howard and Helen Weaver. Harmondsworth: Penguin Books, 1968.

Asimov, Isaac. *Asimov's Guide to Science*. New York: Basic Books, 1972.

— *Inside the Atom*. New York: Amelend-Schuman, 1969.

Ateş, Süleyman. *Yüce Kuran'ın Çağdaş Tefsiri*. Istanbul: Yeni Ufuklar Neşriyat, 1989.

Aydın, Mehmet S. *Din Felsefesi*. 8th ed. İzmir: İzmir İlahiyat Fak. Yayınları, 1999.

Baird, Thomas P. *Scheba's Landing*. New York: Brace and World Press, 1964.

Barrow, John and Frank Tipler. *The Anthropic Cosmological Principle*. Oxford: Oxford University Press, 1986.

Behe, Michael J. *Darwin's Black Box*. New York: The Free Press, 2003.

Beltrami, Edward. *What is Random?* New York: Copernicus Press, 1999.

Berry, Adrian. *Bilimin Arka Yüzü*. 8th ed. Trans. R. Levent Aysever. Ankara: Tübitak Yayınları, 1998.

Bolles, Edmund Blair. *Galileo's Commandment* . New York: W.H. Freeman, 1997.

Bova, Ben. *The Beauty of the Light*. New York: John Wiley and Sons Inc., 1988.

Brock, Thomas P. *Biology of Microorganisms*. New Jersey: Prentice Hall, 1984.

Brock, William. *The Norton History of Chemistry*. London: W.W. Norton, 1993.

Brown, Francis. *A Hebrew and English Lexicon of the Old Testament*. Oxford: 1906.

Bucaille, Maurice. *Mummies of the Pharaohs*. Trans. D. Pannell Alastair. New York: St. Martins Press, 1998.

— *The Bible, the Quran and Science*. Trans. A.D.Pannel. New Delphi: Milat Book Centre, 1995.

Chadwick, Henry. *The Early Church*. London: Penguin Books, 1993.

Chomsky, Noam. *Language and Mind*. New York: Harcourt Brace Jovanovich, 1972.

Cohen, I.B. *Isaac Newton's Papers and Letters on Natural Philosophy*. Cambridge: Cambridge University Press, 1958.

Cohen, Joel. *How Many People Can the Earth Support?* New York: Norton & Company, 1996.

Corbin, Henry. *İslam Felsefesi Tarihi*. 2nd ed. Trans. Hüseyin Hatemi. Istanbul: İletişim Yayınları, 1994.

Craig, William Lane. *The Cosmological Argument from Plato to Leibniz*. West Broadway: Wipfand Stock Publishers, 2001.

— *Theism, Atheism and Big Bang Cosmology*. New York: Clarendon Press, 1995.

Cramer, Freidrich. *Kaos ve Düzen*. Trans. Veysel Atayman. Istanbul: Alan Yayıncılık, 1998.

Crick, Francis. *Life itself: Its Origin and Nature*. London: MacDonald, 1982.

Crosby, Alfred W. *The Measure of Reality*. Cambridge: Cambridge University Press, 1998.

Çakar, Muharrem. *Sebeplilik Problemi ve Allah'ın Varlığı*. 3rd ed. Istanbul: İnkilap Yayınları, 1997.

Çelebi, İlyas. *Islam İnanç Sisteminde Akılcılık ve Kadı Abdulcebbar*. Istanbul:

Rağbet Yayınları, 2002

Dabrowska, Ewa. *Language, Mind, and Brain: Some Psychological and Neurological Constraints on Theories of Grammar.* Washington, D.C.: Georgetown University Press, 2004.

Daley, Roger. *Atmospheric Data Analysis.* New York : Cambridge University Press, 1993.

Davies, Paul. *The Fifth Miracle: The Search for the Origin and Meaning of Life.* New York: Simon & Schuster, 1998.

— *God and the New Physics.* New York: Touchstone Book, 1984.

— *The Last Three Minutes.* New York: Basic Books, 1994.

Davud, Abdulahad. *Tevrat ve İncil'e göre Hz. Muhammed.* Trans. Nusret Çam. Izmir: Nil Yayınları, 1992.

Dawkins, Richard. *The Blind Watchmaker.* London: Penguin Books, 1988.

Deedat, Ahmed, Edip Yüksel. *Kuran En Büyük Mucize.* 3rd ed. Istanbul: İnkilap Yayınları, 1984.

Dembski, William. *Intelligent Design.* Illinois: Intervarsity Press, 1999.

— *The Design Inference.* Cambridge: Cambridge University Press, 1998.

Dennett, Daniel. *Darwin's Dangerous Idea.* New York: Simon & Schuster, 1985.

Denton, Michael. *Nature's Destiny: How the Laws of Biology Reveal Purpose in the Universe.* New York: The Free Press, 1998.

Descartes, Rene. *Philosophical Essays : Discourse on Method; Meditations; Rules for the Direction of the Mind.* Translated, with an introd. and notes, by Laurence J. Lafleur. Indianapolis: Bobbs-Merrill, 1964.

Devlin, Keith. *Goodbye Descartes.* Toronto: John Wiley and Sons Inc., 1997.

Dorman, M. Emre. *Tanrı'nın Varlığının Kanıtlanmasında Kullanılan Modern Deliller: İnsancı İlke Örneği.* Istanbul: Marmara University, The Institute of Social Sciences, 2004.

Drees, Willem B. *Beyond the Big Bang: Quantum Cosmologies and God.* Illinois: Open Court Press, 1993.

Einstein, Albert. *Relativity: The Special and the General Theory.* London: Routledge, 2001.

The Encyclopedia of Islam. Leiden: A.J.Brill, 1971.

Engels, Frederick. *The Origin of the Family, Private Property, and the State.* London: Electric Book Co., 2001.

Fahri, Macit. *İslam Felsefesi Tarihi.* 5th ed. Trans. Kasım Turan. Istanbul: Birleşik Yayıncılık, 2000.

Feynman, Richard P. *The Feynman Lectures on Physics.* Mass.: Addison-Wesley Pub. Co., 1963.

— *The Character of Physical Law*. Cambridge: MIT Press, 1967.

Firsoff, A. V. *The Interior Planets*. London: Oliver and Boyel, 1968.

Flohn, Hermann. *Climate and Weather*. London: World University Library, 1968.

Fülsing, Albrecht. *Albert Einstein*. Middlesex: Penguin Books, 1997.

Gamow, George. *Dünyamızın Hayat Hikayesi*. Trans. Avni Yalakoğlu. Istanbul: Varlık Yayınları, 1963.

— *Thirty Years that Shook Physics : The Story of Quantum Theory*. New York: Dover Publications, 1985

Gell, Murray. *The Quark and the Jaguar*. New York: W. H. Freeman and Company, 1995.

Gilbert, Scott. E. *Developmental Biology*. Sunderland: Sinauer Associates, 1997.

Gleick, James. *Chaos : Making a New Science*. New York: Penguin, 1988.

Golshani, Mehdi. *The Holy Kuran and the Sciences of Nature*. New York: Institute of Global Studies, 1999.

Gore, Al. *Earth in the Balance*. New York: Plume Books, 1993.

Grayling, A. C. *Philosophy*. New York: Oxford University Press, 1998.

Greisch, Jean. *Wittgenstein'da Din Felsefesi*. Trans. Zeki Özcan. Bursa: Asa Kitapevi, 1999.

Gribbin, John. *In the Beginning: the Birth of the Living Universe*. London: Penguin, 1994.

Gürel, A. Osman. *Doğa Bilimleri Tarihi*. Ankara: İmge Kitabevi, 2001.

Han, Fetullah. *God, Universe and Man*. Lahor: Wajidalis Limited, 1982.

Hanson, R.P.C. *The Search for the Christian Doctrine of God: The Arian Controversy*. Edinburgh: T&T Clark, 1988.

Hartle, James. *Gravity: An Introduction to Einstein's General Relativity*. Mass.: Addison-Wesley Longman, 2002.

Hawking, Stephen. *A Brief History of Time*. London: Bantam Books, 1990.

— *The Universe in a Nutshell*. London: Bantam Books, 2001.

Hawking, Stephen and Penrose, R. *The Nature of Space and Time*. New Jersey: Princeton University Press, 1996.

Heilbroner, Robert L. *The Worldly Philosophers*. New York: Touchstone Books, 1992.

Hegel, Wilhelm Friedrich. *Phenomenology of Spirit*. Trans. A. V. Miller. Oxford: Oxford University Press, 1979.

Hobbes, Thomas. *Leviathan*. 3rd ed. Trans. Semih Lim. Istanbul: Yapı Kredi Yayınları, 2001.

Holmes, Hannah. *The Secret Life of Dust*. London: John Wiley and Sons, 2001.

Hopson, Janet L. *Essentials of Biology.* New York: McGraw-Hill, 1990.

Hoyle, Fred. *The Nature of the Universe.* Middlesex: Penguin Books, 1965.

— *A New Model for the Expanding Universe.* Monograph Notes, Royal Astronomy Society, 108, 1948.

Hume, David. *A Treatise of Human Nature.* Oxford: Oxford University Press, 2000.

— *Dialogues Concerning Natural Religion.* Indianapolis: Bobbs-Merrill, 1947.

Hussain, Iftekhar Bano. *The Astonishing Truths of the Holy Quran.* London: Ta-Ha Publishers, 1996.

The Interpreter's Dictionary of the Bible. New York: 1988.

Ibn Sina. *İşaretler ve Tembihler.* Istanbul: Litera Yayıncılık, 2005.

— *Metafizik.* Istanbul: Litera Yayıncılık, 2004.

Ibn Rüşd. *Metafizik Şerhi.* Istanbul: Litera Yayıncılık, 2004.

Jammer, Max. *Einstein and Religion: Physics and Theology.* Princeton: Princeton Press, 1999.

Jaki, Stanley. *God and the Cosmologists.* Washington D.C.: Regnery Gateway, 1989.

Kant, Immanuel. *Critique of Pure Reason.* Trans. Norman Kemp Smith. London: Palgrave Macmillan, 1933.

— *Critique of Practical Reason.* New York: Macmillan Pub, 1993.

— *Religion Within The Limits of Reason Alone.* New York: Harper, 1960.

— *Universal Natural History and Theory of The Heavens.* Edinburgh: Scottish Academic Press, 1981.

Kauffman, Stuart. *At Home in the Universe.* New York: Oxford University Press, 1995.

Kazi, Mazhar. *130 Evident Miracles in the Quran.* New York: Crescent Publishing House, 1988.

Kennett, J. P. *Marine Biology.* New Jersey: Prentice-Hall, 1982.

Kitchen, Kenneth. *The Bible in its World.* Exeter: Paternoster Press, 1977.

Khalifa, Rashad. *Quran: Visual Presentation of the Miracle.* Tucson: Islamic Productions, 1982.

Koyre, Alexandre. *Bilim Tarih Yazıları.* Trans. Kurtuluş Dinçer. Ankara: Tübitak Popüler Bilim Kitapları, 2000.

— *From the Closed World to the Infinite Universe.* New York: Harper, 1958.

Koyuncu, Gufran. *Evrim.* Istanbul: İz Yayıncılık, 1992.

Kuhn, Thomas. *The Structure of Scientific Revolutions.* Chicago: University of Chicago Press, 1970.

Kuran Araştırmaları Grubu. *Uydurulan Din ve Kuran'daki Din.* Istanbul:

Istanbul Yayınevi, 2004.

Landau, L., Y. Roumer. *İzafiyet Teorisi Nedir?* Trans. S. Gemici. Istanbul: Say Yayınları, 1996.

Layzer, David. *Cosmogenisis.* New York: Oxford University Press, 1990.

Leaman, Oliver. *An Introduction to Medieval Islamic Philosophy.* New York: Cambridge University Press, 1985.

Lechte, John. *Fifty Key Contemporary Thinkers.* London: Routledge, 1994.

Lichich, Antonino. *The New Aspects of Subnuclear Physics.* New York: Plenum Press, 1980.

Lidsey, James E. *The Bigger Bang.* Cambridge: Cambridge University Press, 2000.

Lilley, David M.J. *DNA-Protein: Structural Interactions.* Ed. David M. J. Lilley. Oxford: Oxford University Press, 1995.

Lindberg, David. *The Transmission of Greek and Arabic Learning to the West: In Science in the Middle Ages.* Chicago: University of Chicago Press, 1978.

Lange, Friedrich Albert. *Materializmin Tarihi ve Günümüzdeki Anlamının Eleştirisi.* Trans. Ahmet Arslan. İstanbul: Sosyal Yayınları, 1998.

Mader, Sylvia S. *Biology.* New York: McGraw-Hill, 1996.

— *Human Biology.* Dubuque: W. C. Brown Publishers, 1990.

Magee, Bryan. *Yeni Düşün Adamları.* Ed. Mete Tunçay. Istanbul: Milli Eğitim Basımevi, 1979.

Majul, Cesar Edip. *Special Notes.*

Marx, Karl. *Felsefenin Sefaleti.* 3rd ed. Trans. Ahmet Kardam. Ankara: Sol Yayınları, 1990.

Marx, Karl, Friedrich Engels. *The Communist Manifesto.* London: Penguin Books, 1990.

— *Basic Writings on Politics and Philosophy.* New York: Peter Smith Publisher Inc., 1984.

McClelland, J. S. *A History of Western Political Thought.* New York: Routledge, 1996.

Meithe, Tenry, Anthony Flew. *Does God Exist? A Believer and an Atheist Debate.* New York: Harper Collins Press, 1991.

Merriam Webster's Collegiate Dictionary. Massachusetts: Incorporated Springfield, 1993.

Mevdudi. *Tefhimul Kuran.* Istanbul: Insan Yayınları, 1995.

Miller, Albert: *Meteorology.* London: Merrill Physical Science Series, 1970.

Moody, Sally A. *Cell Lineage and Fate Determination.* San Diego: Academic Press, 1999.

Moore, Patrick. *A Guide to the Planets.* New York: Norton, 1954.

Moreland, J.P. *The Creation Hypothesis.* Illionis: Inter Varsity Press, 1993.

Nasr, Seyyid Hüseyin. *Islam ve Ilim.* Trans. Ilhan Kutluer. Istanbul: Insan Yayınları, 1989.

Needham, A.E. *The Uniqueness of Biological Materials.* Oxford: Pelgamon Press, 1965.

Nelson, Gideon E. *Fundamental Concepts of Biology.* New York: Wiley Press, 1982.

Nevfel, Abdurrezzak. *Kuran'da Ölçü ve Ahenk.* Trans. Muzaffer Kalaycıoğlu. Istanbul: İnkılab Yayınları, 1988.

The New American Bible, St. Joseph's Medium Size Edition.

Nordau, Max. *Tarih Felsefesi.* Trans. Levent Öztürk. Istanbul: Ayışığı Kitapları, 2001.

Nurbaki, Haluk. *Kuran-ı Kerim'den Ayetler ve İlmi Gerçekler.* 7th ed. Türkiye Diyanet Vakfi Yayınları, 1997.

— *Kuran Mucizeleri.* Istanbul: Damla Yayınevi, 1997.

Oldroyd, David. *Thinking about the Earth: A History of Ideas in Geology.* London: Athlone, 1996.

Öztürk, Yaşar Nuri. *Kuran'ın Temel Kavramları.* 18th ed. Istanbul: Yeni Boyut, 1998.

Paul, J. Steinhardt. *The Inflationary Universe.* New York: Scientific American, 1984.

Peacocke, A. *Creation and the World of Science.* Oxford: Oxford University Press, 1979.

— *Theology for a Scientific Age.* London: Scm Press, 1993.

Penrose, Roger. *The Emperor's New Mind : Concerning Computers, Minds, and the Laws of Physics.* Oxford : Oxford University Press, 1989.

— *The Road to Reality.* London: Jonathan Cape, 2004.

Plato. *The Republic.* New York: C. Scribner, 1956.

Polanyi, Michael. *Life's Irreducible Structure.* Science 113, 1968.

Politzer, Georges. *Felsefenin Başlangıç İlkeleri.* 6th ed. Trans. Enver Aytekin. Istanbul: Sosyal Yayınları, 1997.

Polkinghorne. J. C. *Faith, Science and Understanding.* New Haven: Yale University Press, 2000.

Postlethwait, John. H. *Biology! Bringing Science to Life.* New York: McGraw-Hill, 1991.

Press, F. and Raymond Siever. *Earth.* New York: W. H. Freeman, 1998.

Pritchard, James. *Ancient Near Eastern Texts Relating to the Old Testament.* Princeton: Princeton University Press, 1950.

Purves, William K. *Life, The Science of Biology.* Utah: Sinauer Associates, 1995.

Qadir, C. A. *Philosophy and Science in the Islamic World*. London: Routledge, 1990.

Ranke, Hermann. *Die Aegyptischen Personennamen: Form, Meaning, History of Names*. J J Augustin, 1988.

Rees, Martin. *Just Six Numbers: The Deep Forces that Shape the Universe*. New York: Basic Books, 2000.

Reeves, Hubert. *İlk Saniye Evrenden Son Haberler*. Trans. Esra Özdoğan. Istanbul: Yapı Kredi Yayınları. 2001.

Redford, Donald. *Egypt, Canaan and Israel in Ancient Times*. Princeton: Princeton University Press, 1992.

Rifkin, Jeremy, Ted Howard. *Entropy*. 2nd ed. Trans. Hakan Okay. Istanbul: İz Yayıncılık, 1997.

Robinson, Daniel. *The Mind*. New York: Oxford University Press, 1998.

Rose, Steven. *Lifelines*. Oxford: Oxford University Press, 1998.

Ross, Hugh. *The Creator and the Cosmos*. 3rd ed. Colorado: Navpress, 2001.

— *The Fingerprint of God*. 2nd edition. New Kensington: Whitaker House, 1989.

Russell, Bertrand. *History of Western Philosophy and its Connection with Political and Social Circumstances from the Earliest Times to the Present Day*. London: George Allen & Unwin, 1961.

— *The Problems of Philosophy*. London: Williams and Norgate, 1912.

Sagan, Carl. *Contact*. New York: Simon & Schuster, 1985.

— *Cosmos*. London: Abacus, 1995.

Salam, A. *Gauge Unification of Fundamental Forces*. Rev. Mod. Phys. 52, 1980.

Sarıoğlu, Hüseyin. *İbn Rüşd Felsefesi*. Istanbul: Klasik, 2003.

Senih, Safvet. *Kuran ve İlimler*. Izmir: Nil Yayınları, 1995.

Siddiqi, Moinuddin. *The Quranic Concept of History*. India: Adam Publishers, 1994.

Silk, Joseph. *Short History of the Universe*. New York: Scientific American Library, 1994.

Slack, J. M. W. *From Egg to Embryo*. Cambridge: Cambridge University Press, 1991.

Smart, Ninian. *Historical Selection in the Philosophy of Religion*. London: SCM Press Ltd., 1999.

— *The Religious Experience*. 5th ed. New Jersey: Prentice Hall, 1996.

Smith, Christopher, Edward J. Wood. *Molecular Biology and Biotechnology*. New York: Chapman and Hall, 1991.

Soykan, Ömer Naci. *Felsefe ve Dil*. Istanbul: Kabalcı Yayınevi, 1995.

Stanley, D. J. *A Natural Sedimentation Laboratory, the Mediterranean Sea.* Cambridge: Dowden, Hutchinson and Ross, Inc., 1972.

Swinburne, Richard. *The Existence of God.* Revised edition. New York: Oxford University Press, 1991.

— *The Evolution of the Soul.* Oxford: Oxford Press, 1997.

Tanzer, Charles. *Biology and Human Progress.* New Jersey: Prentice Hall, 1953.

Taslaman, Caner. *Big Bang ve Tanrı.* Istanbul: Istanbul Yayınevi, 2003.

Tassoul, Jean-Louis, Tassoul Monique. *A Concise History of Solar and Stellar Physics.* Princeton, N.J.: Princeton University Press, 2004.

Taylan, Necip. *Islam Düşüncesinde Din Felsefeleri.* Istanbul: Marmara Üniversitesi Yayınları, 1997.

Thilly, Frank. *A History of Philosophy.* New York: Holt, 1941.

Thurman, H. V. *Introductory Oceanography.* Charles E. Merrill Publishing Company, 1985.

Treadgold, Warren. *A History of the Byzantine State and Society.* Stanford: Stanford University Press, 1997.

Trusted, Jennifer. *Physics and Metaphysics: Theories of Space and Time.* New York: Routledge, 1994.

Tuna, Taşkın. *Uzayın Ötesi.* Istanbul: Boğaziçi Yayınları, 1994.

Ünal, Ali. *Kuran'da Temel Kavramlar.* Istanbul: Kırkambar Yayınları, 1998.

Waldorp, M. Mitchell. *Complexity.* New York: Touchstone Books, 1992.

Warner, Charles E. *Biology and Water Pollution Control.* Philadelphia: Sounders Press, 1971.

Watson, James D. *Molecular Biology of the Gene.* Menlo Park: Benjamin Cummings Press, 1987.

Watson, Lyall. *Supernature.* London: Hodder and Stroughton, 1973.

Weber, Alfred. *History of Philosophy.* New York, Chicago [etc.]: C. Scribner's Sons, 1925.

Webster's New Twentieth Century Dictionary. Simon & Schuster, 1983.

Weinberg, Steven. *The First Three Minutes: A Modern View of the Origin of the Universe.* New York: Basic Books, 1977.

Wittgenstein, Ludwig. *Tractatus-Logico-Philosophicus* Trans. Oruç Aruoba. Istanbul: Bilim/Felsefe/Sanat Yayınları, 1985.

— *Philosophical Investigations.* New York: Macmillan, 1953.

Williams, Ralph. *Molecular Biology in Clinical Medicine.* New York: Appleton & Lange, 1991.

Wolfson, H. Austryn. *Philo: Foundations of Religious Philosophy in Judaism, Christianity, and Islam.* Cambridge: Harvard University Press, 1948.

— *The Philosophy of the Church Fathers*. Cambridge: Harvard University Press, 1970.

Yalçın, Cavit. *Kavimlerin Helakı*. 3rd ed. Istanbul: Vural Yayınları, 1998.

Yazır Elmalılı, M. Hamdi. *Hak Dini Kuran Dili*. Istanbul: Azim Dağıtım, 1994.

Yeniçeri, Celal. *Uzay Ayetleri Tefsiri*. Istanbul: Erkam Yayınları, 1995.

Yılmaz, İrfan. Selim Uzunoğlu. *Alternatif Biyolojiye Doğru*. Izmir: TÖV Yayınları, 1995.

Yüksel, Edip. *Quran the Ultimate Miracle*, Istanbul: Inkılap Yayınları, 1983.

— *Over It Nineteen*, Istanbul: Ad Yayıncılık, 1997.

— *Running Like Zebras*. Unpublished book. 2000.

Zwart, P.J. *The Flow of Time*. Synthese 24. 1972.

Zycinski, J.M., George F. McLean, Jozet Tischner. *The Philosophy of Person: Solidarity and Cultural Creativity*. Washington D.C.: Paideia Press, 1994.